Immigrant Stories ⠶

CHILD DEVELOPMENT IN CULTURAL CONTEXT

Series Editors

Cynthia García Coll
Peggy Miller

Advisory Board

Jerome Kagan
Carol Worthman
Barrie Thorne

Immigrant Stories: Ethnicity and Academics in Middle Childhood
Cynthia García Coll and Amy Kerivan Marks

Academic Motivation and the Culture of Schooling
Cynthia Hudley and Adele Gottfried

Perfectly Prep: Gender Extremes at a New England Prep School
Sarah H. Chase

Forthcoming Books in the Series:

Literacy and Mothering: Women's Schooling, Families, and Child Development
Robert LeVine and the Harvard Project on Maternal Schooling

Immigrant Stories ::

Ethnicity and Academics in Middle Childhood

Cynthia García Coll
Amy Kerivan Marks

OXFORD
UNIVERSITY PRESS

2009

KH

OXFORD
UNIVERSITY PRESS

Oxford University Press, Inc., publishes works that further
Oxford University's objective of excellence
in research, scholarship, and education.

Oxford   New York
Auckland   Cape Town   Dar es Salaam   Hong Kong   Karachi
Kuala Lumpur   Madrid   Melbourne   Mexico City   Nairobi
New Delhi   Shanghai   Taipei   Toronto

With offices in
Argentina   Austria   Brazil   Chile   Czech Republic   France   Greece
Guatemala   Hungary   Italy   Japan   Poland   Portugal   Singapore
South Korea   Switzerland   Thailand   Turkey   Ukraine   Vietnam

Published by Oxford University Press, Inc.
198 Madison Avenue, New York, New York 10016

www.oup.com

Oxford is a registered trademark of Oxford University Press

Library of Congress Cataloging-in-Publication Data

García Coll, Cynthia T.
Immigrant stories : ethnicity and academics in middle childhood / Cynthia García
Coll and Amy Kerivan Marks.
p.   cm.—(Child development in cultural context)
Includes bibliographical references and index.
ISBN 978–0–19–517459–5
1. Children of immigrants—United States.   2. Children of
immigrants—Education—United States.   3. Child development—
Cross-cultural studies.   I. Marks, Amy Kerivan.   II. Title.
HQ792.U5G37 2008
305.23086'9120973—dc22

9   8   7   6   5   4   3   2   1

Printed in the United States of America
on acid-free paper

8/28/09

We dedicate this book to Doris Peralta for sharing with us the celebratory moments and the misfortunes of being an immigrant in this time and place.

Acknowledgments ⁙

We first want to thank the children and the families that participated in the study. Many schools, both public and independent, opened their doors to us and made possible the recruitment of the children, obtaining their grades, and interviewing their teachers. Many thanks to our past research assistants Natalia Palacios, Rebecca Silver, Meghan Lamarre, Dais Akiba, Lisa Dimartino, and Katherine Magnuson, and the many Brown University undergraduates who assisted in data collection. Our special recognition is extended to our current research assistant, Flannery Patton, for her capable work and tireless commitment to seeing this book through to its finish, and to Laura Szalacha, who started us in the path of data reduction and analysis. Thanks to Makna Men and Sokvan Sam for helping us to obtain access to the community permission and to the members of the Cambodian temple for their warm welcoming and acceptance. Many thanks go to Molly Soum for her help in recruiting and maintaining participation of Cambodian families in the study. There were also established investigators in the field who were periodically consulted, such as William Cross, Deborah Johnson, and Sumru Erkut, as well as members of the McArthur Network Successful Pathways through Middle Childhood (McMCN)—Catherine Cooper, Barrie Thorne, Jacques Eccles, Diane Scott Jones, and especially, John Modell, who remained part of the study throughout from its inception.

Our funding sources included the McMCM, the W. T. Grant Foundation, and the Milltemann Family Directorship at the Center for the Study of Human Development at Brown University. Lastly, we thank our own families, including Kevin Marks, for their constant support and encouragement, and where love is a most powerful motivator.

CONTENTS ⠒

IMMIGRANT STORIES ⁜

1 ::

Immigrant Stories: Ethnicity and Education pathways during Middle Childhood

Remember, remember always that all of us, and you and I especially, are descended from immigrants and revolutionists
— FRANKLIN ROOSEVELT, *Delivered before the Daughters of the American Revolution, April 21, 1938*

Give me your tired, your poor, your huddled masses yearning to breathe free, the wretched refuse of your teeming shore, send these, the homeless, tempest-tossed, to me: I lift my lamp beside the golden door
— EMMA LAZARUS, *Inscribed on the Statue of Liberty*

Immigration has been a significant part of the historical forces shaping this country. In the last two centuries, the United States has received distinct waves of people from Europe, Asia, the Caribbean, and Africa, many seeking to move into this country permanently and become full American citizens with all the rights and responsibilities thereof. Two of the largest waves of immigration were observed in the twentieth century, each with distinct characteristics.[1] As a consequence, today, one of every five Americans, more than 55 million strong, is an immigrant or the child of an immigrant.[2]

Immigrants to this country usually come looking for a better life, not only for themselves but also for their children. They may be fleeing poverty, hunger, or persecution or perhaps just seeking better life opportunities for themselves and their family. They come with varying educational and economic assets and many times with skills that are not useful or valued in this country. In turn, each immigrant's experiences are also shaped by the economic, demographic, and political conditions of the receiving communities.

Nevertheless, the "immigrant story" usually told in this country is depicted in monolithic, one-size-fits-all terms. Achieving the American dream is seen as a universal process of assimilation and incorporation whereby immigrants and their children shed their original culture as they successfully acquire the American way of being in the world. Yet, recent research[3] has shown that, while sharing many aspects of the adaptation process, each family and each ethnic group[4] has its own way of succeeding in our land. Moreover, a give-and-take between the incorporation of some aspects of American culture and the retention of some aspects of the original culture is more the norm than the exception.[5] Although the process of immigration is conceptualized in monolithic terms in our public discourse,[6] examination just beneath the surface reveals more nuanced, individualized processes. How an individual experiences this process, and the contexts which are produced by it, depends on a myriad of factors, not the least of which is the developmental stage of the individual.

This book describes children's psychological and academic developmental pathways in middle childhood among three distinct immigrant groups. The groups share space, location, and time in that they are presently living in two small, contiguous, urban centers in the northeastern United States—East Providence and Providence, Rhode Island. Many of the children mingle on a daily basis in local public and independent elementary schools. In these settings, they share a common educational experience that is designed to give them the necessary tools to succeed as citizens in this country.

At the same time, these three immigrant groups differ dramatically in their culture of origin, their local history of immigration, their ascribed ethnicities, their rate of incorporation in the receiving communities, and their ongoing relationship with their country of origin. They represent the diversity of the immigrant experience. One is a refugee group, Cambodians, who left their country in haste because of the fear of death by starvation or persecution, using a rather narrow window of opportunity to escape. The second group is a typical, albeit recent, "European" group, the Portuguese, who have been arriving at these shores since the 1800s and are now visibly incorporated into the power structure of their U.S. community. The third is a more recently arrived group, a transnational community from the Dominican Republic, which benefits from the institutions created by other Latino groups that arrived earlier.

The stories presented in this book try to capture the unique developmental niches[7] that are created by the confluence of economic, historical, and cultural forces over which neither the children nor their families have much control. It is not that they do not have agency nor make proactive decisions in their daily lives; on the contrary, the stories that we will offer here will demonstrate that they are active shapers of their own lives in their own particular ways. For example, children are not only a product of socialization forces but they also respond to multiple socialization agents in unique, individualized ways. Families do not abide by all the rules of engagement that schools provide, and perhaps even rebel against some rules that compete with other important agendas in their lives. For example, parents know that their children need to attend school, but they might ask their older children to take care of younger children when the parents are sick. Parents might also take their children out of school for family celebrations or holiday vacations and may not think that it is important to have a designated time and place to complete homework (in the face of other life demands). Yet their choices and the opportunities that are available to both children and families are very much the product of complex contextual, historical processes beyond their own immediate control. They are not only simultaneously actors and reactors, but also creators of new spaces that mainstream institutions such as schools must, in turn, adapt to and incorporate. This process of mutual adaptation, of resistance and change, is constantly co-created in the daily lives of families, children, schools, and communities. How these processes impinge on or facilitate children's development is the central question guiding this endeavor.

This book thus explores how individual children and their families interact on a daily basis with the contexts they encounter as immigrants and how these interactions affect the ways that the children develop as pupils and young residents of the United States.

Because of the rather strict nature of our existing academic disciplinary boundaries, to study these intersections one must draw from many disciplines, as none of the social sciences traditionally taught and implemented provide all the necessary lenses to capture both the micro and macro complex processes involved. This will not be a traditional developmental psychology book—although this is our own primary discipline—yet it will be based upon numerous developmental theoretical frameworks. In particular, it will conceptualize the individual child not as a sole actor/actress in his or her developmental script but as a reactor and actor/actress interacting and negotiating throughout a multitude of contexts (Cooper, 1999). Developmental processes will not unfold passively with increasing age but will be co-constructed and negotiated as a function of the individual and myriad environmental influences. As a consequence, this book will draw insights into the complexity of the phenomena under study utilizing information obtained from a variety of sources and through various methods. That is why we have included data from children's, parents' and teachers' responses to questionnaires and interviews, school records, observations and interviews conducted by an ethnographer in the immigrant communities, and focus groups of parents from each community discussing the challenges and benefits of parenting in this country. Most social science studies employ only one or two of these methodologies, but not at the depth that we have employed them here. Enormous attention was paid to all these sources of data, not an easy task when you are working with three different communities, languages, and settings. We can now see why most of us stay in our disciplinary cocoon. It is so much easier! Yet, what we have learned about the processes of children's development in context could not have been done without the many different disciplinary lenses utilized.

The stories portrayed in this book are also designed to capture a unique period in children's development: middle childhood.[8] This is intended to fill a gap in the scientific literature on children of immigrants, which has until now concentrated primarily on adolescents and adults.[9] Our desire to study middle childhood arises from a variety of reasons. Many of the developmental processes that have been studied in adolescence may have their origin in middle childhood. Recent research has demonstrated stronger links between later developmental outcomes and developmental status and processes in middle childhood, than those occurring during infancy and preschool.[10] In addition, it is in middle childhood when the near-universal experience of schooling brings children of immigrants in constant contact with mainstream culture. After all, the common school had, from its inception, the objective of incorporating newcomers into our culture.[11] Finally, recent research with other populations provides evidence that individual trajectories in academics that are initiated during middle childhood create pathways that persist into adolescence and possibly beyond.[12] Our suspicion is that these early trajectories might be even more influential in the lives of children of immigrants, because in many cases, their parents lack the know-how or the resources to intervene on their children's behalf or even to recognize the fact that these trajectories pose any risk.

⠃⠃ Critical Tasks for Children of Immigrants During Middle Childhood

In this book, we will explore in depth two developmental tasks of middle childhood that are especially relevant to children of immigrants. These are the beginning of the formation (1) of ethnic/racial attitudes and identifications as children negotiate their inclusion in various social groups from their stance as children of immigrants and (2) of academic pathways as they navigate schools and perform their main developmentally appropriate role as students.

The development of an ethnic/racial identity is a part of the developmental process that underlies a child's other emerging social identities, such as academic, gender, and social roles. Previous research has conceptualized ethnic/racial identity as a multidimensional, organizing self-construct evident in self-labels, attitudes, values, and behaviors (Phinney, 1990, 1992). Most theories dealing with ethnic self-identification suggest that a young child's ethnic identity is largely the result of socialization patterns and emerging cognitive abilities (Corenblum & Annis, 1993; Semaj, 1980). The same can be said for the emergence of social categorizations that help define and create valences associated with group membership (Bialystok, 1999; Bigler & Liben, 1993; Billings, 1999; Black, Dubowitz, & Starr, 1999; Blakeslee, 2002). Many researchers would also agree that sometime in early childhood (i.e., during preschool and early school ages), children are able to categorize people by race and ethnicity (e.g. Ramsey, 1991; Doyle & Aboud, 1995).

These identity theories also assume that by adolescence, individuals are aware of the different groups and categories to which they themselves can claim membership, understand the abstract significance of these identities, and make more self-determined choices about their identities[13] (Knight, Bernal, Garza, Cota, & Ocampo, 1993; Whaley, 1993; Waters, 1990, 1999). Nearly all the work that has dealt specifically with children of immigrants' ethnic/racial self-identification has focused on adolescents' identities and social adjustment (i.e. Rumbaut, 1994a; Waters, 1990, 1999). A similar significant body of research also exists with regard to "minority adolescents," including psychological aspects of ethnic and racial identities (e.g., how proud someone is of his or her heritage; Phinney, 1990; Rotheram-Borus & Wyche, 1994; Rumbaut, 1994a; Waters, 1994). Remarkably, this leaves us with unconnected bodies of knowledge about these processes between preschool age and adolescence and little understanding of how the processes of family migration affect middle childhood developmental milestones such as forming academic pathways and contribute to the formulation of an ethnic/racial identity as part of an emerging sense of self, especially among children of immigrants (Quintana, 1994).

Currently, children of immigrants and native-born families of color in the United States can potentially identify with a variety of ethnic/racial identities or reference groups. These can include ethnic, panethnic, and bicultural categories, or simply the label "American" (e.g., Rumbaut, 1994a). Each one of these identities is theoretically and empirically associated with a different pattern of adaptation or assimilation (Bernal, Saenz, & Knight, 1995; Buriel, 1994; Phinney, 1990; Rumbaut, 1994a; Waters, 1999). In other words, the labels a person selects to describe himself or herself can sometimes tell us about how long they have lived in the United States and how they have integrated—or not integrated—more than one aspect of their cultural and social identities. However, at this point, empirical data, especially with Asian and Hispanic populations, has not informed us of how the young children of immigrant parents determine, define, or understand their ethnic/racial identities (see Bernal, Knight, Ocampo, Garza, & Cota, 1993; Buriel, 1994; Phinney, 1990; Knight et al., 1993).

Therefore, we know little about the processes by which these identities are understood, created, or chosen by young children, the salient contextual factors which are associated with these decisions, or how these decisions are associated with children's academic development and their social relations with others. In this volume, we hope to provide a clearer picture of how a child born into an immigrant family understands and determines his or her own ethnic/racial identities in reference to other aspects of the self. To do this, we will try to understand the lives of children from the three immigrant groups— Cambodian, Portuguese, and Dominican—as they vary greatly in their ascribed "racialized" identities. For example, the Portuguese are easily categorized by others as white after the first generation; Cambodians are always considered by the majority culture to be Asian regardless of generation; Dominicans can vary from very light to dark skin, so they might be ascribed by others as Latino and/or black. Additionally, these groups are among the larger immigrant groups in the school systems that we are studying, and the lack of information on these groups has been found to lead to existing educational interventions and strategies which are inadequate (see Collignon, Men, & Tan, 2001). Our findings can inform not only the academic literature but hopefully also the local schools, as well as others who are struggling to provide culturally appropriate services to these children and their families.

Furthermore, children form these emerging identities at the same time that other attitudes toward their own group and other social groups are being formed. These attitudes can range from positive (e.g., black people are nice) to negative (e.g., Cambodians are stupid). They can also include perceptions of discrimination, which can be used to explain inclusion or exclusion of self and others into particular social interactions (e.g., a student perceives that the teacher is not calling on her because the teacher does not like Dominicans). Many of these perceptions are shaped by children's daily experiences in multiethnic schools.

This brings us to the second task of middle childhood considered in depth in this book: the establishment of academic pathways. As school officials and scholars of education know, children's early successes or failures in school often persist or become enlarged in subsequent school years. Children of immigrants experience many challenges that might get in the way of academic success and prevent them from succeeding in school (Kao, 1999). They tend to have many siblings and large families, often live in poverty, and their parents might have little education or awareness of the educational system and/or knowledge of English (Hernandez & Darke, 1999). Because of poverty or the parents' lack of specific school-related knowledge, many children of immigrants do not have literacy-rich home environments or attend preschools or out of school programs that could contribute to their school readiness and eventual successes. Their parents usually have very little understanding of what they can or should do on behalf of their children's educational success (García Coll et al., 2002). Many of the children themselves are also English-language learners, so learning academic English in order to learn disciplinary content (math, science, history, etc.) becomes yet another challenge to surmount. And often parents' lack of fluency in English allows them to be of little help to their children in this regard.

Children of immigrants also attend particular kinds of schools. Often, they attend large, inner-city schools and schools where, according to their parents, teachers don't maintain discipline in their classrooms and where the family's involvement in education is not encouraged (Nord & Griffin, 1999). In our own study, we have observed that as parents realize that the schools are not preparing their children well, many will try to enroll their children in independent or parochial schools if they can find the extra financial resources to do so.

Yet these immigrant households are "rich" in other ways—ways that have only begun to be documented in the literature (see García Coll & Magnuson, 1999). Parents have specific funds of knowledge (Moll, Amanti, Neff, & Gonzalez, 1992) that, even if devalued by contemporary American society, can inspire in the child a sense of pride attached to their family's country of origin—their culture, their extended family, their landscape. As expressed by a Dominican boy, "I like being Dominican; I like speaking Spanish." Children's pride in their family's culture can also serve as a buffer[14] against experiences of denigration that occur due to the fact that they are not white or their status as offspring of immigrants.

These families also place high value on family life and their children's education (Shields & Behrman, 2004). A significant percentage of the children we studied, in each of the three immigrant groups, spend most of their out of school time with their families rather than with their peers. Parents tell us that they worry that as their children acculturate and lose their family's native language, their children will acquire "American ways" that will lead to lack of respect for other family members, and ultimately, to drugs, premarital sex, and vandalism. They also hold high educational expectations for their children: 98% of Dominicans, 88% of Cambodians, and 85% of Portuguese parents told us that they expect their children to go to college. Even if they do not know how to promote their children's educational success, these families value and encourage hard work and high academic achievement. The parents in our study share an American dream, to see their children live successful, well-educated lives, but also share the uncertainty as to how this dream can be achieved. As we will see later in this book, for the Cambodians, this actualization of the American dream is made even more difficult by their immigration to the United States as refugees.

As we mentioned earlier, achievement in the early years of schooling is crucial because early learning provides the basis for future success in school and beyond. After all, you have to learn how to read in order to be able to use reading as a learning tool. Academic pathways start early: attitudes and achievement levels as early as first grade are related to educational outcomes even in high school (Alexander, Entwistle, &

Horsey, 1997; Huston & Ripke, 2006; Stipek, 2005). However, early academic achievement is not only measured by grades and tests scores, but by the attitudes that children express toward school and learning—what researchers have oftentimes called academic engagement (Alexander, Entwistle, & Kabbani, 2001; Finn, 1993; Finn & Rock, 1997; Greenwood, Horton, & Utley, 2002). First, children need to buy into the rules of the school setting; they must behave from now on in ways compatible with the school setting to meet school expectations and be rewarded. And when competing needs arise—doing homework or going out to play—children must learn that their most important task is to do everything possible to do well in school. They have to envision their future academically and occupationally and have high aspirations and expectations for themselves. A positive academic pathway would be shown not only by high grades and test scores but also by positive attitudes toward school and high educational expectations for the future.

So what has published research so far shown about the academic pathways of children of immigrants? Not much during middle childhood. Research on the psychosocial and academic orientation of children of immigrants has been conducted almost exclusively with adolescents. In general, these studies suggest that the adolescents are doing relatively well in spite of their families' relatively low socioeconomic status and their relative unfamiliarity with the school system. Past studies show that youth from immigrant backgrounds are physically and psychologically healthier, engage in less risky behaviors, work harder and have higher achievement in school, and have more positive social attitudes than their peers (e.g., Blake, Ledsky, Goodenow, & O'Donnell, 2001; Fuligni, 1997; Harris, 1999; Hernandez & Charney, 1998; Hussey et al., 2007; Jutte, Burgos, Mendoza, Ford, & Huffman, 2003; Kao, 1999; Kao & Tienda, 1995; Berry, Phinney, Sam, & Vedder, 2006; Portes & Rumbaut, 2001; Rumbaut, 1995; Ruiz-de-Velasco & Fix, 2000; Steinberg, Brown, & Dornbusch, 1996; Schwartz & Stiefel, 2006; Suárez-Orozco & Suárez-Orozco,1995, 2001). In spite of all the challenges to their academic success, many first and second-generation immigrant groups are outperforming their peers. However, several studies have found that the more these adolescents become acculturated to mainstream American culture, the more they exhibit negative attitudes toward school and lower academic achievement (Fuligni, 1997; Portes & Rumbaut, 2001; Rumbaut & Portes, 2001; Suárez-Orozco & Suárez-Orozco, 1995)

In other words, there are two interesting phenomena at hand. First, immigrant children are exhibiting greater academic, behavioral, and psychological resilience than their native peers, despite multiple environmental risk factors. Second, as acculturation takes place—whether within one individual or over successive generations—outcomes worsen. Individually, as well as taken together, these findings are often referred to as the "immigrant paradox."[15] This "paradox" is difficult to explain because as children and families acculturate to the United States, they typically acquire greater wealth, social capital, and skills in communicating in English, all of which are very important resources usually associated with better academic outcomes. Clearly, more research is needed to understand how and why the immigrant paradox develops.

Though these past studies are revealing, several caveats do exist. First, these findings vary dramatically by immigrant group: The children in some immigrant groups tend to excel in academics while others do not. Also, within pan-ethnic categories such as "Hispanic" and "Asian," there is wide variability in culture and family capital as well as educational outcomes (Erkut & Tracy, 2002; Rumbaut, 1994a, 1995). The processes by which most members of some groups succeed and many members of other groups do not are still not well understood.

The main objectives of this book are to understand how the variability of academic outcomes within and across national groups of children of immigrants occurs, the role of acculturation in promoting (or inhibiting) academic success, and ethnic identity processes and attitudes in middle childhood. Do our three groups of children—Cambodians, Portuguese, and Dominicans—provide examples of the immigrant paradox? Who succeeds in school and who does not—and why? How are aspects of families and schools involved in the development of ethnic identity, cultural attitudes, and academic achievement? How are families and school processes interrelated, if at all?

Guiding Principles of Our Conceptual Approach and Methodologies

As mentioned above, this study employs theoretical perspectives that situate children's development within many contextual influences, a necessary conceptual approach in the study of children of immigrants. In particular, the frameworks of Bronfenbrenner (1986), García Coll et al. (1996), and Modell (2000) guide the overall conceptualization of this study.

Bronfenbrenner (1979, 1986) has argued that children's development is influenced not only by the family system but also by the other important institutions with which the child and family interact. Bronfenbrenner's ecological model points out the importance of the interconnection between nested contexts: how circumstances in one context (e.g., immigrant family) can moderate the impact of another context (e.g., neighborhood school) on developmental processes. Moreover, both persons and contexts are seen not as static but as continually evolving, one as the function of the other and vice versa. So, for example, as a child develops a sense of self as a student and learner, he or she will act differently in the classroom, which will in turn influence the teacher's behaviors toward and expectations of him or her as a student. The emphasis moves away from static unidirectional influences to person–process–context interactions over time. In our case, a child of an immigrant family is not seen as passive but as an active and selective agent, who constructs, based on one's interactions with his or her various salient contexts over time, new ways of interpreting and acting. Thus, individual differences within the same context (i.e., school) are expected as a function of the particular processes that each individual partakes in his or her interaction with that context.

But children of immigrants also become part of a larger stratification system that uses their "race," ethnicity, socioeconomic background, and gender (along with other aspects of their lives) to categorize them (see García Coll et al., 1996; García Coll & Szalacha, 2004), and allows or denies them access to certain resources critical to their development. These larger societal processes are expressed on a daily basis in the various contexts that the child navigates (see Thorne, 2005). According to García Coll and colleagues, two particularly critical institutions for children are schools and the adaptive cultures that arise as immigrant enclaves develop in the United States.

Schools are highly segregated environments in this country, reflecting to a certain degree residential patterns that are distinctly differentiated by race/ethnicity and social class.[16] Schools not only differ in their ethnic/racial/socioeconomic composition but in turn are given differential resources critical to children's development (Frankenberg, Lee, Orfield, 2003). In general, inner-city schools with higher concentrations of poor, minority students tend to have fewer or less optimal resources than their counterparts. Among the variables that are critical for the development of positive academic outcomes in children of immigrants are the percentage of children in a school who are from families that live below the poverty line (measured as those who qualify for free lunches) and the percentage of children from minority versus white backgrounds (Portes & Rumbaut, 2001).

In contrast, ethnic enclaves are important sources of support for recent immigrant families, and immigrants from different enclaves differ in their knowledge and nature of interactions with mainstream institutions such as schools (Portes, 2000). The school and neighborhood contexts in which these children live can at once inhibit and promote children's academic and social development (García Coll et al., 1996). For example, an ethnic enclave may be linguistically isolated, inhibiting an immigrant child's English literacy skill development. On the other hand, this type of neighborhood context might promote positive social skill and self-concept development by creating a buffer between the child and the negative effects of racism and discrimination in the larger cultural context. Similarly, segregation by language skills in a particular school classroom can provide a good learning environment for an ESL student, yet it might also isolate the student from mainstream peers and inhibit him or her from acquiring important cultural capital.

Finally, Modell (2000) notes that the sociohistorical context of development does not have a unique and solely unidirectional influence on children, but that the processes of immigration and their adaptations also change the contexts of schools, neighborhoods, and communities. These multidirectional processes create particular developmental niches (Super & Harkness, 1986) that are reflective of larger sociohistorical processes such as labor markets, immigration policies, and historical group migration patterns. These larger historical patterns result in different group migration histories and modes of reception, yet individual families and children will actively use and shape the larger historical processes. As such, individual families and children from immigrant groups that differ in their migration and incorporation patterns will be both reflections and shapers of these patterns. (In thinking about immigrants, one must never forget how frequently the migration itself was undertaken in significant part in order to improve children's opportunities, or, even when not undertaken for this reason, calling forth immigrants' very most urgent and profound efforts.) As such, we would expect differences in modal adaptations not only *between* immigrants groups but also *within* each immigrant group.

These processes reflect three broad theoretical notions that are crucial in understanding the adaptations and outcomes of children from immigrant families. One is the notion of path dependence: the progressive narrowing of options brought about by previous actions and decisions. This fits nicely with the notions of how during middle childhood, academic pathways and attitudes—formed and maintained through interactions between the individual child and the multiple surrounding contexts—lead to certain outcomes in middle and high school (Alexander et al., 2001). The second notion is the important role of social capital (social connections that create access to important resources) and the ethnic culture in shaping developmental outcomes. The final concept is that of the "structural embeddedness of individual action," whereby individuals are seen as actors within contexts that provide or exclude them from opportunities for optimal growth and development.

Reflecting the interdisciplinary lenses described above, this study values the contribution of mixed methods (Greene, 2001; Greene & Caracelli, 1997; Tolman & Szalacha, 1999; Weisner, 2005). Mixing qualitative and quantitative methods, which reflect very different epistemological traditions (i.e., assumptions, requirements, and procedures), represents a real paradigm shift in the behavioral sciences. This theoretical shift has come about with a realization that each method has its own limitations and that the use of methods anchored in both traditions provides a better understanding of complex social phenomena. Although the bulk of the data for this study was gathered primarily through "standard" quantitative and qualitative methods, the study was designed with a mixed method approach from its inception, therefore deriving a rich variety of data from multiple sources.

Organization of This Book

This book is designed to portray the experiences of children of three distinct immigrant groups as they navigate middle childhood. The next three chapters provide the background of the study. In Chapter 2, we examine more carefully the immigrant context as a major source of influence in children's developmental pathways. In Chapter 3, we consider what is known about the two main developmental tasks of middle childhood that constitute the focus of this book: ethnic identity and academic pathways. Chapter 4 elaborates the conceptual framework for the study and, along with appendices, provides a road map of the multiple methodologies used in the study. Chapters 5, 6, and 7 discuss the situation of each immigrant group: Cambodians (Chapter 5), Dominican (Chapter 6), and Portuguese (Chapter 7). Chapter 8 presents a comprehensive analysis of the three groups simultaneously, eventually comparing the somewhat-similar, somewhat-distinct processes by which these groups' children progress into middle childhood. Finally, Chapter 9 presents our conclusions and thoughts for future scholarship with children of immigrants.

2 ::

Why Study Children of Immigrants?

The children of today are the citizens, workers and parents
of America's future, and no other group of American
children is expanding more rapidly that those in
immigrant families

—DONALD HERNANDEZ

:: The Contexts of Immigration

The United States is commonly referred to as a country of immigrants. There is, of course, no question that other populations were here before. Various Native American nations and previous colonizers had populated this continent for centuries. But the country that we refer to as the United States of America was founded by immigrants to these lands. And thus the process of immigration has always been closely tied to the history of this country. We argue that this process is an integral part of the developmental niche of children of immigrants and, following contextual developmental theoretical frameworks, an important consideration in understanding these children's development.

Foreigners from every conceivable corner of the world have come to these shores and have crossed its historically fluctuating boundaries. Depending both on the policies of the day toward immigration and the factors pushing citizens from their countries of origin, various groups have dominated the distinct waves of immigration that have made this country what it is today (Rumbaut & Portes, 2001). Initially, the preponderance of immigrants came from northern European countries; shortly thereafter, most came from southern Europe and other parts of the world. More recently, the majority are from Mexico, Central and South America, the Caribbean, and Asia (Shields & Behrman, 2004). The need for cheap or free labor has also brought distinct and sometimes continuous waves of African, Chinese, Filipino, Mexican, and Puerto Rican[1] workers among others. These most recent waves of immigrants are not from northern European ancestry and therefore are more ethnically and racially distinct; in the United States they are typically considered "nonwhite." Regardless of the reasons for immigration or the country of origin, many immigrants stay in the United States, and their children are either by birthright or by their parent's naturalization, citizens of the United States. For them, this country is home.

Immigrants come to this country for a variety of reasons. They are also categorized differently by our policies. They can be considered illegals, sometimes coming on tourist visas and staying and sometimes dangerously crossing our borders. They can be refugees fleeing war and persecution or governments that we classify as our enemies. They can also be "voluntary,"[2] choosing to come to this country seeking a better life for themselves and their children; they might also be sought after by our government for their specific work skills. Therefore, immigrants vary in class, education, language, culture, race, and ethnicity, making them a very difficult group to categorize or characterize as a whole (Kasinitz, Mollenkopf, & Waters, 2004; Rumbaut & Portes, 2001; Suárez-Orozco & Todorova, 2003). Their life context here also varies tremendously not only as a function of what they bring (and leave behind) but also of the unique characteristics of the receiving communities in which they settle.

In the second half of the twentieth century, the United States experienced one of the largest waves of immigration in its history. The increase in immigration to the United States can be seen as part of a global pattern of large-scale immigrations (Coatsworth, 2004; Suárez-Orozco, 2004; Suárez-Orozco & Qin-Hilliard, 2004) and the growth of transnational communities.[3] As a consequence of the growth of the immigrant population in the United States, the 2000 census indicates that one in every five children in the United States is the child of one or two immigrant parents (Shields & Behrman, 2004). In addition, children in immigrant families are the fastest growing segment of the population: Since 1990, their numbers have increased seven times faster than the number of children in native-born families (Hernandez, 2004). Their numbers contribute to one of the largest demographic shifts in the United States where ethnic and racial minorities in aggregate are projected to become the numerical majority sometime during this century.

Recent immigrants, like many of their earlier counterparts, tend to live in urban centers (Jensen, 2001). Unlike their predecessors, however, they are not only concentrated in a few gateway states (California and New York), but their numbers have also grown rapidly in nearly every state (Hernandez, 2004). Another interesting analysis is provided by the examination of their growth in proportion to their population in a particular state. Analyzed this way, Rhode Island (the state where this research was conducted) ranks third in the nation (after California and Hawaii) in the concentration of second-generation immigrants relatively to the size of the general population in the state (Jensen, 2001). Both concentration and large numbers can contribute to the development of ethnic enclaves, which have the potential of providing critical social capital for newcomer families and their children (Portes, 1995; Perez, 2001; Portes & Rumbaut, 1996; Rumbaut & Portes, 2001).

But growth and concentration can also have negative consequences. Even while our country's history is so closely linked to immigration, the public attitudes and ensuing public policies toward immigrants have shifted dramatically over time (Rumbaut & Portes, 2001).[4] It has been argued that these changes in attitudes and policies are a reflection of the perception of the immigrant populations at the time (Perea & García Coll, 2008; Stepick, Grenier, Castro, & Dunn, 2003). These attitudes may be in part due to the perceived threat of the new immigrants to the well-being of particular communities and the nation as a whole. For example, existing residents of a community may feel threatened by the idea of extending economic opportunities and government resources to new-comers or undocumented workers.[5] In the United States, attitudes have been shifted over time from welcoming to rejecting, as have the public policies (Suárez-Orozco & Suárez-Orozco, 1995). These shifting attitudes are referred to by Stepick et al. (2003) as "American Ambivalence." They assert that "Americans are always of two minds about immigration . . . Two attitudes have revealed themselves in the public debate: open generosity versus nativism and racism. The United States has always kept the door open or attempted to close the door" (Stepick et al., 2003, p. 11). Whether there are two minds or shifting minds, many scholars are in agreement that Americans' perceptions of immigrants are varied and complex and have changed over time.

In addition, public attitudes have varied toward the process of incorporation of immigrants into society at large. Policies have ranged from promotion of total incorporation and assimilation as the goal, to exclusion, rejection, and segregation. A good example to gage these historical shifts is a closer examination of the changes in language instruction policies in our public schools (see Perea & García Coll, 2008). Bilingual education programs have ranged from English language immersion to dual language, where proficiency in both languages (and therefore bilingualism and biculturalism) is desired. Over time, we have seen historical shifts in language instruction policies that reflect the desire for immigrants' complete assimilation to allowing bilingualism/biculturalism and more recently back to assimilation.

Moreover, native ethnic minorities and immigrants from different generations also clash as they share their daily space in segregated schools and neighborhoods (Kasinitz et al., 2004; Stepick et al., 2003). In the United States, the likelihood of living in a segregated neighborhood or attending a segregated school has continued to rise, especially for Asian and Hispanic families (Logan, Stowell, & Oakley, 2002). While attending school with primarily children of a similar race or ethnicity has some positive affects, such as fostering a sense of belonging, racial segregation in schools often translates into economic segregation (Orfield & Lee, 2005)—which is a risk factor for various markers of academic success. Various studies have linked schools with a large minority population, high percentages of students eligible for federally subsidized lunches as well as inner-city schools as being linked to lower academic performance among children of immigrants (e.g., Perez, 2001; Portes & Rumbaut, 2001).

These school environments shape not only how successful children are in their academic pursuits, but also their motivations and aspirations to learn and their sense of self as a member of an ethnic/racial group. For example, student demographics in a school can affect academic attitude development through social mirroring. In a segregated school, children of immigrants develop academic attitudes and identities within a network of native minority peers. Native minority children may hold, in contrast to the "immigrant optimism" of first-generation parents, the belief that a positive academic identity will not translate into upward mobility (Zhou, 1997b). This belief can lead to a peer culture which does not reward those who have adopted an identity based in academic achievement and striving. Thus, in this school context, children of immigrants find themselves in the precarious position of choosing between devaluing an academically focused identity in reaction to peer culture and adopting pro-school attitudes and running the risk of being ostracized by peers (Zhou, 1997b).

In addition, in these settings, children might for the first time face negative ethnic/racial stereotypes and diminished expectations because of their immigrant status and ethnic background (Fuligni, Witkow, & García, 2005). The welcoming or rejecting attitudes are not only formed by institutional policies or the dominant culture but also from other "oppressed" groups that now have to share their limited resources with newcomers. Since prejudice, racism, and discrimination are conceived as relevant to children's developmental outcomes (García Coll et al., 1996), these public attitudes and policies, as well as other aspects of the context of immigrant reception, are part of the unique developmental niches that immigrant families provide to their children in this country (Harkness & Super, 1994).

The family demographics of the "new" immigrants also contribute to the unique developmental niches of their children (also called the second generation). Children of immigrants (as compared to children in native-born populations) are more likely to live in two parent households and also have other relatives and nonrelatives in their homes (Hernandez, 2004). These families are also overrepresented among the poor: The overall poverty rate is 49% compared to 34% for children in native-born families. Probably as a consequence of these two factors, 47% of children in immigrant families as compared to only 11% of children in native-born families live in overcrowded housing.

These structural aspects of immigrant families present several interesting puzzles. Among the native-born population in this country, poverty among families with children is usually associated with single heads of households. In contrast, immigrant families have a higher percentage of two parent families and higher rates of employment, yet they remain poor (Nightingale & Fix, 2004). Forty-four percent of children in two-parent immigrant families are poor as compared to 22% in the native-born population. Perhaps the observed low levels of education, limited job skills and consequent employment in low wage positions, and language barriers of their parents contribute to the higher incidence of poverty among children of immigrants. Since growing up in poverty is considered a high-risk condition for health, mental health, and education outcomes,[6] this is a major aspect of the unique developmental niche of children of immigrants.

But generalizations about immigrant families and their children have to be carefully interpreted. For example, in his detailed analysis of the demographic and life circumstances of immigrant families based on the 2000 census, Hernandez (2004) reports some of his findings not only as a function of immigrant/native born but further separated by high/medium/low parental education. His analyses are striking because many of the risk factors associated with immigrant families— overcrowded housing, unemployment, low education, poverty, and language barriers—are only found in immigrant groups who have, as a predominant characteristic low parental education.[7] So closer examination of the data not only supports the importance of parent education as a major determinant of many important aspects of the child's developmental niche, but also suggests the heterogeneity among immigrant groups and the need to conceptualize the contexts of immigration as determined in part by the parents' country of origin and the overall characteristics of such immigration (Hernandez, 2004; Rumbaut & Portes, 2001). In our studies, we are careful to acknowledge both the commonalities among immigrant groups, as well as the unique aspects of children and families that are related to children's academic experiences and ethnic identity development.

Children of Immigrants: Risks and Assets

Despite their increase in numbers and their unique context, we know very little about the developmental outcomes of children of immigrants, particularly during middle childhood. Importantly, we also know little about children's development in context, interacting with and as a function of their unique developmental niches. Several scholarly practices contribute to this fact. As we noted in the introduction, most studies of immigrants have been conducted with adults. Of the extant knowledge based on youth, most of the studies have been conducted with adolescents, leaving many unanswered questions about developmental processes before this age.

In addition, because immigrants become part of ethnic groups in their process of incorporation into the social stratification in the United Sates (Rumbaut & Portes, 2001), many studies do not differentiate immigrants from native born or native born who have immigrant backgrounds by generation. So groups of people with different cultures, countries of origin, and immigration patterns (i.e., Filipinos and Chinese) become part of the same ethnic group (i.e., Asian), when they settle in this country. Thus many studies use large, broad, and unspecified ethnic/racial categories such as Latinos, Asians, or blacks, and include an unspecified number of children of immigrants who are not studied as a function of their parents' immigration to this country. This is problematic given the extant research that finds strong generation effects within ethnic groups (e.g., Suárez-Orozco & Suárez-Orozco, 1995)

Moreover, much of the extant research of children of immigrants (or immigrant children) is also limited in scope and in the range of developmental outcomes explored. Many of these studies utilize theoretical frameworks that conceptualize immigration solely as a negative influence on development without considering the possible benefits of growing up bilingual and bicultural in this country. For example, children have often told us of the rich cultural experiences they have as bicultural children, knowing multiple languages and traveling abroad.

In this and other research we have conducted with adolescents (Marks, 2008), students comment that being bicultural provides them diverse social and family experiences that give them unique perspectives in the classroom when studying history, languages, and literature, experiences which help make them "open" to new ideas and social experiences. We also know little about the potential protective factors of indigenous cultures against high-risk lifestyles associated with downward assimilation[8] (Fuligni & Hardway, 2004; García Coll & Magnuson, 1997; Rumbaut & Portes, 2001). There may be particular ways by which families maintain traditional values or cultural practices that can prevent children from feeling socially isolated or becoming involved in "risky behaviors" (e.g., drug use, school truancy). Our lack of understanding about such protective processes is due in part to the prevalent conceptualization in this country that cultural differences from the white majority culture are sources of risk rather than potentially multifaceted (i.e., they contribute both resources and vulnerabilities) or primarily positive processes (García Coll & Magnuson, 2000). In particular, studies of normative processes and of successful pathways of development (as opposed to studies focusing on problems), balanced between strengths and weaknesses, are lacking.

In addition, when academic studies use broad race and ethnicity categories solely to compare immigrants versus nonimmigrants (or immigrants from different national origins to one another), serious limitations are placed on how we understand developmental processes and outcomes (Cooper, García Coll, Thorne, & Orellana, 2005). When groups are compared this way, categories like ethnic/racial/country of origin/generation are used as proxies for contextual processes that are neither clearly conceptualized nor articulated, nor in most cases, directly measured. For example, comparing Asian to Latino parents' involvement in their children's education may provide some information regarding broad differences in parenting practices; however, we will know little from such an analysis about which cultural characteristics, language processes, or interactions between the family and school may be primarily responsible for any differences. Further, an analysis by national origin may show that parents from different nationalities are very different within panethnic groups and cannot adequately be grouped by "Asian" or "Latino" categories. In other words, the limitations of relying solely on this comparative approach are many, including obscuring variation within groups, emphasizing differences between groups, and neglecting similarities between groups (García Coll, 1990; García Coll et al., 1996; McLoyd, 1990, 1998). Given these limitations, interpretations of such comparative findings can also be faulty as group differences can easily lend themselves to be interpreted as hierarchical (one group is better than other) or group membership can be used as the sole explanation (rather than in association with other processes) for the differences observed.

It is important to note that we are *not* advocating against a comparative approach when studying multiple immigrant groups; in fact, such an approach is vital to the research presented in this volume. Rather, we are advocating for a comparative approach that is sensitive to within group variation and acknowledges—through multilevel analysis and a variety of measures—the complexity of processes underlying differential outcomes. We therefore believe that a mixed method of inquiry using both comparative and within-group analyses along with a serious assessment of the processes associated with group membership are necessary in order to advance the field. This book therefore tries to strike a balance between comparative (i.e., etic) and within-nationality-group (i.e., emic) perspectives (see Berry, 1999).

Theoretical Frameworks

In spite of all the limitation of the extant literature, there is an emerging interdisciplinary scholarship that is beginning to document the unique developmental niches of children of immigrants and their developmental processes. Because of the importance of educational attainment in the life course of children of immigrants, much of this scholarship is examining the potential influences of developmental contexts on academic success in various immigrant populations. Moreover, this recent scholarship has utilized comprehensive theoretical frameworks that are cognizant of the complexities of how immigration contexts can shape developmental niches and outcomes. We will first examine these frameworks and then present some of the emerging generalization and limitations of this work.

The work of Portes and Rumbaut (Portes & Rumbaut, 2001; Rumbaut & Portes, 2001) introduces some important conceptual refinements into this area. Their work rests on the premise that conventional theoretical models of acculturation and ethnic self-identification, based on earlier immigrant waves of Europeans and their descendents, do not apply to the experiences of the most recent immigrants (Portes & Zhou, 1993; Rumbaut & Portes, 2001). In their framework, there are marked variations in the acculturation processes of different groups that lead to very different developmental outcomes. This is in part due to the fact that recent newcomers who are overwhelmingly non-European (mostly from Latin America, the Caribbean, and Asia) are easily marked not only by language and culture but by non-European "racially" defined features. In addition, these newcomers are being incorporated into a more complex, post-industrialized society that requires higher educational attainment than earlier populations to live out of poverty. This cultural landscape is also not ruled solely by forced assimilation campaigns but by identity politics and ethnic revivals that are in part a product of the civil rights movement. Therefore, the processes of assimilation and its developmental consequences are not seen as linear, uniform, or straightforward, and they can be quite heterogeneous as a product of the interaction between the particular immigrant population and its context of reception.

Instead, the notion of segmented assimilation (see Portes & Zhou, 1993; Portes & Rumbaut, 2001) is introduced by these investigators as a way of capturing this emergent phenomenon, "in which outcomes vary across immigrant minorities and in which rapid integration and acceptance into the American mainstream represent just one of the possible alternatives" (Rumbaut & Portes, 2001, p. 6). The families' preimmigration and post-immigration characteristics, the context of their reception, generational differences, cultural and economic barriers, and the family and community resources to confront such barriers all contribute to the heterogeneity of outcomes. For example, families' social capital and their access to ethnic communities that are successful in accessing important resources to support their children's education are seen as critical (Portes, 1998; Portes & Rumbaut, 1990; Portes & Zhou, 1993; Zhou, 1997a). But, access to such an enclave will depend on past immigration policies and resettlement efforts, which will, in part, determine the size, placement, or even existence of enclaves available to an individual. For those without the support of ethnic enclaves, which provide hiring opportunities and a buffer from ethnic/racial discrimination in the larger workforce, pre-immigration capital, such as level of education will be far more important to an individual's assimilation pattern and economic success in the United States (Portes & Rumbaut, 1990).

In addition to family and ethnic community characteristics, the socioeconomic and ethnic composition of the schools also make a difference in education experiences of immigrants' children, since they serve as proxy for segregation[9] and the differential access to critical resources (García Coll et al., 1996; Portes & Hao, 2005; Portes & MacLeod, 1999). Given the many factors that contribute to such contextual processes, variability in developmental outcomes is more the norm than the exception. However, selective acculturation and fluent bilingualism are conceptualized in this framework as positive developmental outcomes (Portes & Rumbaut, 2001).

Similar conceptual sophistication is observed in the work by Suárez-Orozco and Suárez-Orozco (1995, 2001) in which the examination of developmental processes in immigrant contexts takes into account not only the structural properties of this context but also the interplay of these factors with the subjective experience of the individual. Like other theoretical frameworks that deal with developmental outcomes in minority children in the United States (García Coll et al., 1996), the premise of their work is that children of immigrants will experience not only structural barriers in accessing critical resources but also prejudice and discrimination, what they term "negative social mirroring." As Suárez-Orozco (2004), asserts, "The exclusion can take a structural form (when individuals are excluded from the opportunity structure) as well as an attitudinal form (in the form of disparagement and public hostility)." (p. 181) Thus, in their framework, a major task for these children is to forge an identity that enables them to withstand and overcome these barriers while developing positive adaptations. As in the work of Rumbaut and Portes, there are a variety of identities and adaptations that are possible, and these are highly context dependent and fluid (Suárez-Orozco & Todorova, 2003). Identity is not "achieved" but is a continuous process, which can range from and shift between rejection of their ethnicity and complete identification with it, independent of attitudes toward the mainstream culture. In several of their studies, transcultural/bicultural identities seem to lead to the most optimal developmental outcomes. In recent work exploring identification patterns in immigrant adolescents from 13 different countries, not only was "integration" of dominant and ethnic cultural identities the most common type of identification, but this type of identification was associated with better sociocultural and psychological adaptation (Phinney et al., 2006).

This type of identification may contribute to positive outcomes as it "does not require [the individual] to choose between cultures but rather allows them to incorporate traits of both cultures while fusing additive elements" (Suárez-Orozco, 2004, p. 192).

Biculturalism might be an adaptive response in children of immigrants given the complexity of growing up in a family which is not historically (or perhaps in the present) part of this country's mainstream culture. One of the striking aspects of the developmental niches of children of immigrants is the discontinuity between their worlds. There can be striking contrasts between their parent's original country and their own, the family left behind and their present household, the values espoused by their parents and those espoused by their peers and their school (Kasinitz et al., 2004; Suárez-Orozco & Suárez-Orozco, 2001). Not only do children of immigrants have to deal with structural and attitudinal barriers, but also they must adapt to multiple contexts that may have competing values and goals. The work by Phelan and colleagues (Phelan, Davidson, & Yu, 1993; 1998) introduced the notion of how adolescents from diverse backgrounds have to learn how to negotiate the multiple worlds of family, school, and peers and how individuals can differ in their success in doing so. Cooper and colleagues (Azmitia, Cooper, García, & Dunbar, 1996; Cooper, 1999; Cooper, Dominguez, & Rosas, 2005) have extended this work and conceptualized this particular developmental niche with what they term a "challenge" hypothesis, whereby the challenges of poverty, racism, and other obstacles can motivate children to succeed. Although many of their studies are with groups that are considered ethnic minorities in the United States, their framework seems rather pertinent to children of immigrants as well.

In this model, developmental successes can be a product of strong alliances across worlds (i.e., parents and teachers) that permit children to access and coordinate resources that will support them in overcoming the challenges they face. Both challenges and resources can be located in the multiple worlds composed of family, peers, schools, and communities. In addition, development is not seen as linear: Children might succeed at some points in their development and/or in some contexts and not others; the mobilization of resources will help children to "come back on track" when their developmental pathways deviate to less optimal outcomes. So the fact that a special after-school program might help a child not be retained in the present grade is seen as collaboration across worlds designed to keep a positive developmental pathway. And in the process, children will construct identities that will incorporate the dreams, values, and goals that they acquire throughout their adaptations to their multiple worlds.

Waters and colleagues (Kasinitz et al., 2004; Waters, 1990, 1994, 1999) also use many similar theoretical positions in their work on second-generation youth in NYC. They emphasize the importance of identity, the importance of the racial/ethnic characteristics of the group/individual in their acculturation and identity process, the need to learn how to navigate multiple worlds, and the fluidity of all these processes and their developmental consequences as a function of individual agency and particular contexts. In addition, a factor that is emphasized in their work more than in others is the strong influence of other ethnic minority groups in these processes. Most acts of prejudice and discrimination in daily life experienced by second-generation ethnic groups come from other ethnic minority groups and not from mainstream individuals or institutions. As a consequence their "choices" of identities are not only a function of ascribed identities by the white, mainstream culture but also the product of a social comparison process with other minorities and other generations of their own racial/ethnic group. As Waters (1994, p. 802) argues, "The daily discrimination that the youngsters experience, the type of racial socialization they receive at home, the understanding of race they develop in their peer group and at school affect strongly how they react to American society. The ways in which these youngsters experience and react to racial discrimination influences the type of racial/ethnic identity they develop." More recently, Kasinitz et al. (2004, p. 10) assert that "one cannot help but be impressed by the sheer complexity of the business of constructing racial/ethnic identities. The second generation lives in a world of new and shifting ethnic divisions of which outsiders may be only barely aware."

These identities have important developmental consequences since youth gravitate to groups with whom they share a common identity. Thus, the academic and long-term prospects in life for the second generation are determined not only by existing structural opportunities—the quality of schools and neighborhoods and job opportunities—but also by what groups they belong to, what these groups do (or don't do), and what resources they have access to because of their ethnicity (Portes, 1998; Portes & Hao, 2005; Portes & Rumbaut, 2001; Portes & Zhou, 1993; Rumbaut & Portes, 2001; Stepick et al., 2003). Mainstream institutions, especially educational institutions, are seen as "sorting mechanisms," but parents' and their children's individual agency, social capital, and networks react, respond, and try to modify them. Ethnic enclaves are seen as double-edged swords, which might in some cases enable and in other cases deny the immigrant family and their children access to critical resources. The child's emerging and shifting identity, which results in part from the ethnic socialization they receive from family, peers, and the institutions themselves, permeates not only their individual intentions, but also their success in navigating these complex mechanisms. Perhaps because so many immigrant families end up living in segregated neighborhoods with little chance for social mobility (and therefore their children end up going to similarly segregated and relatively deprived schools), the social comparisons with other ethnic groups and the ensuing identities and group memberships which deny or provide access to resources, become incredibly important for their life course.

Other scholars who champion the role of ethnic identity in other developmental outcomes with particular emphases in the consequences for the life course are Ogbu and colleagues (Fordham & Ogbu, 1986; Ogbu, 1991, 1994, 2004). These scholars coined the phrase "oppositional cultural frame of reference or identity" to refer to the system of attitudes and behaviors that members of certain minority groups (immigrant and native born) adopt as a reaction to their mode of incorporation, reception, and ensuing prejudice, and discrimination that they perceive coming from white Americans.[10] This system, which is quite established in adolescence, reflects the adaptation of oppressed groups to the competing demands of excelling academically to get ahead and yet feeling that doing so will in one way result in acculturation into a white cultural frame of reference or "acting white." Unfortunately, adopting an oppositional frame or identity leads students to disengage from the academic processes, and buy into a value system and kinship that disdains academic achievement. Fordham and Ogbu's argument is that this is the main mechanism behind the poor academic outcomes observed in some ethnic groups. This argument has been heavily contested by others but again highlights the gravity of understanding racial/ethnic identity processes to appreciate academic experiences and outcomes among racial minority youth.[11]

The final work to be mentioned here is the research by Fuligni (Fuligni, 2001; Fuligni, Alvarez, Bachman, & Ruble, 2005; Fuligni & Pedersen, 2002; Fuligni, Tseng, & Lam, 1999). In this framework, a child's sense of obligation toward his or her family is a distinctive feature of family relations in immigrant families and a particularly strong motivator for adolescent's achievement. Because of family cultural prescriptions, adaptations in a new culture, and motivations for migrating, adolescents in immigrant families integrate their role and membership in the family as a part of their sense of self. Importantly, that identification serves as a motivator. As Fuligni, Alvarez, et al. (2005) assert, "A sense of family obligation appears to enhance the youths' motivation to achieve by providing meaning and purpose behind their efforts to succeed in the American school system" (p. 265).

What are the commonalities among all the theoretical frameworks employed in recent scholarship on children of immigrants? Aside from emphasizing complexity, they consistently emphasize the role of ethnic/racial identities in conjunction with contextual factors (such as structural barriers) in permeating developmental outcomes.[12] As in other developmental frameworks, individual agency and context are crucial parts of any analysis. An emphasis on heterogeneity of outcomes is also present as the combination of these two sources of influence—individual and context—can lead to a myriad of developmental outcomes. There is also an emphasis on the fact that community environments can range from hostile to unconditionally supportive, but that most contexts, including peer relationships among immigrant group members, can bring both assets and vulnerabilities to individual children. Even acculturation itself can lead to a variety of developmental outcomes and can have very different pathways and consequences, depending on what cultural groups a child or family can acculturate to.

Empirical Evidence

Though most of the extant scholarship has been conducted with adolescents and young adults, we can use this work as a foundation to reach some conclusions about the developmental outcomes of children of immigrants. In general, these studies suggest that many children of immigrants are doing surprisingly well in spite of their families' relatively low status in the social stratification system of this country and their relative isolation and unfamiliarity with mainstream institutions. For example, youth from immigrant backgrounds are reported by their parents and by themselves to be physically healthier than youth from native-born populations (Harris, 1999; Hernandez, 1999; Mendoza & Dixon, 1999). This is in spite of the fact that they are less likely to have health insurance and make fewer visits to a regular healthcare provider (Brown, Wyn, Yu, Valenzuela, & Dong, 1999). Similar findings have been observed for mental health outcomes and services (Hough et al., 2002; Crosnoe, 2006a). Asian and Latino second-generation youth are more likely to have engaged in deviant behaviors than foreign-born youth (Bui & Thongniramol, 2005; Martinez & Valenzuela, 2006; Rumbaut,1997). Similarly, the rate of use of marijuana and alcohol has been found to be higher in U.S.-born than immigrant adolescents of comparable races/ethnicities (Blake et al., 2001). Delinquent behavior is also observed less frequently in Asian-American adolescents and young adults than in white Americans (Lorenzo, Frost, & Reinherz, 2000; Lorenzo, Pakiz, Reinherz, & Frost, 1995). White Americans also report more sexual partners by late adolescence/young adulthood than do Asian-Americans (McLaughlin, Chen, Greenberger, & Biermeier, 1997). Moreover, although they might feel less accepted and efficacious in school settings, first- and second-generation adolescents do not differ in psychological well-being from native-born youth (Chang, Morrissey, & Koplewicz, 1995; Chiu, Feldman, & Rosenthal, 1992; Harris, 1999; Kao, 1999). Finally, children of immigrants in general work harder and have higher grades in school, have higher math test scores, have more positive academic attitudes, and are less likely to drop out than their peers (e.g., Fuligni, 1997; Glick & White, 2004; Kao & Tienda, 1995; Portes & Rumbaut, 2001; Pong & Hao, 2007; Rumbaut, 1995, 2000; Schwartz & Stiefel, 2006; Suárez-Orozco & Suárez-Orozco, 1995, 2001).

However, there are several caveats to these generalizations. First, these findings vary dramatically by immigrant group, since among panethnic categories such as "Asian," there is wide variability in outcomes (Hernandez, 2004; Hernandez & Charney, 1998; Kao, 1999; Rumbaut, 1994a, 1995; Rumbaut & Portes, 2001). In addition, the processes by which some groups succeed and others do not are still not well understood. Nevertheless, the circumstances of departure and arrival, the actual immigration processes, and the particular immigrant group's position on a continuum of racialized and ethnic realities in the United States have been posed as important determinants for children's development (Portes & Rumbaut, 2001; Rumbaut, 1997; Suárez-Orozco & Suárez-Orozco, 1995; Waters, 1990, 1999).

In addition, not all adolescents from immigrant backgrounds succeed in school, even if broad ethnic groups appear to do so, on average. Several studies have found that the more acculturated adolescents are, the more negative are their attitudes toward school and the lower their academic achievement (Fuligni, 1997; Portes & Rumbaut, 2001; Rumbaut & Portes, 2001; Suárez-Orozco & Suárez-Orozco, 1995). In addition, with more acculturation, the physical and mental health outcomes worsen, and engagement in risky behaviors becomes more likely[13] (Cachelin, Weiss, & Garbanati, 2003; Harker, 2001; Harris, 1999; Kaplan, Erickson, & Juarez-Reyes, 2002; McQueen, Getz, & Bray, 2003; Pumariega, 1986; Rumbaut, 1997). Phrases like "oppositional" or "adversarial identities" are used to describe adaptations that children of immigrants might take on as they progress through school especially during adolescence (Ogbu & Simmons, 1998; Portes, 1996; Suárez-Orozco & Suárez-Orozco, 2001). These oppositional ethnic identities have been associated with lower academic achievement among children of immigrants (Fuligni, 1997; Kao & Tienda, 1995; Ogbu & Simons, 1998; Rumbaut & Portes, 2001; Suárez-Orozco & Suárez-Orozco, 1995, 2001). Finally, consistent gender differences in educational outcomes are found for children of immigrants as well. In general, immigrant girls tend to outperform immigrant boys in academic endeavors as measured by attitudes, grades, and graduation rates (Portes & Rumbaut, 2001; Suárez-Orozco & Qin-Hilliard, 2004; Waters, 1996). Thus, nationality and other sources of individual differences such as acculturation, ethnic identity, and gender have been identified as important correlates of other developmental outcomes, though the processes behind these mechanisms are barely understood.

The variability in outcomes and explanatory factors suggest the following series of questions: When and under which circumstances do children of immigrants form and maintain positive attitudes toward school and themselves as students? Why do some immigrant children succeed academically while others, in the same schools, do not? Are there particular child, family, school, and/or community characteristics that support more positive or different adaptations? As in any other developmental stage, there are some social and psychological processes that are more salient than others, with strong implications for later developmental outcomes. Given our studies of children of immigrants, we were particularly interested in examining academic pathways and early ethnic and racial identity development. Chapter 3 aims to establish the importance of understanding these processes in our populations. Given the paucity of research in middle childhood and the limitations of the extant knowledge of the developmental outcomes of children of immigrants, the need for scholarship in this area is imperative. This necessity is compounded by the growth of this population and thus the pressing need for evidence-based practices and policies to deal effectively with the unique circumstances of these populations.

3 ⊞

The Developmental Tasks of Middle Childhood

To begin to capture the complex contextual influences on children of immigrants' identity development and academic pathways, we have chosen to focus our studies on the period of development often referred to as "middle childhood." This period, ranging roughly between the ages of 6 and 12 years, is a crucial time in children's development (Eccles, 1999; Huston & Ripke, 2006). Yet, most of the literature has tended to neglect this developmental period. We know a fair amount about the first 3 years of life, about preschoolers, and about adolescents (unfortunately, in the latter stage, mostly about their problems), but little about the normative processes in middle childhood. Before we could begin our studies, then, we needed to build a thorough understanding of what developmental processes and milestones are currently known to be important to children of this age and consider how to apply these past developmental studies to our research with children of immigrants.

Why is increasing our knowledge about middle childhood important? We contend that pathways that are created, initiated, or maintained during middle childhood put children onto certain life trajectories and not others. Many life course research projects start such analyses in adolescence, since trajectories and decisions made in that developmental period (i.e., continue education, start work, start parenthood, etc.) are clearly implicated for later life trajectories (e.g., MacMillan & Eliason, 2003). In contrast, we propose that patterns established and decisions made in middle childhood are just as critical in determining later outcomes. This is, in considerable part, because it is during middle childhood (in contemporary American society, and in many others) that children pass from the nearly exclusive institutional charge of their family to a set of social arrangements in which families share responsibility for their child with schools (most prominently), churches, juvenile justice agencies, and the manifold voluntary organizations who seek to serve children by their own guiding principles.

As such, middle childhood is universally characterized by children's first sustained encounters with different institutions and contexts outside of their family (Eccles, 1999). During infancy and the preschool years, children can be exposed to multiple caregivers or preschool teachers on a regular basis, and marked social class, racial, and ethnic differences are observed in the use of out-of-home day care and preschools (Flanagan & West, 2004). But by the age of six, all children, regardless of race/ethnicity or social class, have to attend school. Moreover, they have increasing roles in other social institutions (e.g., church or temple) and in out-of-school activities (e.g., organized sports), opening the windows to many possible regular interactions with others outside of their immediate family. Finally, in many of these arenas, parents are not expected to be present: Children are becoming their own agents. Therefore, it is during this period that children begin to navigate their own ways through societal structures, which, for children of immigrant backgrounds, can be quite distant from their home environments (Moll & Greenberg, 1992; Delgado-Gaitán, 1987) and which, increasingly as the children grow older, have their own rules for proper behavior, their own patterns of positive and negative sanction.

We therefore contend that context matters—that the tasks of middle childhood will be magnified, exacerbated, or ameliorated (and, indeed, are to some extent defined) by contextual influences and demands. From a developmental perspective, there are many social, emotional, and cognitive developmental tasks associated with middle childhood, all of which take place in the various social contexts noted above. We emphasize two tasks that are particularly salient to children of immigrants: the development of cultural[1] attitudes and identifications and of academic pathways. As we describe these tasks in detail, it is of great importance to keep in mind the variability of developmental contexts (e.g., the qualities of schools that differ by neighborhood) across the ethnic groups we are studying, as the characteristics of families, schools, and neighborhoods vary greatly among the participants in our investigation. Ethnic composition in neighborhoods, and thus schools, varied dramatically among the three groups. While the Portuguese children attended schools in which they were the ethnic and racial majority, Dominican and Cambodian youth attended schools that were ethnically diverse and had low SES. Differences in neighborhood and school context derive from differences both in immigration histories (refugee vs. immigrant status and the ability to join an ethnic enclave) and in human capital (where families could afford to live).

⠃ Cultural Attitudes and Identifications

As posited in the previous chapter, the "new" immigration waves consist primarily of people who are not, not even eventually,[2] considered "Caucasian," "white," and/or Anglo-Saxon and who are easily marked not only by their cultural traits (e.g., language, religion, etc.), as earlier waves were, but by "racialized nonwhite" characteristics such as skin color and facial features. In this country, children of immigrants become members of ethnic groups, as ethnicity is something ascribed by the receiving community (Portes & Rumbaut, 2001). For example, typical American ethnic/racial categories such as "Asians" or "Latinos" do not make sense to recent arrivals of these countries. They think of themselves, instead, in terms of nationalities (e.g., Vietnamese, Argentinean, etc.) as they come to think of themselves in terms that refer to categories beyond their own families. But these categories are readily available to the majority to identify such groups, although such categories change over time and across contexts (Cooper et al , 2005).

So how do children develop *cultural attitudes and identifications*? We know from previous research that as early as 3 years of age, children in the United States can not only make categorical distinctions based on racialized features, but they also know the social valence of such categories (i.e., Bigler & Liben, 1993; Clark & Clark, 1947; Katz & Kofkin, 1997; Hirschfeld, 1995), although wide individual and group differences are observed. In addition, we also know that knowledge of the social construction and valence of a category like male or female does not necessarily imply internalization of membership in that category as part of their own identity (see Ruble et al., 2004). We now know that several steps are necessary to form stable identities: Initially the child must be *aware* of the category as distinct from others; then she or he must be able to *identify* himself or herself and others as members of the category; then there has to develop for him or her *stability* of the category membership over time; finally, there is typically some *consistency* of category membership across superficial transformations, such as immediate social context (e.g., from home to school). Forming a stable identity through active exploration of roles and group membership is important for psychological well-being and stability. Beyond simply formation, it is important to understand whether the various aspects of social identities are stably evaluated as positive and negative (*valence*) and whether it is *salient* (i.e., important) and *central* (i.e., more important or as important as other identities) to the self-concept.

Ethnic/Racial Identity

In contrast to the amount of research in the development of gender identity (see Ruble, Martin, & Berenbaum, 2006, for a review), there is relatively little research regarding ethnic/racial identity development prior to adolescence (see Phinney, 1990, for a review of the literature during adolescence). This is perhaps a function of the fact that most theoretical models of ethnic/racial identity emphasize its development during adolescence and adulthood (e.g., Cross, 1995; Helms, 1995; Phinney, 1993), following the earlier theorists who place overall identity formation as one of the main developmental tasks of adolescence (e.g., Erickson, 1963). In both the theoretical and empirical literature, achieving a stable and positive ethnic/racial identity is critical for overall psychological well-being.

But scholars who have conducted ethnic/racial identity research with children during early and middle childhood, as well as those who have investigated the development of other social identities during the middle childhood period (including gender identity, see Ruble et al., 2004), have found early signs of "identity work" (Thorne, 2005). Children are actively trying to make sense of who they are in terms of race, ethnicity, and culture and of how they feel and act accordingly, much earlier than we had previously imagined. For example, Connolly (1998) found that 5- to 6-year-olds discuss race, gender, and other social groupings in a sophisticated manner, actively negotiating and renegotiating their identities as in the following example (p. 110):

Jordan: I'm West Indian—I'm English and I'm half-White, ain't I?

Paul: Yeah, but then if you say that d'you know what?— you're an *Indian*!

Jordan: No! . . . Are you still my friend, then?

Paul:	Not if you talk like India! No—talking like an Indian!
Jordan:	I bet I am!
Paul:	If you do, I'm not, we're not playin' with ya!
[Observer]:	Why's that, Paul? Don't you like. . .
Paul:	We don't like Indians!
[Observer]:	Why?
Paul:	We don't like Indian talkers!
[Observer]:	Why?
Jordan:	[*indignantly*] Well, I ain't a Indian!

In this example, Jordan demonstrates knowledge of his membership in several ethnic and racial groups. Importantly, we observe in this discourse a sort of negotiation demonstrating the importance of peer social interaction in shaping the valence that Jordan may attribute to his "Indian" identity. To maintain his friendship with Paul, Jordan rejects the "Indian" label that he initially uses to describe himself. We are only recently beginning to appreciate the ways in which children (and individuals in general) come to understand and ultimately accept and employ ethnic and racial identity labels. The dynamic roles of parent and peer cultural socialization (as exemplified in the exchange between Jordan and Paul above) are now considered extremely important to forming ethnic identity.

We are also learning more about the stages children go through to learn about ethnic and racial categories. In a literature review, Ruble et al. (2004) characterize the saliency of ethnic identity in middle childhood by noting "that identification with social groups, especially gender and ethnicity or race, is likely to be quite significant to children by middle childhood" (p. 63). Specifically, although children as early as 3 years of age can label racial groups and those between 4 and 5 years of age can use such labels to identify themselves and others (Morland, 1958; Ramsey, 1991), it is not until 7 or 8 years of age that they show not only awareness but also constancy[3] of identity. Starting in middle childhood, children can not only *identify* themselves with an ethnic/racial category, but they show increasing *stability* by inferring from prior experience that their (and others) membership in that category will not change over time, and they show constancy, by inferring that minimal perturbations (e.g., makeup, dressing, etc.) will not change that membership either (Aboud & Doyle, 1993; Ocampo, Knight, & Bernal, 1997). Also their explanations of why they are members of a particular ethnic/racial group get more complex and abstract over the period of middle childhood (Bernal et al., 1993). This increasing understanding and knowledge about one's ethnic and racial membership may be fostered by cultural socialization in the home. Children whose families engage in cultural socialization[4] have been shown to possess a greater knowledge of cultural traditions, show preference for ethnic behaviors, and have more salient and positive ethnic identities (for a review of the literature, see Hughes, Rodriguez, Smith, Johnson, & Stevenson, 2006).

What theoretical frameworks guide the research on early ethnic/racial identity development? Most investigators combine a social identity theory approach (i.e., Tajfel & Turner, 1979) with a cognitive developmental framework (Kohlberg, 1969). In other words, investigators conceive of collective identities as serving a number of different purposes (feelings of inclusion, belonging, differentiation, and bases for social comparison) that have significant interpersonal and personal consequences (Ruble et al., 2004). They also suggest that cognitive developmental skills account for at least part of age cohort and individual differences observed in these processes.[5]

The clearest example of such a theoretical model is presented by Bernal and colleagues (Bernal & Knight, 1997; Knight et al., 1993). In this model (see Figure 3.1), socialization forces both within and outside the family are thought as important influences on the child' ethnic identity. However, these influences are moderated by the development

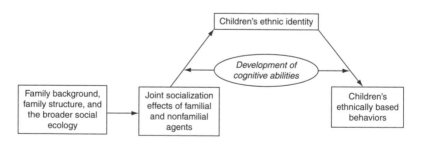

FIGURE 3.1.
A social cognitive model of the development of ethnic identity and behaviors among Mexican-American children.

Source: From García, Jorge G., and Maria Cecilia Zea. *Psychological Interventions and Research with Latino Populations,* published by Allyn and Bacon, Boston, MA. Copyright © 1997 by Pearson Education. By permission of the publisher.

of cognitive abilities such as abstract reasoning and multidimensional classification abilities. As cognitive abilities mature, the child's understanding of his or her own ethnic identity (and that of others) becomes more adultlike over time. Three stages are described (see Bernal, Knight, Garza, Ocampo, & Cota, 1990) by contemporary American scholars:

- Preschool: Where ethnic labeling is based on simple, concrete description of appearance, physical attributes, and behaviors; there is a lack of understanding of the complete meaning of ethnic labels, of ethnic constancy or behavioral preferences, or of the feelings associated with membership in a particular ethnic group.
- Early school level (6–8 years of age): where ethnic labels have more complete meaning and children have a rudimentary understanding of the constancy of their own ethnicity and the behavioral consequences of ethnic membership.
- Later school level (8–10 year olds): where there is a higher percentage of correct self-identification, ethnic constancy, and higher ethnic knowledge, preferences, and behaviors.

There are several important implications of these theoretical models and the ensuing empirical work in the development of ethnic/racial identity during childhood, adolescence, and adulthood.[6] One is the notion that children, adolescents, and adults achieve a more advanced state or stage in their development of an ethnic identity with the passage of time. Although most researchers do acknowledge great individual variability in terms of when the stages are achieved, there is this embedded notion of "progression" toward a "better" (i.e., more nearly adultlike) end point, from which there is perhaps no turning back. Reversals to earlier stages or states are thought of as regressions or instability in the system in the midst of a transition. Fluidity and instability of identity is considered in its extremes even pathological. The notion of the culmination of development into one right, final identity is quite strong in this tradition.

In contrast, other more sociological or social psychological traditions incorporate notions of multiple identities (Akiba, Szalacha, & García Coll, 2004), biculturalism (LaFromboise, Coleman, & Gerton, 1993), hybridity (Walker, 2001), situationality (Bailey, 2002) and the concept of multiple "right" choices with perhaps differential consequences for the individual (Rumbaut, 1994a; Waters, 1990). These frameworks do not emphasize the attainment of a stage or of a "correct" identity but the fluidity of these identifications as a function of the social historical context (i.e., pre–civil rights era) and of more immediate contexts (i.e., with your same-ethnicity peers vs. others). As Phoenix (1998) asserts, "There is widespread agreement [which we think is a bit of an exaggeration on Phoenix's part] that identities are plural and intersecting, rather than singular; decentered, rather than organized around a core; dynamic, rather than statistic; historically located, rather than timeless; relational and contingent, rather than absolute; productive of diverse subjectivities and potentially contradictory" (pp. 860–861).

The research presented here is guided by a combination of the various traditions of study of ethnic/racial identity. It assumes that ethnic identity in middle childhood is a work in progress and that the inclusion of children assessed both longitudinally and at different ages will give us a sense of both stability and change in the phenomena during middle childhood. Making predictions based on the developmental literature, we hypothesized that younger children would differ from older children in that they would be less "accurate" in their choices of labels that will apply to them. We also hypothesized that their explanations of why they selected the labels they did would increase in complexity and abstraction with age. For example, older children were more likely to explain to us their family heritage and attribute labels to cultural routines or visits to the family's culture of origin, whereas younger children were more likely to provide ambiguous or seemingly unrelated answers. (For example, one ambiguous answer by a younger child to the question, "Why did you select this label?" was, "I have a horse.") Also, following developmental predictions, we were expecting that these identity choices were going to be related to ethnic and racial in- and out-group social preferences.

Following nondevelopmental traditions, we allowed children to select from a multitude of possible identities (many "right" and many "wrong"). We expected that children would be able to choose multiple labels and multiple identities (as role, gender, etc.) as their own. We also explored their projected affective states as a function of the situation and with people "like them" or "unlike them" (i.e., in the classroom, the playground, the lunch room, in the family, etc.), expecting that both situational and relational context would have an impact on their affective state. Finally, given the importance of the larger sociocultural and historical context, we are not only contributing to the growing literature that places identity work earlier than adolescence but we are studying these processes in three distinct immigrant groups who differ dramatically in their context of immigration and their ascribed ethnicities. We also add to the equation the ethnic/racial composition of their neighborhood of residence and their school, two other contexts that have been hypothesized as important for the development of academic competencies.

Finally, there is a whole other set of literature that relates ethnic/racial identity with various aspects of school performance. As described above, there are major developmental changes in ethnic identity processes, including self-evaluations (in-group preferences and self-esteem), motivations (information seeking and personal choices), and interpersonal (out group) preferences (see Ruble et al., 2004). In various theoretical perspectives, various aspects of ethnic identity development have been associated with academic pathways during adolescence (Ogbu, 1987; Ogbu & Simmons, 1998; Spencer, 1999) and college (Steele, 1997). Specifically, it has been posited that social identities may contribute to or hinder academic performance (Bernal, Saenz, & Knight, 1995; Okagaki, 2001). For example, Rumbaut (1994a) found that middle schoolers (with at least one immigrant parent) who identified themselves as American (rather than hyphenated American or in terms of parents' national origin) had more mediocre academic performance and reported less academic effort. Fordham and Ogbu, contrastingly, have suggested that a "raceless" identity is developed by many high-achieving African-Americans (Fordham, 1988), while others may develop an "oppositional identity" that is related to poor academic performance (Fordham & Ogbu, 1986; Ogbu, 1987, 2004). Although the "acting white hypothesis" has been contested (e.g., Arroyo & Zigler, 1995; Ainsworth-Darnell & Downey, 1998; Spencer, Noll, Stoltzfus, & Harpalani, 2001), we explore how children's attitudes toward school and academic achievement are related to their evolving ethnic identity.

In-Group and Out-Group Preferences

So middle childhood becomes the time when children are beginning to seriously explore the meaning, for their own lives, of the notion of membership in racially/culturally/ethnically defined groups, the valence of such membership for themselves and others, and the implication of such membership for interactions and relationships with members of groups. For most children, this is not only because of cognitive advances but also because of changes in their social contexts (Ruble et al., 2004). As they navigate through different worlds, such as schools and after-school programs (Bigler, Jones, & Lobliner, 1997; Cooper, Jackson, Azmitia, &

Lopez, 1998), children in middle childhood increase their awareness and probability of encounters with members of other ethnic/racial groups (Aboud & Doyle, 1993; Ruble et al., 2004). These novel school experiences introduce to the child new ways of behaving and thinking about race and ethnicity, socialization which had largely taken place within the family context earlier in childhood (Hughes & Chen, 1997; Hughes et al., 2006; Knight, Bernal, Cota et al., 1993; Knight, Cota, & Bernal, 1993; Knight, Bernal, Cota, Garza, & Ocampo, 1993). Moreover, as children enter middle childhood, they are becoming increasingly more sensitive to the societal meaning and to the implications of specific ethnic and racial labels, and therefore, their group memberships have more functional consequences not only for their own identity formation and behaviors but for the ways in which they evaluate other groups (Ruble et al., 2004). Previous studies have shown that there are links among the qualities of ethnic/racial identities and adolescents' social preferences and biases (Aboud, 2003; Kinket & Verkuyten, 1997).

So ethnic identity has important implications for other behavioral, cognitive, and affective systems, such as social interactions and perceptions of self and others. In particular, changes with age in attitudes toward one's own, and, derivatively, other groups are related to the child's evolving conceptions of whether or not they belong to certain groups. Grouped under the concepts of in-group and out-group preferences, these attitudes include both positive (favoritism, attachment) and negative attitudes (prejudices) toward their own group and toward members of other groups. These attitudes can be accompanied by behaviors of inclusion, exclusion, and discrimination. The leading theory in this field, social identity theory (e.g., Tajfel, 1978; Tajfel & Turner, 1979; Turner, 1982), proposed that a comparative/competitive motivation leads people (namely adults) to maximally evaluate differences between their own groups and others. Tajfel (1978) argued that children must be able to categorize ethnic/racial groups and then be able to identify with one (establish some sort of ethnic identity) in order to show both in-group and out-group attitudes. The motivation underlying these perceptions and attitudes is to enhance the child's own self-esteem by belonging to a comparatively superior group. This is accomplished by maximally differentiating groups leading to optimally distinct grouping and self-identification with one group. In other words, this theory posits that increased perception of between-group differences and within-group similarity is accompanied with more in-group preference and more out-group prejudice and vice versa.

The early work of Clark and Clark (1939; 1947) with black children showing preferences for white dolls (which has been replicated with other minority groups[7]) was interpreted within this theoretical stance. Preference for the white dolls was interpreted as indicating self-hate or deprecation in light of the negative comparison with the dominant out group. More recent studies have also shown that as early as 3 years of age, we can find in-group preference and out-group prejudices in white children (Aboud, 1988; Bigler & Liben, 1993; Doyle & Aboud, 1995; Katz, 1983, 2003; Katz & Kofkin, 1997; Yee & Brown, 1992). Though most of this social psychology research has been conducted with adults, we also know through experimental manipulations that children between the ages of 6 and 11 who are randomly assigned to arbitrary group memberships display in-group favoritism (Bigler, Brown, & Markell, 2001; Bigler, Jones, & Lobliner, 1997; Nesdale & Flesser, 2001; Vaughan, Tajfel, & Williams, 1981). It is very important to note here that much of the past research regarding in- and out-group preferences have equated selecting or preferring an in-group member to being biased (or prejudiced) against an out-group member. Finally, we know that certain categories (e.g., gender, race) have more perceptually salient criteria if category membership is thought of as having a biological basis (Hirschfeld, 1996; Bigler, 1995) and that white children in the United States hold more biases than minority children (Katz, 2003) even if some minority groups, such as African-American children, are more aware of race than their majority peers (Ruble et al., 2004).

As mentioned above, others have questioned the reciprocal association posited between in-group and out-group preferences. Several authors (Aboud, 2003; Brewer, 1999, 2001; Cameron, Alvarez, Ruble, & Fuligni, 2001) have forcefully argued that it is important to differentiate in-group preference from out-group prejudices or out-group preference from lowered in-group evaluations (Crocker & Major, 1989; Rosenberg & Simmons, 1971; Tropp & Wright, 2003). This is important because developmentally these processes might or might not be related: Children might first prefer their own groups without disliking out groups (Aboud, 2003). For example, there is evidence that in-group preference does not automatically lead to negative attitudes toward the out group (Aboud, 2003; Nesdale & Flesser, 2001) and that the association might be a function of the amount of intergroup contact (Aboud, 2003). In addition, there is evidence that the relationships between in-group and out-group preferences might differ as a function of group status and social conditions (Ruble et al., 2004). In-group preferences seemed to be stronger and appear earlier in white or dominant groups than in minority groups (Aboud & Skerry, 1984; Corenblum & Wilson, 1982; Rice, Ruiz, & Padilla, 1974; Doyle & Aboud, 1995; Morland & Hwang, 1981; Newman, Liss, & Sherman, 1983; Spencer & Markstrom, 1990). In-group and out-group preferences are also sensitive to school ethnic/racial composition (Aboud, 2003; Carlson, Wilson, & Hargrave, 2003; Joyner & Kao, 2000), to functional use by adults (Bigler, 1995; Bigler et al., 1997), to group size (Brown & Bigler, 2002), and to cultural constructions of self and others (Tropp & Wright, 2003). Finally, there is evidence that preference or lack of negative appraisal of the out group does not translate into either self-hate or negative attitudes toward the in group among contemporary Americans (Spencer, 1984; Tropp & Wright, 2003).

Finally, there seem to be age differences in the intensity of these in-group and out-group feelings and attitudes. In-group preference seems to develop earlier and stronger than out-group attitudes (Aboud, 2003). It also appears that these developmental processes might be curvilinear, meaning that they start by age 3 and might peak at age 7–8 and thereafter diminish (Yee & Brown, 1992; Doyle & Aboud, 1995). Other studies have observed a rise of positive out-group attitudes in middle childhood (Bigler & Liben, 1993; Clark, Hocevar, & Dembo, 1980), and these attitudes are associated with more balanced in-group attitudes.

Given the extant literature, we decided to measure in-group and out-group social preferences in two contexts: in school and at home. We asked children how they would feel interacting in a series of situations at schools (e.g., at lunch time, in the playground), and at home. Given the distinction between in-group and out-group preferences, we followed the recommendation by others to measure these processes separately from each other. As social preferences are often linked to social biases that in turn may lead to prejudiced behaviors, we also wanted to include in our study a series of interview questions that would ask children about their experiences with and perceptions of ethnic or racial discrimination.

⠃⠃ Perceptions of Discrimination

She should not treat me differently because I am Portuguese
Eight-year-old girl, child of Portuguese parents

So by middle childhood, children have developed awareness and, often, attitudes and feelings about their own race/ethnicity and that of others. Some of these developmental processes arise as early as 6 months of age (see Katz, 2003) but many more are still evolving and have been responsive to both internal cognitive processes and social circumstances. One such process that seems to initiate in middle childhood is that of perceiving discrimination based on these categories.

Discrimination refers to the directing of unfair actions or behaviors toward another individual solely because of his or her membership in a particular group. In other words, it is the enactment of prejudice or bias on the basis of group membership, making these attitudes and perceptions visible in the social environment. By middle childhood children may have witnessed many different types of discrimination: from a teacher neglecting to call on a child from a certain background to name calling and hostility toward a certain child or group on the playground. Discriminatory acts can range from mild to virulent and from subtle/ambiguous to clearly open and hostile (Brown & Bigler, 2004).

Important to our research is not simply a child's exposure to acts of discrimination, but rather how children understand those acts. Perceptions of discrimination[8] refer to "how and when children come to understand that they or other individuals may be the target of discrimination within a situation" rather than "the *objective* experiences of being the target of discrimination" (Brown & Bigler, 2005, p. 533). So you might perceive a discriminatory act as such or not; you can also perceive discrimination toward others, even members of your own group, even if you have not experienced direct discrimination (Taylor, Wright, & Porter, 1993; Verkuyten, 1998; 2002). Member of majority groups can perceive discrimination toward others, especially those of different nationalities, ethnicities, and race, even if they have never experienced discrimination themselves. In both minority and majority populations, individuals are more likely to perceive discrimination in a situation involving other members of the group than in a situation involving themselves (Verkuyten, 2002). This discrepancy between perceptions of discrimination toward others versus discrimination toward oneself has been documented in both children and adults; such a discrepancy may be a sort of protective response, guarding an individual from the negative feelings associated with seeing oneself as a victim of discrimination (Brown & Bigler, 2005). For this reason, in our research, children were asked to interpret a *fictional* interaction between individuals in a school contexts; this allowed children to interpret scenarios that were likely familiar to them in their day-to-day environment (i.e., a teacher refusing to call on a student in the classroom) without having to comment on their own treatment or perceived social evaluation.

Perceptions of discrimination are related to other aspects of cultural attitudes and identification. Higher ethnic identity exploration and more negative attitudes toward out groups have been associated with perceiving more discrimination, although a stronger sense of belonging to one's own group was associated with more positive attitudes and these were related to less perceived discrimination toward out groups (Romero & Roberts, 1998). (One could imagine the inclination to discriminate proceeding from a sense of having oneself been discriminated against, or vice versa.) Higher ethnic centrality is related to less perceived discrimination to both group and self, but only in boys (Verkuyten, 2002). Ethnic self-esteem has been found to be related negatively to perceptions of discrimination (Verkuyten, 1998), such that the worse a person feels about their ethnic identity, the more the individual feels they have been the victim of discrimination. However, several theorists have warned us (e.g., Cross, 1991; Phinney, 1989) that these associations might not be in place until late adolescence, as other studies have failed to find associations between various aspects of ethnic identity and perceived discrimination in middle adolescence (Phinney, Madden, & Santos, 1998; Verkuyten, 2003; Verkuyten & Brug, 2002). In addition, individuals in the United States who speak less English and have spent less time in the United States perceive more discrimination (Felix-Ortiz, Newcomb, & Myers, 1994; Romero & Roberts, 1998) Accordingly, type of ethnic identification is also associated with levels of perceived discrimination: Identifying as "American" is associated with the lowest levels of perceived discrimination, while identifying with a national label is associated with the highest, and adolescents who identify with the label "black" have far higher proportions of perceived discrimination than those who identify as "Hispanic" or "Asian" (Rumbaut, 2005).

We know that by the age of 10, most children (92%) attribute social behaviors such as name calling, unequal sharing of goods, and social exclusion to being a member of a particular ethnic or racial group (Verkuyten, Kinket, & van der Wielen, 1997). Studies of minority children 10 years and older and adolescents consistently report instances of discrimination with verbal insults and slurs, suspicion of wrongdoing, or social exclusion as the most frequent ones (Fisher, Wallace, & Fenton, 2000; Rumbaut, 1994a; Quintana, 1998; Simons et al, 2002; Wong, Eccles, & Sameroff, 2003). These experiences are with adults and peers in both public places and in educational settings, although clear variations are perceived depending on national origin (i.e., African-American and Latinos perceive more institutional racism, but Asian students perceive the most peer discrimination (Fisher et al., 2000)). There seems to be a trend of increasing perceptions of discrimination with age although there is only one longitudinal study (Rumbaut, 2005), so most of the evidence is based on cross-sectional studies (e.g., Romero & Roberts, 1998; Szalacha et al., 2003). In Szalacha's work with Puerto Rican youth, while only 12% of 6- to 8-year-olds perceived discrimination directed toward themselves, 49% of 13- to 14-year-olds did. In Rumbaut's study (2005), adolescents' experiences of discrimination increased for all groups; for example, while 68% of those self-identified as "black" perceived discrimination in the first year of assessment, 80% of this group perceived discrimination three years later.

So the question is how early do children start perceiving discrimination based on their race/ethnicity? We know that other types of perceptions of discrimination, such as those based on gender, are found as early as age 5; children at this age can attribute teacher's behavior to discrimination, although these attributions are more infrequent and inconsistent than those observed in 10-year-olds (Brown & Bigler, 2004). Unlike perceptions of gender bias which appear early in childhood, perceptions of discrimination based on race and ethnicity emerge in middle childhood. For example, Hughes and Johnson (2001) found that even if third through fifth graders are aware of being treated unfairly by peers, only 12% attributed race/skin color as the cause. Similarly, in the study by Szalacha et al. (2003), where children were asked specifically if they had been treated badly *because* of there ethnicity, only 12% of first through third Puerto Rican graders reported that they had. In the present study, we attempted to measure perceptions of discrimination against the in group in addition to perceptions of discrimination against the self.

So why is it important to study perceived discrimination in middle childhood? Aside from the fact that this is the period in which these perceptions initiate, perceptions of discriminations have traditionally been tied up with various outcomes in adolescence and middle childhood including self-esteem, depression, and academic adjustment (Erkut, Szalacha, Alarcon, & García Coll, 1999; Fisher et al, 2000; Jasinskaja-Lahti & Liebkind, 2001; Liebkind, Jasinskaja-Lahti, & Solheim, 2004; Patchen, 1982; Rumbaut, 1994a; Verkuyten, 1998). For example, in the study by Szalacha et al, 2003, individuals who reported perceived discrimination, even if they are a small percentage of the population of first to third graders studied, reported higher levels of depression, stress, and behavioral problems, as well as lower global self-esteem.

In our three-group developmental study, we were interested in assessing perceptions of discrimination in a series of hypothetical situations that involved children of the same immigrant group as the respondent. We have data not only across the three immigrant groups but also in two consecutive years to assess it longitudinally. Finally since academic performance is one of our ultimate areas of interest, we assessed the relationship between perceptions of discrimination and academic outcomes.

⁑ The Beginnings of Academic Pathways

> Typically, children enter the middle-childhood years very optimistic about their ability to master a wide array of tasks and activities, including their school work.. ... By age 10 however, children are typically far less optimistic and there is much stronger relation between their self-ratings and their actual performance ... this decline ... continues to adolescence, when it may lead students to avoid certain courses or to withdraw from school altogether
>
> (Eccles, 1999, p. 35).

As indicated in the previous section, there is a universal experience in middle childhood for children in the United States: Regardless of geographic location, class, or ethnicity, children now spend a large percentage of their day and year in school. Rather than working in apprenticeship positions among their same-gender elders as observed in some other historical and current cultures (Rogoff, 1990, 2003), children in our culture are expected to acquire many of the basic tools to succeed in their adult life in schools amongst teachers and peers.

Two processes are of interest to us concerning children's developmental tasks during middle childhood in schools: One is the formation of positive attitudes toward school (which are, it is hoped, associated with behaviors) that will facilitate learning. The other are standard indicators of actual academic achievement, measured through grades, teacher reports, and standard test scores. We consider both to be critical in maintaining positive academic pathways through middle childhood, which with time become predictive of long-term academic outcomes.

Research has shown that academic attitudes and pathways that take shape in elementary grades are not only important contributors to academic achievement in this particular developmental period but continue to contribute to academic attainment in middle school and beyond (Dauber, Alexander, & Entwistle, 1996; Alexander et al., 1997). We also know that the mastery of many of the basic skills of reading, writing, and numeracy acquired during the elementary years constitute the building blocks for lifelong achievement (Alexander & Entwistle, 1988; Alexander, Entwistle, & Horsey, 1997; Marks, Fleming, Long, & McMillan, 2000; Marks, McMillan, & Hillman, 2001). Thus, the development of positive attitudes toward school and positive school-based achievement during middle childhood can have implications for these children's future life trajectories.

What set of attitudes are critical to learning in school? Children at this age are developing a sense of competence, that is, they are forming ideas about their own abilities, the domains of accomplishment they value, and the likelihood of doing well in these domains (Eccles, 1999; Entwistle, Alexander, Pallas, & Cadigan, 1987; Skaalvik & Hagtvet, 1990). They also need to feel engaged in the process of learning in the classroom, to adopt the values of schools (such as believing that following rules and performing well in school are important personal goals), to have high aspirations and expectations of themselves now and into the future, and to feel like others are supportive of those goals.

These attitudes are thought of as critical to children's engagement in school, which in turn is one possible contributor to student academic achievement and behaviors in the classroom (Schmader, Major, & Gramzow, 2001). School engagement has been identified as a crucial variable in maintaining a high level of academic achievement (Connell, Spencer, & Aber, 1994; Peel, Powell, & O'Donnel, 1997; Steinberg, Lamborn, Dornbusch, & Darling, 1992). These findings have been replicated with adolescents from immigrant families (Fuligni, 1997).

Historically, the nature and purpose of schooling has changed, and thus intellectual involvement and investment are now essential ingredients for problem solving, analyses, and other higher level cognitive processes that are necessary for becoming an effective learner (Blumenfeld et al., 2005). Engagement is expected to be a function of both child characteristics and contextual influences, including support from adults at home and in school (Blumenfeld et al., 2005; Connell et al., 1994).

A widely replicated finding is the decrease of engagement as children enter higher grades in school (Eccles, 1999). Specifically, a decrease in engagement has been observed between third and fourth grade, partly attributed to increased level of difficulty in the curriculum, higher teacher expectations, and more social comparison with peers (Blumenfeld et al., 2005). This drop in engagement continues through middle school and beyond (Graham, 2000; Seidman, Aber, Allen, & French, 1996; Vandivere, Gallagher, & Moore, 2004).

What contributes to children's engagement in school? One contributor to school engagement that has been widely documented is the student's perceptions of his or her own teachers. Student's perceptions of teachers include dimensions such as teachers' respect, caring, and support for students. Several studies have documented how students who perceive their teachers positively in these dimensions tend to be more academically and socially engaged, as measured by both students and teacher reports (Furrer & Skinner, 2003; Goodenow, 1993; Skinner & Belmont, 1993; Mansfield, 2001; Roesser, Midgley, & Urdan, 1996; Ryan & Patrick, 2001; Wentzel, 1994, 1997, 1998; Wentzel & Wigfield, 1998). In addition, these associations have been found in both elementary and middle school, even though children report that teachers are less nurturing in the upper grades (Feldlaufer, Midgley, & Eccles, 1988; Midgley, Feldlaufer, & Eccles, 1989). Finally, studies have shown the predictive power of teacher perceptions not only in academic engagement but also in academic achievement (Furrer & Skinner, 2003; Muller, 2001; Roeser et al., 1996). Students who perceive their teachers as more caring and supportive tend to not only be more engaged in school but also have better grades at the present and in the future.

Children's own and their perception of others' aspirations and expectations for their success in school now and in the future (especially from parents and peers) have also been identified as contributors to school engagement and positive academic outcomes. Children's own expectations and aspirations of their present and future scholastic competencies have been associated with school outcomes (Asakawa, 2001; Ensminger & Slusarcick, 1992; Haller & Portes, 1973; Kim, 2002). Children's perceptions of parents' and peers' expectations ("My parents expect me to do well in school"; "My friends want me to do well in school") are also found to be positive predictors of academic attitudes and outcomes (Gill & Reynolds, 1999; Wentzel, 1998). These associations seem to be stronger in children from diverse backgrounds or less acculturated backgrounds where family obligations are seeing as a strong motivation in school achievement (Asakawa, 2001; Au & Harackiewicz, 1986; Canniff, 2001; Fuligni, 1997, 2001b).

Finally, another possible contributor for children of color in the United States, inclusive of children from immigrant backgrounds, is the child's increasing perception of racism in his or her environment. Experiences of exclusion, devaluation, invisibility, discrimination, and racism are considered important potential sources of influence on children's interactions and reactions to "mainstream" institutions, including schools (Szalacha et al., 2003). Previous studies have found that as early as fourth grade and throughout their school years, including college, students who perceive racially motivated barriers affecting their own group report being less engaged in school (Okagaki, Frensch, & Dodson, 1996; Schmader et al., 2001). During later grades, especially in high school, perception or awareness of racism has been identified as a major obstacle for the engagement of minority students—in both the United States and Europe—in academic processes that would lead to positive outcomes (Fordham & Ogbu, 1986; Ogbu, 1991; Verkuyten & Brug, 2003; Verkuyten & Thijs, 2004)

School attitudes and academic achievement in elementary school are good predictors of children's long-term academic achievement (Skinner, Zimmer-Gembeck, M. J., & Connell, 1998) and their eventual completion of school (Connell et al., 1994). Moreover, as the literature shows, children's perceptions of their own competencies and of the perceptions of their teachers, families, and peers are implicated in children's engagement and academic outcomes in school. To date, no study has studied both academic attitudes and outcomes in depth before the onset of adolescence amongst children of immigrants. We will document longitudinally how academic attitudes and outcomes evolve over time as a function of child, family, and school characteristics and will test for the mediating role of ethnic identity and perception of racism in such outcomes.

▪▪ The contexts of middle childhood

Following developmental frameworks that emphasize the role not only of the individual child but of contextual circumstances (see description of theoretical frameworks, Chapter 1), our research looks at the development of ethnic identity and school attitudes and achievement as a function of several contextual influences. The context of immigration is a major source of influence: understanding what immigrant families bring and maintain, how they are received, and how they use resources to promote positive developmental outcomes in their children are fundamental questions that give origin to this work.

In particular, there is literature to support that family academic socialization amongst immigrant families is a major influence on children's attitudes and success in school (Asakawa, 2001; Bempechat, Graham, & Jimenez, 1999; Carter & Wojtkiewicz, 2000; Chao, 2000; Shumow & Miller, 2001). Although most immigrant parents have high aspirations and recognize the importance of their children's success in school, many do not engage in the educational activities that are characteristic of middle class, mainstream families (Asakawa, 2001; Suárez-Orozco, & Suárez-Orozco, 2001; Delgado-Gaitán, 1992). Immigrant parents might not, for example, see themselves as their children's primary teacher, so they might not engage in formal learning strategies such as teaching letters or numbers, reading books together or after-school entry, been part of the Parent Teacher Organization, checking homework, or becoming strong educational advocates for their children.

These academic socialization patterns are not only due to the lack of familiarity with the educational system in this country. Parents of different ethnic groups also differ in beliefs about child rearing, expectations of their children's schooling, and in self-reported and observed parenting strategies around teaching and academic achievement (Okagaki & Sternberg, 1993). The importance of these socialization practices is that they have been associated with children's academic achievement from preschool to adolescence although these associations differ from one ethnic group to another (Asakawa, 2001; Steinberg et al., 1992).

Immigrant families also differ in how much they maintain traditional cultural practices such as native language and customs and how much cultural socialization[9] they impart to their children. Studies of cultural socialization document how much families from seemingly similar cultural backgrounds differ in their practices (see Hughes & Johnson, 2001, for a review)). Families can maintain religious, cultural, and linguistic practices; they can also prepare children for being treated as "other"; they can also foster biculturalism[10] in their children. These practices can be associated with both ethnic/racial identity development and academic attitudes and outcomes.

As most studies of children of immigrants have been conducted with adolescents, our knowledge of these processes during middle childhood is quite limited. This book is intended to fill this gap.

4 ::

The Children of Immigrants:
Development in Context (CIDC) Study

In order to study ethnic identity and academic pathways among children of immigrants, we first had to conceive of a theoretical framework and set of methodologies that would meet our study's specific goals and needs. To do this in a way that would explain both individual and group similarities and differences in developmental processes across our Cambodian, Dominican, and Portuguese groups, we adopted a "mixed methods" approach for our research. Using theory and methods from sociological, anthropological, and psychological disciplines, we created a "mixture" of concepts and measures suited to understand our research questions from both *qualitative* (i.e., descriptions used to characterize developmental processes and contexts) and *quantitative* (i.e., specific psychological processes captured using scales and numbers), across our diverse group of children of immigrants. This chapter is an integrative presentation of our theory and related methodologies that served as the basis for our study; results from our study are described in detail in further chapters. We conclude this chapter with some important practical information to describe how we went about collecting our data (please see Appendix A for quantitative descriptive information on measures used throughout the study).

To begin, we present our overarching theoretical framework for the study in Figure 4.1 As the study is focused ultimately on understanding academic pathways, the construct "Academic Achievement" serves as the ultimate "dependent variable" in our theoretical model. In other words, we believe that aspects of children's developmental contexts and ethnic attitudes and identification leads to (or influences) Academic

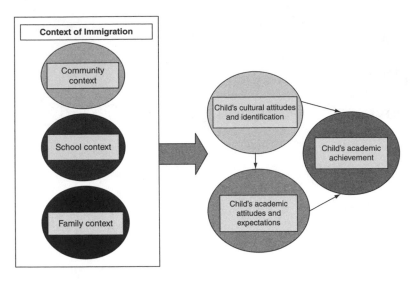

FIGURE 4.1.

Framework for understanding effects of contextual factors on childhood attitudes and academic achievement.

Achievement. Another important note is the Context of Immigration box on the left side of the model. Here, we have stacked Community, School, and Family contexts together, all under the frame of the Context of Immigration. By stacking them in this way, we also imply an ecological ordering (such as that proposed by Bronfenbrenner, 1986), whereby families interact with schools inside of the larger community— all of which takes place under the larger historical and social context of immigration.

As expressed in Chapter 1, this framework is informed by several theoretical viewpoints that derive from various disciplines. From contemporary developmental psychology theories, we derive the notion of multiple contextual influences (Bronfenbrenner, 1986) inclusive of an adaptive culture and inhibiting/promoting environments (García Coll et al., 1996). From developmental theories, we also derive the notion that children and families are active participants and cocreators of their own developments, and therefore, individual differences will emerge in developmental pathways. From sociology (Portes & Rumbaut) and social history (Modell), we derive the notions that larger sociohistorical contexts (such as the Context of Immigration) matter, and that of individual family adaptations, which we measure, will be a function of these larger external forces. Importantly, because we believe the Context of Immigration is so important to understanding development and is so varied by ethnic group we conceived of our study in *parallel design*,[1] considering how developmental contexts would influence ethnic attitudes and identification and academic pathways *separately* for each ethnic group.

◼◼ Measuring the Contexts of Development

Following these theoretical frameworks, much effort was dedicated in this study to assess not only developmental process in the children but also many components of the children's environments. Again, in most standard developmental research, context is either minimally measured, sometimes nominally inferred from group membership, or indirectly studied through children's or parents' reports. In addition, in most instances, only one context is measured, usually the family or the school context.[2] Given the array of developmental outcomes under investigation in the present study—ethnic attitudes and identification and academic outcomes—three primary contexts were assessed in this study: (1) the immigrant context measured through ethnographies of the communities with particular reference to the children's outcomes and measures of cultural socialization by children and families, (2) other aspects of family functioning considered relevant to the developmental outcomes of interest, and (3) various aspects of schools including markers of the school environment (e.g., rates of student interpersonal conflict, teacher grievances, percent of students on reduced or subsidized lunch programs), student demographics, and teacher characteristics. It is important to consider the larger immigration and receiving community contexts of development of children of immigrants, as these in turn shape family and school contexts and inform how children and parents approach and interact within their proximal contexts.

This comprehensive approach reflects our notions that developmental outcomes are embedded in multiple contexts, and outcomes and contexts are mutually affecting each other.[3] For example, children's ethnic identification might be influenced by the maintenance of family cultural socialization derived from their country of origin, the cohesiveness, and strength of the local immigrant community; or its isolation from mainstream American institutions; or the ethnic and racial distribution of students in their school and classroom. Similarly, children's academic outcomes might be a function of their parents' literacy activities at home, the presence of members of their immigrant community that can provide bridges between the home and school, or the level of training of their teachers. Daily interactions across contexts shape the developmental processes of interest. These daily interactions also affect the contexts upon which children and families operate. Given their importance, we embarked in an assessment of three contexts in as much depth as our resources permitted us.

Community Context

Before one examines what elements of community context are most important in shaping the developmental outcomes of immigrant children, it is important to understand what about the initial immigration process determined the type, size, and nature of the community context in which these children were raised.

The mode of incorporation under which the parents of these children initially entered the United States is of great importance when looking at community variables and the outcomes of first and second-generation youth. Different ethnic and national groups face different modes of incorporation, and these modes are highly dependent on the political and economic climate of the United States at the time of entrance. As Portes and Rumbaut express, "for immigrants the most important contexts or reception are defined by the policies of the receiving government, the conditions of the host labor market and the characteristics of their own ethnic communities" (1990).

Each of these factors contributes to the ways in which one assimilates as well as the ultimate success or difficulty of the assimilation process. For example, immigrant groups who receive substantial government aid may have a very different experience than immigrant groups who enter the United States without the presence of supportive governmental programs. Governmental programs such as the Cuban Loan Program enacted by Kennedy in the 1960s is a good example of the role that governmental support plays in the transition of immigrant individuals (Portes & Zhou, 1993). In her article on segmented assimilation, Zhou (1999) points out that due to the initial governmental support that many Cuban families received, many of the children of these Cuban immigrants were able to go to college, and as a result, the percentage of Cuban professionals and executives in the late 1980s was on par with that of the native population.

In addition to governmental attitudes, the ethnic characteristics, size, and cohesiveness of the receiving community is of great importance in outcomes of immigrant parents and therefore their children as well. A strong ethnic enclave can act as protection against the stressors of cultural change and economic and social discrimination that confront many immigrant individuals when they enter the United States (Portes & Rumbaut, 1990). Immigrants who enter into strong receiving communities may gain ready employment through chains of preexisting immigrant-owned businesses and may gain a voice in community concerns through prominent community members.

However, the greatest benefit of these communities may not only come in the way of financial or political gains but in its social rewards for the individuals. Strong ethnic enclaves may provide for children of immigrants through social capital. This concept, first defined by Coleman (1988), involves a system of relationships within a community that facilitates positive outcomes for its members, visible at both a family and community level. As Portes and Rumbaut (2001) note, social capital is different than human capital as "it depends less on the relative economic of occupational success of immigrants than on the density of ties among them" (p. 65).

These ties are particularly important for children of immigrants as they may benefit from what Coleman (1988) referred to as *closure*, a phenomena wherein the ties between community members, especially parents, strengthen parental supervision and the ability of parents to continue to be knowledgeable of their children's lives. This closure within a community may also strengthen the transmission of cultural values to the children through the congruence of the parent cultural values and those of the community.

The insular quality of a strong ethnic community that may benefit children through a greater system of community supports and may buffer individuals within from the discrimination in the greater society, may also hinder the child's full incorporation into mainstream American culture. As Zhou (1997a) points out, ethnic enclaves where many immigrant children are raised are often "linguistically distinctive neighborhoods where their native tongue is used more commonly than English." (p. 87) This linguistic distinction may place a barrier between the child's experience of their own immigrant community and the larger American cultural arena—a barrier that could make the transition to school and jobs in the greater community more difficult as the children age.

Lastly, the physical characteristics of the neighborhood may prove important to the educational and identity development of these youth. Historically and presently, there is a concentration of immigrant families in inner cities—neighborhoods that are often plagued by unsafe conditions and pervasive poverty. Growing up in poverty is a risk factor for all children (Duncan & Brooks-Gunn, 1994; McLoyd, 1998) but may present specific developmental obstacles for children of immigrants. As Zhou (1997b) speculates, "The creation of concentrated low-income neighborhoods has had social consequences for people who live in [them] ... particularly the young people who form their expectations of the world from what they see around them." (p. 986) In other words, living in poor conditions may not simply be a hazard to children on a physical level but may alter the way that they perceive the larger society and their role within it. Taking this one step further, "Social isolation and deprivation can give rise to oppositional culture" (Zhou, 1997b, p. 986; Suárez-Orozco & Suárez-Orozco, 2001; Portes & Zhou, 1993). Thus, for children of immigrants growing up within poor, cramped conditions may cause the optimistic outlook of immigrant parents to be less readily seen in their youth.

School Context

Aside from the family, school[4] is perhaps the most critical arena in which development during middle childhood occurs and where children's futures are shaped. Schools are the first major institution that children of immigrants encounter on their own and in which major socialization, outside of the house, occurs with profound consequences for the future status of those children in the social stratification system of our country (Portes & Rumbaut, 2001; Suárez-Orozco & Suárez-Orozco, 2001). This is particularly true for children of immigrants: Schools are where these children are exposed daily to mainstream culture, and as such, schools serve as agencies of acculturation. In addition, schools shape not only what these children learn, but also their motivations and aspirations to learn.

But schools differ dramatically from one another in terms of the type, quality, and quantity of resources to support children's development. Researchers with the Harvard Civil Rights Project have documented a growing trend toward resegregation, and the emergence of a substantial group of American schools composed entirely of children of color which they label "apartheid schools." In fact, Frankenberg et al., (2003) report that almost three-fourths of black and Latino students attend a school that is predominately minority. More often than not these schools are mired in enormous poverty, limited resources, and have a high concentration of social and health problems which are associated with lower academic achievement (Orfield, 2001; Suárez-Orozco, 1987).

However, a segregated school environment that is inhibiting due to limited educational resources and concentration of poor students may, at the same time, be promoting if it is supportive of the child's emotional and academic adjustment (García Coll et al., 1996). It is possible that in such segregated environments, children of immigrants might feel extremely supported by the mere fact of being surrounded by others like themselves. Studies find that school connectedness (the extent to which children feel cared for by others in and the extent to which they feel part of their school) is greatest for minority students in ethnically segregated public schools and least for those attending integrated schools (McNeely, Nonnemaker, & Blum, 2002).

Finally, teacher characteristics have been found to be important for children's academic attitudes and outcomes. Studies have shown teacher quality, including teacher level of education and experience, to be important for the educational outcome of students (Darling-Hammond, 1999, 2000; Rice, 2003; Wenglinsky, 2000). Furthermore, teachers' attitudes and beliefs concerning their own ability to motivate and teach are of importance when looking at outcomes. Bandura pointed out that it is not only the self-efficacy (or the belief that one can succeed) of the students that is important but the self-efficacy of the teachers as well. Bandura writes, "Teachers' beliefs in their personal efficacy to motivate and promote learning affect the types of learning environments they create and the level of academic progress their student achieve" (Bandura, 1993).

Teacher–student relationships also play important roles in students' academic achievement. Studies have found correlations between the quality of teacher–student relationships and academic achievement; relational negativity between teachers and students is shown to have detrimental effects on behavioral and academic outcomes throughout the elementary and middle school years. (Birch & Ladd, 1997; Hamre & Pianta, 2001) Positive teacher–student relationships may be helpful in building a child's sense of self-efficacy—something that seems particularly important in the case of immigrant students. Kao (1999) found that first and second-generation adolescents had significantly lower feelings of self-efficacy and higher feelings of alienation from their school mates compared with children in native-born families.

The ethnic similarity or dissimilarity of the teachers and the students is of great importance as well, especially in the case of ethnic minority students. Dee (2004) has found that same-race teacher and student pairing, as well as greater representation of minority teachers in schools (Bali & Alvarez, 2003; Crosnoe, 2005; Dee, 2004) leads to more positive educational outcomes for minority and Caucasian students alike.

Lastly, teachers' impressions of students can be a powerful influence on student achievement and attitudes toward education. Research indicates that beginning as early as kindergarten, teachers are likely to perceive poor and low-SES students as disadvantaged both behaviorally and academically; these beliefs are apt to translate into differential treatment of poor children in the classroom (e.g., calling on low-SES students less or giving them less positive feedback; Mcloyd, 1998; Marks & García Coll, 2007). Studies on teacher expectancy effects have found that teacher expectancy effects can explain some of the variance in academic achievement between individual students (Jussim & Harber, 2005), something that may be especially true for minority students (Gill & Reynolds, 1999; Jussim, Eccles, & Madon, 1996).

Family Context

Families are complex systems, and thus we focus on multiple dimensions of families that have been theoretically and empirically linked in previous work with the children's outcomes of interest. The first set of family characteristics that we document, are sociodemographic characteristics (i.e., income, education, and occupation) which are considered social address variables[5] (Bronfenbrenner, 1986). Nonetheless, these family characteristics provide not only markers of general contextual family influences on children's development, but more importantly they act as proxies for both cultural and academic practices

Family Context

- Family immigration and demographic characteristics
- Cultural socialization
- Educational values and practices
- English Language Comfort

and opportunities that can (or cannot) provide certain critical experiences for the children. Numerous studies have found associations between "background" variables and children's developmental outcomes in both immigrant and nonimmigrant populations (Bradley & Corwyn, 2002; Duncan, Brooks-Gunn, & Klebanov, 1994; McLanahan & Sandefur, 1994; McLoyd, 1998; Portes & MacLeod, 1996, 1999; Portes & Rumbaut, 2001).

But we also needed to obtain indicators that reflect more proximal aspects of family processes that are relevant to both emerging ethnicities and academic outcomes. Cultural socialization is the fundamental process by which families can exert influence on children's ethnic attitudes and identifications and attitudes toward their own group and others (Boykin & Toms, 1985; Hughes & Chen, 1999; Hughes et al., 2006; Knight et al, 1993; Phinney, Romero, Nava, & Huang, 2001; Quintana & Vera, 1999). Hughes and colleagues, in a recent review article, define cultural socialization as "practices that teach children about their racial or ethnic heritage and history; that promote cultural customs and traditions; and that promote children's cultural, racial and ethnic pride either *deliberately or implicitly*" (p. 749). Many studies have attested that cultural practices are salient aspects of childrearing across many minority cultures in the United States and that they are one of the most prevalent ways that parents engage in cultural socialization (Hughes et al., 2006). Examples of cultural socialization include exposing children to cultural artifacts and rituals, use of native language, and sharing of information about their country of origin. In transnational communities, regular communication and contact with relatives who live in the country of origin, and visits for vacations, weddings, and other family rituals contribute to the child's knowledge and attachment to their parents' country of origin.

Similarly, there is literature to support that academic values and practices are a major influence on children's attitudes and success in school (Carter & Wojtkiewicz, 2000; Shumow & Miller, 2001). Sometimes there is a disconnect between the academic values that parents have and their practices, and this, at many times, seems to be the case in immigrant families. Although most immigrant parents have high aspirations and recognize the importance of their children's success in school, many do not engage in the activities that are characteristic of middle-class, mainstream families (Suárez-Orozco & Suárez-Orozco, 2001; Delgado-Gaitán, 1992). For example, many do not participate in organized school activities such as open houses and parent–teacher conferences or belong to the parent–teacher associations. At home, they might not be able to read to their children or check their homework. This could have a negative effect on the educational outcomes of their children, as studies have demonstrated positive relationships between literacy activities at home and literacy skills in both preschool and the elementary grades (see Dickinson, Snow, Roach, Smith, & Tabors, 1998; Jordan, Snow, & Porche, 2000; Nathenson-Mejia, 1994; Snow, 1993). In addition, parents of different ethnic groups differ in beliefs about childrearing, expectations of their children's schooling, and in self-reported and observed parenting strategies around teaching and academic achievement (Okagaki & Sternberg, 1993). The importance of these socialization practices is that they have been associated with children's academic achievement from preschool to adolescence, although these associations differ from one ethnic group to another (Britto, 1999; Steinberg et al., 1992).

Finally, the parents' comfort with the mainstream culture is another source of socialization for the child. We have two marker variables for this aspect of family life: the main caregiver's comfort with English and their perceptions of the neighborhood. We would predict that parents who have less educational experience in the United States, and often, less English language comfort, would have academic socialization practices that will be less conducive to academic achievement in the traditional way defined by school (e.g., not providing a particular quiet place to do homework).

We predict that children from families with stronger ethnic and academic socialization will possess stronger and more salient ethnic identities with positive ethnic esteem and stronger school engagement. We postulate that these are the actual mechanisms upon which family characteristics become a source of influence for both cultural attitudes and identification and academic attitudes and achievement.

Cultural Attitudes and Identification

One of the fundamental arguments of this book is that cultural attitudes and identifications are major developmental tasks of middle childhood for children of immigrants. We conceptualize ethnic identities (see Cooper, García Coll, Thorne, & Orellana, 2005) as socially constructed and historically situated, meaning that the social construction by the child is in response to/incorporates extant racial/ethnic categories, but these categories are fluid and continually under revision (e.g., as a function in part of new waves of immigration). We also see ethnic identifications as situationally dependent, which means that the identity's saliency and centrality as well as the child's satisfaction with belonging to these categories might change from home to school or other hypothetical situations. We also use the word *identities/identifications* (instead of *identity/identification*) because we believe that children have multiple identities that reflect various socially important dimensions such as race, ethnicity, nationality, and also gender, roles, and religion. Finally, we conceptualize that the evolution of identifications is developmentally mediated and multidetermined—family, school, and ethnic enclave experiences interact with developmental processes to create more complex and more "accurately" defined identities and deeper knowledge of the dominant societal views. For example, it is expected that children whose parents are more recent immigrants, maintain more cultural practices, and are part of a strong ethnic enclave and a school with more multicultural characteristics will have more salient and central ethnic identities and higher ethnic satisfaction, more positive attitudes toward the in-group and will perceive less discrimination. However, as children develop and have more interethnic/racial contacts, the saliency, centrality, and satisfaction related to their ethnic identities might vary, in addition to their in-group and out-group preferences and awareness of discrimination. Those who can be assimilated into a socially accepted white racial category (e.g., Portuguese) might have more racial (white) versus ethnic identities, and might feel better about their racial identities and perceive less racial discrimination.

Another area that we consider an important part of the children's cultural attitudes and identification is their in-group and out-group preferences. We believe that positive in-group attitudes are another sign of a healthy ethnic identity development, something that might buffer them from negative consequences derived from experiences of discrimination (Mossakowski, 2003; Phinney, 1990; Phinney, Ferguson, & Tate, 1997). We also conceptualize out-group attitudes as critical for children of immigrants as they adapt to school settings where most of the adults represent and enact mainstream values, while their peer groups are perhaps primarily members of other minority groups. But given the age group (middle childhood) under study, we conceptualize these attitudes as preferences in friendships and for playmates or companions across a variety of situations and settings (school and home). As indicated by previous literature (Aboud, 2003; Brewer, 1999, 2001; Cameron et al., 2001), we also ascertained independently whether they had preferences for the in group and for the out groups separately. We therefore expected that preferences for the in group would be independent from preferences for the out groups.

Academic Attitudes and Expectations

Academic attitudes and expectations have been found to shift dramatically over time and to be associated with academic outcomes

(Blumenfeld et al., 2005; Fuligni, 1997; Simmons & Blyth, 1987; Sirin & Rogers-Sirin, 2005). We believe that, among children of immigrants, academic attitudes and expectations will also be influenced in part by students' ethnic attitudes and identities. As with other populations, several studies have found that immigrant children enter the United States with very positive attitudes toward school and education (Fuligni, 1997; Kao & Tienda, 1995; Portes & Zhou, 1993; Suárez-Orozco & Suárez-Orozco, 1995, 2001). However, by adolescence, phrases like "oppositional" or "adversarial identities" are used to describe the adaptations of children of immigrants and other children of color toward school and education (Ogbu & Simmons, 1998; Portes, 1996, Suárez-Orozco & Suárez-Orozco, 2001).

These findings are disturbing since positive attitudes toward school have been identified as a crucial variable in maintaining a high level of academic achievement (Connell, Spencer, & Aber, 1994; Peet et al., 1997; Steinberg et al., 1992). Historically, the nature and purpose of schooling has changed, and thus intellectual involvement and investment are essential ingredients for problem solving, analyses, and other higher-level cognitive processes that are necessary for becoming an effective learner. School engagement has also been identified as a major contributor to academic success Engagement is expected to be a function of both child characteristics and contextual influences, inclusive of support from adults at home and in school (Blumenfeld et al., 2005; Connell, Spencer, & Aber, 1994).

⠘ Methodology

As promised at the beginning of this chapter, we include here a description of our specific methods, study design, and procedures that allowed us to obtain our research information. In 1995, we started to design a longitudinal study that would address our research questions and started to create and pilot test questionnaires appropriate for 6- to 12-year-olds and their parents, from three immigrant communities. Armed with our research questions, our academic knowledge about immigrant children, in general, and about our geographic area (as a large secondary center for recent immigrants) and its schools, we embarked on our journey of discovery.

❖ Recruiting a Sample: Who Gets in, Who Doesn't . . .

One of the first issues that we encountered was how to identify and access the families that we wanted to have as participants in the study. From the 1990 census and our local knowledge of the immigrant communities, we decided to concentrate in three particular immigrant groups: Cambodian, Dominicans, and Portuguese. These groups were chosen because they are the biggest national groups within the broader categories they represent: Asian, Latino, and traditional white European. They also represent very different modes of incorporation: refugees (Cambodian), "voluntary" immigrants but one more recent (Dominicans), and another part of a long-term migration wave (Portuguese). Finally they differ in their ascribed ethnicity (as Latinos, white European, and Asian), home culture and language, racialized features, timing and process of immigration, and compatibility with the receiving communities (Bailey, 2000a, 2000b, 2000c). These are all factors that have been previously identified as important to describe immigration contexts in the United States (Portes & Rumbaut, 2001; Rumbaut & Portes, 2001).

We knew that certain immigrant groups tended to live in particular sections of our metropolitan area, but a door-to-door approach was going to be too costly and inefficient, given the available resources. We settled on recruiting through local schools, both public and independent:[6] After all, children between 6 and 12 years of age are universally[7] in formal education settings, and thus accessing these communities through these means would not introduce any particular biases.

But as with any decision of this nature, considerations arose. Because of our interest in placing these children's journeys through middle childhood in the context of their own immigrant group's local history, sampling all children in a school or classroom regardless of their parent's immigrant status was not going to be efficient. Although the schools (two school districts including 26 public schools and four independent, mostly parochial schools) were chosen with *a priori* knowledge that they had high concentrations of children of immigrants, these varied tremendously by the country of origin of the children.

Moreover, if we examined school census lists, broad categories such as Asian (including Cambodians, Laotians, and Hmong), Latino (including Puerto Ricans, Dominicans, and Central Americans), black (including African-Americans, Africans, and West Indians), and white (including recent immigrants) were used. These categories[8] suggested panethnic affiliations but not definite nationality membership by any specific group. So in order to identify children from specific immigrant groups, we had to oversample schools whose census categories suggested a high concentration of immigrant families using the available census of panethnic groups.

After developing, pilot testing, and creating final versions of questionnaires for children between the ages of 6 and 12 years and their parents,[9] in the fall of 1998, we started the present study: a longitudinal study of over 300 families with children in either the first or fourth grade at the time of recruitment. To reflect immigration as a major context of these families' (and their children's) lives, only families from three specific immigrant groups were chosen to be in the longitudinal study: Dominican, Portuguese, and Cambodian.[10] The oversampling of children from these three immigrant groups and exclusion of children from other immigrant groups were done deliberately in order to allow for a more in-depth assessment of each group's context, experience, and developmental outcomes.

To qualify to be in the study, at least one of the parents of the first or fourth grader had to be born in the country of origin (Cambodia, Dominican Republic, and the Azores), so not all families identified as belonging to the particular immigrant groups qualified to be in the study (some had been born in this country). This was done because of the importance of generation and acculturation[11] in the outcomes and processes being measured in this study and our particular interest in the experience of children of immigrant parents.

Although standard methods of recruiting school-based samples were initially employed (informed consents were sent home with children for parents to sign), our approach had to eventually become more flexible and responsive to culturally defined patterns of interaction with schools and authority figures. Initially, undergraduate and graduate students trained to conduct ethnographic observations in classrooms went to schools where the school census suggested there were large concentrations of Asian, Latino, and white children. Aside from conducting classroom observations, the observers recruited participants by distributing consent forms to the entire classroom (regardless of immigrant background membership) or leaving consent forms with teachers or principals to be distributed to the age appropriate classes. Thus, through this whole-classroom method, we ended up recruiting and obtaining consent for participation in the study from a larger cohort of children than the one that was finally included in the longitudinal sample representing only the three immigrant groups of interest.

However, using this recruitment strategy was not enough. Only 24% of the Cambodians children and their families approached through the classrooms consented to be in the study, compared to 56% percent of the Dominicans and 37% percent of the Portuguese respectively. Cambodian and Portuguese key informants were consulted to explain the lower consent rate obtained for those groups and to suggest other venues for recruitment. Issues of trust in authority figures (i.e., bad experiences with signing papers during the Khmer Rouge in Cambodia) and/or busy and demanding family lives (more so for the Dominican and Portuguese parents) were getting in the way of obtaining consent for participation in the study. It was clear that a face-to-face approach by familiar community members was needed in order for us to recruit more families.

Using student total enrollment lists for all schools (which contained parents' place of birth, and/or student placement in ESL classes which were made available either by the school districts or by the independent schools themselves), families were again contacted through telephone to obtain consent and set up interviews. These phone calls were made by multilingual research assistants (many of whom were community members themselves), who made it known at the beginning of the phone call that they could speak English and/or Khmer, Spanish, or Portuguese. For the Portuguese and Cambodian groups, research assistants also made home visits to encourage and increase the participation within these groups. The contact with familiar community members who attested to the value of the study for the community resulted in the recruitment into the study of families that had initially turned us down through the standard classroom recruitment procedures, as well as others who had not been initially approached. This two-tier method was still targeting the same population: children of first-generation immigrants from the three immigrant groups who where in either first or fourth grade in local public and independent schools.

The final sample—those identified through classrooms and/or school lists who gave informed consent to be in the study—consisted of 772 first and fourth grade students classified by their schools as white, Latino, black, Asian, and "other." Because these students were identified by panethnic labels used by the schools—Asian, whites, and Latinos—we interviewed all of them in order to identify subsamples of

Portuguese, Dominican, and Cambodian first- and fourth-graders who would meet the criteria of having at least one parent born in the country of origin. From this, then, a longitudinal sample of Portuguese ($n = 122$), Dominican ($n = 140$), and Cambodian ($n = 142$) were recruited (See Table 1). The children from each immigrant group were roughly equally divided by grade (Portuguese: 62 first-graders, 66 fourth-graders; Dominican: 70, 70; Cambodian: 70, 72) and gender (Portuguese: 58 females, 64 males; Dominican: 75, 75; Cambodian: 73, 69). The first- and fourth-grade cohorts were each comprised of approximately the same proportion of males and females, as gender differences have been found historically in academic pathways.[12] The Cambodian and Portuguese samples had the largest percentage of children born in the United States, 88% and 85% respectively, in contrast to the Dominicans (72.3%), ($X_{(2)} = 10.1$, $p < .01$).

⚙ A Mixed Method Approach to Data Collection

Thus, our study was designed to capture the children's experiences throughout the whole age range of middle childhood (6–12 years of age) by recruiting from local schools Cambodian, Dominican, and Portuguese children in first and fourth grades and interviewing them yearly (in first, second, and third grade, or fourth, fifth and six grade). We also obtained individual school records for those 3 years, interviewed their parents in the second year of the study (when children were in either second or fifth grade), and obtained questionnaires from teachers in third and sixth grades (see Figure 4.2).

From the conception of the study, and throughout questionnaire development, pilot testing, and data collection, analysis, and interpretation, we sought to integrate qualitative and quantitative methods.[13] This approach was necessary given the complexity of the developmental phenomena under study, the lack of standard measures in this age range, and the serious commitment to measuring developmental pathways in context. This approach created unique demands, both practical and analytic, and required an interdisciplinary approach to the conceptualization and conduct of the study. As such, we were obligated to go beyond standard developmental research methodologies such as administering questionnaires and/or conducting interviews and observations, and incorporate methodologies used in other disciplines such as anthropology and sociology.[14]

◈ Measuring Contexts and Developmental Outcomes

Community Context

During the first year of data collection, as we were identifying and recruiting potential subjects and interviewing them in schools in order to identify a longitudinal sample of Cambodians, Dominicans, and Portuguese, an ethnographic study[15] was carried out in each of the three communities under study, reflecting our emphasis on the importance of understanding the community context in which developmental outcomes occur (see Bailey [2000 a,b,c] for each of the ethnographies written by him). As mentioned previously, often in developmental research, a social address approach is used in which membership in an ethnic, racial, and/or immigrant group is used as a proxy for an explanatory variable. This approach has many limitations, as context is not directly measured but inferred.[16] From the inception of the study, we were committed to understand immigration context not only as inferred from group membership but also by data generated by a systematic ethnographic study of each community. In addition, census and any other publicly available data that would provide insights into the three immigrant groups were collected. These data sources gave

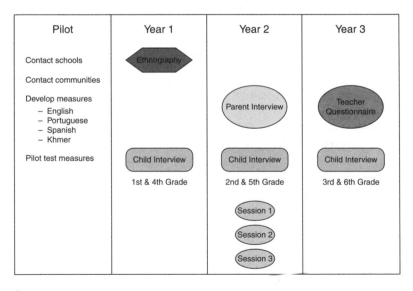

FIGURE 4.2.
Study design and measures.

us the absolute and relative size in each respective city, the main reasons for migration, the actual migratory patterns, characteristics of their ethnic enclave, and the relation with mainstream institutions for each immigrant group. Information on individual perspectives on the feeling of belonging, perceptions of neighbors, and community resources was obtained through questions within the parent and child interviews.

School Context

To assess the school context, we relied on data collected by organizations like Rhode Island Infoworks (Information Works, 1999, 2000, 2001), as well as our own ethnographic data collected based on interviews with teachers, administrators, and counselors at the eight schools with the highest numbers of participants from our study. Schools were assessed in terms of the number and ethnicity of students and teachers and the school's overall performance on standardized tests on math, writing, health, and reading. The economic background of the students attending the schools was indirectly assessed through the percentage of students who qualify for free lunches (and of this percentage how many students were white, black, Hispanic, Asian, or Native American). To investigate the type of education provided by the school, we looked at the percentage of the school population enrolled in ESL, Bilingual, and Special Education classes/programs, as well as student attendance and class size (Information Works, 1999, 2000, 2001).

In the third year of the study, we sent questionnaires to the child's homeroom (third grade) or English teacher (sixth grade). In these questionnaires, teachers answered questions about their background (education level, etc.), beliefs about learning and teaching, and questions comparing the child (whom they taught) to their peers in class in regards to both social and academic skills. Teacher characteristics were analyzed in terms of the number of years the teacher had been working the field of education, the amount of time they had been employed at the school, and the level of education that they currently possessed.

Family Context

In the second year of the study, primary caregivers were contacted through phone to arrange for an undergraduate or graduate student or a bilingual community member to meet with them for an interview (see Appendix A for individual items and measures). These interviews took place in the homes of the participants in the language of their choice. They usually ranged from 2 to 4 hours.

The parent interview was an essential component to our understanding the family context, including sociodemographic characteristics, cultural socialization, and academic attitudes and practices of each child. Most sections of the parent's interview called for the parent to choose between given responses (e.g., "Do you speak English with people at your child's school?" "Yes or No"; followed by, "How comfortable are you doing this?" "Very comfortable," "Comfortable," or "Uncomfortable.") In most cases, these more structured questions were followed by an opportunity for the participant to give a more open response (e.g., "Do you like this neighborhood?" "Yes or No;" followed by "Why or Why not?"). Other sections called for the parents to speak freely on topics such as how they would handle a situation; for example, parents were asked to give open responses to questions such as, "What would you do if the school work seems too easy for [*child's name*]?"

Developmental Outcomes

The immigrant community, family, and school contexts were used as ways to contextualize and explain the child's cultural attitudes and identifications, academic attitudes and expectations, and the child's academic outcome. The yearly child interview was a central part of the study design and it was created to assess the child's cultural attitudes and identification and academic attitudes and expectations through the child's own responses to a variety of predetermined questions and prompts (see Appendix A for specific items and measures). Two years of piloting was required to finalize the interview protocol for all three immigrant groups.

Age and culture appropriate measures were developed to investigate cultural identification and attitudes such as issues of ethnic esteem, pride, centrality, and salience, as well as in-group and out-group perceptions and perceived racism. Many different types of questions and tasks were employed in the interview to get at each of these constructs. For example, in the first year of the study, using an adaptation of the multidimensional measure from Erkut, Alarcón, García Coll and colleagues, children were shown cards on which different labels were written (Erkut, Alarcon, & García Coll, 1998). Labels referred to a role, an ethnicity/panethnicity, a religion, or a multiethnic label (see Appendix B for examples of labels used.) Given the child's ethnicity, labels specific to their particular background, including hyphenated labels (e.g., Asian-American), specific nationality labels (e.g., Chinese) and their hyphenated American derivatives (e.g., Dominican-American), were included.[17] For example, any or all of the following could apply to Cambodian children: Cambodian (national label), Khmer (ethno-linguistic label), Southeast Asian (panethnic label), Asian (panethnic label) and Asian-American (hyphenated label). The interviewers read each label to the children and asked if that word was "about them" or "not about them." Continuing to use the label cards, children were asked to rank the labels in order of importance to further explore the construction of the label as well as which (of the most important labels) made them happiest and why. They were also asked if they wish they could get rid of any of the labels from the list, and if so why this was the case.

Other measures employed cards in similar ways. For example, in a measure to assess cultural identification based on one developed by Alarcon, Szalacha, Erkut, Fields, & García Coll (2000), children were given a set of skin tone–colored cards and asked to choose the color most like their skin tone. This was followed by questions about the difficulty of this task, the child's feelings about their skin color, if the child would choose another skin color if they could (If the response was "yes," children were given the chance to choose a color they preferred from the colored cards) and why. In questions regarding feeling—in this task and others—children responded to interviewer prompts by pointing to a spot along a drawn scale presented to them before the questions. One end of the scale signified very happy (demarcated by a smiley face at one end) and the other represented very sad (frowning face on the opposite end; see Appendix A).

For many sections, children were encouraged to give more open responses to follow up questions about why they had chosen their response, much like the parent interview, and in some sections they were asked to provide free explanations. For example, to look at perceived discrimination, children were given several hypothetical situations in which there was some sort of racial discrimination involved. Subjects were asked to pretend they were one of the characters and, after listening to the story, the children were asked what they would do about this problem and why it happened.

In addition to cultural socialization and identification, the children's interview sought to explore the child's perceptions of teachers, school values and engagement, academic aspirations and expectations, and school-related stress. For most of these measures, children were asked to respond using prefixed responses. For example, to measure school values children were asked: How important is it for you to get good grades? Children responded with either "very important," "pretty important," "in between," "not very important," or "not at all important."[18] (See Appendix A for more examples.)

In sum, we included both open- and closed-ended questions in our child and parent interviews and in the teachers' questionnaire. Thus, sometimes respondents had a series of answers from which to select one; in others, answers were open and recorded verbatim. This was another way that mixed methods were employed in this study.

Data Reduction and Analyses

The intermingled use of both qualitative and quantitative methods created some particular challenges in the data analyses. For example, many of the open-ended responses from both the parent and children's interviews were subsequently coded quantitatively. While reducing qualitative data with quantitative coding is neither new nor unusual in a mixed methods approach, we also incorporated quantitative data in some qualitative coding schemas. For example, students' grades and individual teacher's quantitative ratings and qualitative reports were coded qualitatively in order to capture each child's academic achievement longitudinally. The end result of this qualitative analysis being the child placed into one of five academic pathways representing the child as either "excelling," "positive," "mixed," "negative," or "abysmal" across the three years of the study. These paths represent a qualitative assessment of multiple data points across various domains (e.g., grades, teacher reports), in order to capture the phenomena of school achievement in a more nuanced way than if we had relied solely on the quantitative measures (such as Grade Point Average (GPA) or standardized test scores). For example, a child who was classified as "excelling" had predominately A's (only a maximum of two B's were allowed in the third year) and only positive comments on the teacher questionnaire and/or top ratings on behavioral items in the report card. On the other hand, a child who was classified as "abysmal" had predominately D's and F's, was failing or had already failed a grade, had only negative comments from the teacher (1 and 2) or on their report card, and their teacher's comments revealed frustration and/or that she or he had given up on the child. These pathways served as a major dependent variable in this study.

In addition, after ending the data collection phase, three focus groups of other parents and key members of the community were conducted for each of the immigrant groups. Preliminary findings were presented, and the community members were asked to generate their own explanations for our findings. A substantial amount of qualitative data was generated that was used to inform our interpretation of the study findings.

The diversity of methodologies and instruments used in our studies reflects both the diversity of the populations which we are studying, as well as the complexity of our theoretical frameworks on development. Because developmental processes among children of immigrants are contextualized, mixed method approaches are not only suited, but are critical for this and future studies.

5 ::

The Cambodian Community: Small, Isolated, and Resilient

Given the theoretical frameworks guiding the present study, our start-ing point to understanding children's development is to examine the community context that most Cambodian families are part of. The local Cambodian community is the product of a larger historical process that brought Cambodians as refugees to the United States during a rela-tively short period of time, primarily between 1980 and 1986 (see Bailey, 2000a[1]). These migrations followed the decimation of the Cambodian population by war (both as a product of their involvement in the Viet-nam War and ongoing civil war), starvation, persecution, and targeted executions of its most educated citizens who were seen as a threat to the oppressive regime. Eventually, hundreds of thousands of Cambodian survivors of the Khmer Rouge genocide fled to Thailand during 1979 and 1980, where they were placed in refugee camps. Tens of thousands were subsequently resettled as refugees in the United States and other countries (e.g., France and Canada). Since the most educated and afflu-ent Cambodians had either been killed or fled in earlier years, many of the refugees who came to the United States were the most disadvan-taged. They were disproportionately poor, less educated, and had suf-fered most from the emotional and physical trauma of the Khmer Rouge.

The relatively large number of Cambodian refugees who came to the United States in that historical period was made possible by the sign-ing of the 1980 Refugee Act by President Jimmy Carter, which drastically increased the number of refugees allowed entrance to this country. Current census data gives us a sense of the size and growth of this pop-ulation. Cambodians are considered both locally and nationwide as part of the Southeast Asian panethnic group.[2] According to the 2000 U.S. census, a total of 1,814,301 persons reported being Southeast Asian, of whom 206,052 also reported being from Cambodia (Yang, 2004). According to the Census of 1990, the Cambodian community in Rhode Island had just over 3,600 members, a number that grew to over 4,500 by 2000, a relatively small sized community with a relatively slow rate of growth compared to others. Providence, the city from where the sample for this study was drawn, had 3,124 Cambodian residents in 1990 and about 3,500 in 2000 (U.S. Census Bureau, 1990a, 1990b, 2000a, 2000b). Although the local Cambodian community makes up a relatively small portion of the city's population (Providence has over 150,000 residents), it represents a majority of the Cambodian population in the state. Cambodians are also concentrated in the part of the city that is commonly known as the South Side, where Latino (including the Dominican population), blacks, and other recent immigrants populate the many multifamily houses. Although gentrification and urban revitalization is occurring at a faster pace in this city in the last 10 years, this part of the city is considered to have many of the poorest neighborhoods in Providence. Thus, Cambodians are a relatively small community who live in a highly concentrated, poverty-stricken area.

The experience of coming to the United States was quite different for Cambodians than for Dominicans or Portuguese (Bailey, 2000a), who are the two other groups included in this book and who are considered voluntary migrants.[3] Most of the Cambodian parents in our study fled from Thailand for survival reasons. Many thought that their settlement in refugee camps in Thailand was temporary and that they would eventually return to their homes. They did not leave their country thinking that they would never come back. They did not choose to migrate; they had no choice but to migrate. In some instances, they were the sole survivors of their families and came to the United States as refugees because they could not return to Cambodia for safety reasons. They ended up in the United States because they had no other choice. These experiences are exemplified by the immigration history of one of our families in the study, as described below.

> The Loch family's story is very much like that of many other Cambodian refugee families. Jorani and Nimol are the mother and father of four American-born children. Both Jorani and Nimol were born and raised in Battambay, Cambodia. However, in 1979, they escaped from

Cambodia to Thailand with the help of the United Nations, as a result of the war raging around them. After 5 years in Thailand, they immigrated to Philadelphia in 1984. And just 1 year later, they moved to Providence, where they currently live. Although Jorani says that she was interested in learning English, she makes it clear that the fundamental reason for the family's move to the United States was war. They escaped hurriedly, and when reminiscing, Jorani states, "[I] ran to the United States. No time to get something." She had very little control over the journey and in the interview was asked if at the time she knew how long she would stay in the United States. Jorani simply states, "No. I did not know anything."

The local Cambodian community in Providence is a product of this particular kind of transnational migration, and in addition, it is also the product of the area's identification as a federal resettlement site (Bailey, 2000a). Providence was selected by the government because of the availability of religious and charitable organizations that sponsored refugees, and characteristics such as the availability of jobs, a low crime rate, and affordable housing made it suitable to receive a large wave of new immigrants. Refugees who qualified for resettlement needed to have local sponsors before they could resettle. Therefore, in contrast to immigrant groups who use family reunification to migrate and/or to gravitate to ethnic enclaves for resources and supports, Cambodians were primarily sponsored by institutions, especially during the period of greatest refugee resettlement, 1980–1986. Thus, local social service agencies filled many of the roles for Cambodians that for most groups of immigrants to the United States, in the nineteenth and twentieth centuries, were served by relatives or the immigrant community itself. Unfortunately, by the 1990s, most of the federal funds available for resettlement had been used, and therefore, many social services exclusively designed for the Cambodian population ceased to exist.[4]

Perhaps because resettlement was guided by sponsorship and not by earlier migration waves, the Cambodian community has not followed the traditional development of an ethnic enclave and the subsequent development of local ethnically based institutions to support their integration and access to critical resources (Bailey, 2000a; Portes, 1995). For example, unlike many other linguistic ethnic enclaves, the Cambodians in Providence have no local Cambodian or Cambodian-language media (newspapers, radio, or television), except for video rentals. There is also a noticeable lack of demonstrated engagement in local politics: There are no Cambodian elected officials, precious few appointed ones, and little representation of other kinds in local government. The Cambodian entrepreneurial/small retail business presence is also small compared to that of the Dominicans and Portuguese. In particular, given the growth of global communication, many immigrant communities in the United States keep close ties with their communities of origin. However, many typical ethnic institutions are missing altogether among the Cambodian community in Providence. As expressed by Bailey (2000a):

> Noticeably absent from the Cambodian business community are the international/transnational services typical of immigrant communities with on-going and circular migration: long distance calling centers, money wiring services, freight forwarding agencies, and travel agencies . . . While immigrants such as Dominicans regularly call the Dominican Republic, visit the island on special family occasions (weddings, funerals, etc) and on regular vacations, send remittances, ship things back and forth, re-migrate, sponsor an on-going stream of relatives, etc., the Cambodian community is in most ways cut off from their original homes in Cambodia. They have been isolated through years of warfare and genocide starting in 1970, years spent in refugee camps, persecution by a hostile regime in Phnom Penh until the 1990's, and the short window of time during which refugees were accepted as refugees (e.g., at Khao I Dang camp) in Thailand and resettled in the US. (p. 14).

Perhaps because of the lack of new immigration, the loss of family members, and the lack of relations between Cambodia and the United States until just recently, there is no evidence of cultural renewal in this community as measured by new arrivals, visits, or ongoing communication and transactions with the country of origin.

However, there are signs of entrepreneurial efforts and community-based organizations that support the maintenance of traditional Cambodian culture and practices. There are various Cambodian-owned restaurants, retail stores, and food markets that carry Cambodian traditional foods and goods; the food markets and some hair salons have become informal "community centers," the main place for communication and exchange of information, with regard to jobs (Bailey, 2000a). There is also an active temple as well as a Cambodian Society which serve as the anchors of the community and conduits of Cambodian Buddhism and culture between the older and younger generation.

Although not necessarily based on their own particular culture, there are other community organizations that have provided ongoing support to Cambodian families. There are pan-Southeast Asian organizations like the South East Asian Development Corporation and other social service organizations, such as the International Institute, that have historically provided support to these families. But unlike the recent Portuguese immigrants who joined a large, centuries-long established strong community, and the Dominicans who arrived to discover a growing, yet relatively stable Latino community that recognized a strong kinship with them, Cambodians did not join an established community representing their nationality and do not share a language with any of the available Southeast Asian national groups. This isolation from a local and strong ethnic enclave, other similar national groups who share a language and the mainstream culture, will be evident in family life as reflected in our interviews with parents and children.[5]

According to Bailey (2000a), the physical and cultural distance between Cambodian refugees and their country of origin and the lack of a strong ethnic enclave have other consequences for family life. Specifically, children are not exposed to newly arrived relatives or other community members who have just visited the country of origin, which would allow them to maintain connections through others to their parents' original home culture. As Bailey asserts,

> There is no on-going stream of migrants or circular migration re-invigorating the original "Cambodian" aspects of the community. Children have little/no contact with newly arrived cousins/peers, so Cambodian culture, language, and values are only represented by parents. Given the stark cultural differences between Cambodia and the US, parents can seem even more out of touch with reality to the younger generations than is typical in immigrant situations. Flourishing immigrant communities can recreate institutions and attitudes from the home country, inculcating youth with a common cultural memory based on shared language and customs (pp. 15–16).

According to Bailey, this discontinuity between family life and outside culture and values contributes to a wider generation gap between Cambodian parents and youth. According to one of his informants, this generation gap contributes to many of the problems observed by the elders in the youngest generations:

> For many years, we have had problems with gang activities, drop out, the whole teenage, junior high school and high school generations. The reason why we think there were problems came down to the fact that it's lost culture . . . They don't remember what the authentic Cambodian culture is, you know what practices, what family rules are. So they become rebellious (Bailey, 2000a, p. 15).

Many of these problems are perceived as school related. Although Cambodian parents are grateful and appreciative of their children's access to public education, they also recognize that it is in school and in the peer group that their children learn some dangerous "American ways." Most Cambodian children attend public schools (95%), although other minority families who can afford parochial and independent schools for their children choose them (see Table 3). About 10% of the local elementary school population from which the participants were recruited is considered Asian, with Cambodians accounting for more than half of this figure. Initially, children go to local elementary schools, where, with the exception of one school, they are one of the smallest minority groups in attendance. These same patterns are replicated in middle schools and beyond.

The schools that they attend are prototypic of inner-city schools.[6] These schools are all considered "low achieving" by the State Department of Education (Information Works, 1999, 2000, 2001). Only 24% of students in the schools that Cambodian children are attending reached proficiency or state standards in math and 34% in writing.[7] The students are also predominantly poor and minority: 94% of the students qualify for free lunch and 89% are non-white. Most teachers are females and European-Americans (82%). Cambodian children are also part of larger classes as compared to Portuguese children (24 vs. 21 students). Only one aspect of the schools that Cambodian children are attending is not prototypical of inner-city schools: their teacher qualifications. A majority of their teachers (76%) had at least a master's degree compared to teachers of Dominican (50%) or Portuguese (44%) students (χ^2 28.4, $p < .001$).

If we consider that less than 2% of the Cambodian parents spoke primarily in English to their children, an important attribute of the schools would be instructional provisions for their English Language Learner

(ELL) status. The availability of instruction that took into account their ELL status varied considerably from school to school. If the child had limited English proficiency, English as a second language (ESL) classes were available in some schools, but not others. Bilingual Cambodian/English instruction was not available anywhere. In actuality, only 22% of the schools that Cambodian children attend have ESL services. Unlike bilingual classes where students in the class share a common language, ESL classes sometimes have as many languages as students. The sense of linguistic isolation, at least until English proficiency is attained, is profound in these classes.

As in local government and other aspects of public and community life, there was also very little representation of Cambodian adults in the children's schools. In the whole Providence district (serving approximately 26,000 students), there was one Cambodian assistant principal, five teachers, and three social work employees. At some point, there had been 25 Cambodian Teacher Assistants systemwide, but they were cut as part of local school reform efforts. Thus Cambodian children see few adults in the school context who reinforce traditional Cambodian culture, language, and practices.

In sum, because of the circumstances of migration and reception and the original characteristics of Cambodian refugees, the Cambodian community provides a unique developmental niche for their children. Culturally, the Cambodian community does not embody the strengths seen in the Portuguese and Dominican communities of our study. Specially, there is neither media nor constant influx of recently arrived immigrants to contribute to a vibrant community. Yet, some sense of community is imparted by several Cambodian institutions as the temple, the Cambodian Society, and a myriad of small local businesses. In addition, the schools and neighborhoods that they live in are prototypical inner-city institutions, reflecting the high segregation of poor nonwhite communities into particular sections of the city. Cambodians are culturally and economically segregated from mainstream culture, except for their daily contact with white, middle-class teachers.

⠿ Cambodian Families: Contexts for Children's Development

Aside from communities and schools, we see children's development as a function of family environments. Cambodian families present a unique context for their children's development. In general, families can be seen through the lenses of their demographic characteristics, the values they espouse, and the activities they engage in with and on behalf of their children.

▪▪ Family Immigration and Demographic Characteristics

Immigration and demographic profiles are used as distal indicators of more proximal family processes. They help us categorize families as particular niches for children's development (see Table 4 for the demographic characteristics of the sample). Most Cambodian parents in our study were in their mid-30s at the time of interview and both were born in Cambodia (see Table 4). On average, they have been in the United States since 1984. Forty nine percent of the parents arrived between 1983 and 1985, reflecting the small window of opportunity for immigration for this group. Fifty one percent came directly to Rhode Island, while the rest immigrated into the state after arriving in another city, reflecting the resettlement history of this group. Most of them came to this country as adolescents or very young adults after spending some time in refugee camps in Thailand. As exemplary of the last waves of immigrants out of Cambodia, 80% came from towns and rural areas as opposed to cities.

From a sociological perspective, with regard to human, social, and cultural capital,[8] the Cambodian families in our study present a mixed profile for promoting developmental competencies in their children. Most of the families (74%) have both parents present, a factor that has been identified as protective for children's development.[9] On the other hand, Cambodian families are larger, on average, than the other families in our study, a product not just of more two-parent families but of more people, usually children, in the household. Our sample has more household members (5.4 people on average) than the Cambodian population in Providence (4) but resembles that of the Cambodian population nationwide (5). In our sample, having more children is associated with migration from towns and the countryside as opposed to the city, suggesting the importance of pre-immigration characteristics to family size. Large household size has been associated with lower academic achievement in other populations.[10]

There are several additional demographic indicators that place Cambodian families at high risk for being unable to foster optimally their children's development. One of the main assets that parents bring to their children's education is their own level of formal education.[11] Cambodian families in our study have extremely low levels of formal education, on average only 4 years, reflecting the disruption caused by war and the rural origins of this population.[12] Eighty two percent of the sample has had no education in the United States, perhaps another source of unfamiliarity for these parents on how to negotiate this educational system. Actually, 27% have had no formal education at all, and all these individuals come from towns and the countryside and not from the city. In addition to low levels of formal education, and perhaps partly as a function of these levels, a majority of these families now live in a context of poverty[13]. Sixty eight percent live with incomes below the 1999 poverty line.[14] Only 26% of the families had two parents employed, and only 16% of those employed are considered skilled workers. Only a quarter of these families own the homes they live in, although the majority has only had one or two addresses since the child entered school. These indicators of pervasive poverty are important as it has been clearly established across many populations that living in poverty is one of the most consistent and powerful correlates of children's poor developmental outcomes.[15] Thus, even if Cambodian children live in two-parent families, some of the derived benefits associated with this protective factor need to be understood in conjunction with two caveats—their family's profile of low educational attainment and poverty. According to the literature in human development, both these are at-risk contexts for their children's development.

> Since arriving in the United States, Jorani and her husband have worked in the jewelry business for a total of 8 years combined (Jorani for 3 years and her husband for 5 years). Friends recommended them each for the jobs. They are currently unemployed, however. Jorani quit to care for her children, and she explains that Nimol stopped working because he got sick. To make ends meet, they are aided by welfare, and their current household income does not exceed $5,000 per annum. This money must be spread across seven people. The seven people in the house are Jorani, Nimol, their four daughters (ages 2, 4, 6, and 10) and Jorani's mother (aged 60).

But families living in poverty differ tremendously in other dimensions that are important for children's development, especially families from immigrant backgrounds, as discussed in Chapter 2. Cambodian families have other distinct characteristics, including cultural and educational values and practices that are pertinent to the developmental outcomes of our interest: their children's ethnic attitudes and identification and their academic achievement.

⠶ Cultural Socialization

Parents' language maintenance (in this case Khmer) and other family cultural routines and practices have been associated in other populations with children's own cultural attitudes and identification.[16] In turn, strong ethnic socialization and strong ethnic identities have been associated with an array of positive developmental outcomes.[17] When we interviewed the Cambodian primary caregivers about their language use and their cultural routines, we ascertained a sense of relative cultural isolation from mainstream American culture resulting in low cultural capital (Bourdieu, 1986). Cambodian parents strive for a family life congruent with some of the traditional values of Khmer culture but do not provide a strong foundation in the mainstream American culture. In terms of language use, Cambodian parents reported rather low comfort with regard to speaking English across various contexts (see Table 5 for actual numbers and statistical analysis). The interviews revealed the low level of comfort most parents felt speaking English with neighbors, teachers, and in other public spaces. They also spoke very little English with their children. Over 86% of the Cambodian interviews were conducted in Khmer, at the interviewee's request. Nationwide, 40% of Cambodians reported that they do not speak English well or at all, and 26% of the households were reported as linguistically isolated (Yang, 2004). From census data, 88% of Cambodians nationwide and 97% of Cambodians in Rhode Island report speaking a language other than English at home (U.S. Census Bureau, 2000b, 2000c). It seems that a larger percentage of the local Cambodian community has limited English proficiency in comparison to these national statistics.

Both children and parents also reported relatively frequent engagement in cultural routines at home such as listening to Khmer music, watching Khmer videos/TV, reading Khmer publications, eating ethnic foods, singing songs or playing games, and going to temple (see Table 5 for actual values and statistical analyses). On average, Cambodian parents and children engaged in each of these practices twice a week. Cambodian parents also report encouraging their child to feel good about their Cambodian heritage and perceive little racism toward their children. Thus, Cambodian children are growing up in home environments that are linguistically and culturally reflective of their parents' country of origin and encouraging of their own participation and identification with that culture, even though these memories of Cambodia are not refreshed by new arrivals and other news of life and culture there.

> Jorani is not comfortable speaking English. She only speaks Khmer at home and avoids having to interact with others in English. Her family has strong connections to Khmer culture, and she says that in particular they all enjoy eating Khmer food, watching Khmer TV, and listening to Khmer music. They are also always looking forward to celebrating the traditional Khmer New Year. Some of their family customs are not traditional though. For instance, they are not a particularly religious family. No one in the family attends temple or church, and they have no religious items in their home. A particularly salient example of Americanization is their expressed enjoyment of typical American fast food. They eat from McDonalds and Burger King almost as often as they eat Khmer food, at least 3–4 times a week.

The observed mixture of native cultural practices and acculturation is clearly the norm with many families of immigrant backgrounds.[18] But what is interesting about the Cambodian experience in Providence is, as previous mentioned, unlike other immigrant groups that are part of strong ethnic enclaves and/or continuing waves of immigration, these home-based language and cultural routines that children are part of are not often experienced or reinforced outside the home. In our sample, as expected, most Cambodian parents have not returned to their country of origin (only 13% had visited Cambodia) unlike a majority of Dominican (89%) and Portuguese (71%) parents who have returned to their home country.[19] Most Cambodian parents (83%) plan to stay permanently in the United States. Likewise, there is no steady wave of new Cambodian immigrants or Cambodians in position of power in the public light that exposes the children to significant role models who are more connected to their families' original culture (Bailey, 2000a). Finally, like their parents, the children do not visit Cambodia and therefore do not get to experience firsthand the culture in the country of origin.

Jorani's disconnect from Cambodia is not by choice as it rarely is with the Cambodian refugee population. When asked if she would like to visit Cambodia and where she would go, Jorani quickly replied, "Yes. See my home." She explained that it would be wonderful to return and to take her children with her. She said, "[my children] need to go and see my country." She knows, however, that it would be incredibly difficult to realize this dream. She no longer has any direct ties to the country. She has no other relatives or Cambodian friends in the United States, and she has not maintained any contact with family or friends still in Cambodia.

Both the parent interviews and the ethnographic study point out the relatively small numbers of Khmer-oriented institutions outside of the temple and the activities organized around Cambodian holidays, such as New Year. In addition, most Cambodian parents, living dispersed as they are throughout the South Side, report that they do not feel like they belong in the neighborhoods they live in, that their neighborhood is not their community, and that their neighbors are predominantly of other ethnicities (Table 2 for actual values and statistical tests). In fact, they feel like they neither have a community nor are part of community-based organizations.

Jorani currently lives on a "Spanish block" and says that she is unhappy there. She describes it as being too noisy and makes it clear that the neighborhood is not her community in any way. It is not the first time that she has felt this way. The family has actually moved 2 times since her child started school, having spent only 4 months in their current rented apartment.

In sum, Cambodian children are raised in a family context that reflects on a regular basis the parents' cultural knowledge from the home country and their adaptation to a new setting without much reinforcement from others outside the immediate family. The relative isolation of these families, both from other Cambodians and from their neighborhoods and mainstream American culture, has important consequences for the children's comfort with their own ethnicity and other ethno-cultural processes, as we shall see later in this chapter.

⬛ Educational Values and Practices

Research has found that parents differ in their educational aspirations and their involvement in their children's formal education.[20] Additional research has shown that these differences in values and practices are associated with their children's educational outcomes.[21] In spite of their relative cultural isolation from mainstream institutions, Cambodian families have high educational aspirations for their children, a value that has been identified as part of traditional Khmer culture and of immigrant families in general.[22] When asked about their aspirations for their children's future, 86% of Cambodian parents reported that they wanted their children to complete a college education, and 81% identified career goals for their children where the careers required education beyond college, such as becoming a physician or an attorney.

Jorani has high academic expectations for her daughters. When asked about her daughter, she said that she wants her to graduate from college, and the only major deterrents that she fears are "bad friends and gangs." Jorani hopes that her daughter will be a doctor, but having received little formal education herself, she is unsure of the exact steps that need to be taken to achieve that goal. When asked how many years her child must dedicate to school to receive a medical degree, she guessed "5 years." Jorani feels that there is a strong correlation between morality and education, and being convinced of her daughter's strong moral values might be what helps convince her that her daughter will in fact succeed. When asked what makes an adult a good person, Jorani responded, "Respect, tradition, and culture. Do well in school." For her, the American educational system is a dependable pathway that leads to a good job.

The importance of parents espousing such attitudes is suggested by the fact that parents' high educational aspirations and expectations for their children have been associated in other populations with their children's own higher academic aspirations, expectations, and achievement, thus parents' aspirations typically have constituted a protective factor for their children's development.[23]

These high aspirations and expectations, however, do not translate into a high level of parental involvement of Cambodian parents in their children's formal education or the provision of supports and resources in the household (see García Coll et al., 2002 for a detailed analysis). In all aspects of parental involvement, from beliefs about involvement to providing a place to study, rules about behaviors, checking homework, and number of meetings with a teacher, having a computer, and a place to do your homework and where books are kept, Cambodian parents have very low levels of involvement (See Table 6 on educational values and practices). Only half of Cambodian families (vs. 96% of Portuguese families and 92% of Dominican families) reported active involvement in their children's education (see Table 6 for actual values and statistical tests). Differences were observed in all aspects of parent involvement: ideology, school based, home rules, and provision of educational resources. In addition, perhaps as a function of their low level of education and/or their isolation from mainstream culture, Cambodian families do not display home literacy practices that have been identified elsewhere as promoting literacy and school achievement among children.[24] These include parent's independent reading habits as well as those of their children, shared reading practices, and the number of children's and other books at home (see Table 7 on family literacy activities). Most of these indicators are rather low, the highest being the reading habits of the children themselves.

Jorani sees the importance of education in the life course and has very high expectations for her children. Nonetheless, she believes that parents should be minimally involved and that most teachers do just fine; therefore, it is not necessary that she contact the school regularly. There is not a particular school that she would want her child to be in, and when asked if she is involved in her child's education, she states, "No. I'm not educated." In fact, she admits that if her child's schoolwork seemed too easy, she would not do anything about it. She puts great trust in the abilities and intentions of the teacher. She said that she would meet with her child's teacher if the teacher requested it but she feels just "ok" about having this communication. She stresses that in her own home there are no communication problems with her children. If she chooses to she can talk to her child about "schoolwork, everything, everyday."

How do we reconcile the discrepancy between high educational aspirations and low parental involvement and literacy practices observed amongst Cambodian parents? Both cultural beliefs and barriers contribute to the discontinuity between high educational aspirations and low parent educational involvement and literacy practices observed in these families. Traditionally, teachers in Cambodia were absolute authority figures in the realm of academic pursuits (Bailey, 2000a; Collignon et al., 2001), and parents neither were expected to nor thought it appropriate to play a role in their children's formal education (Ebihara, 1985; Hopkins, 1996; Smith-Hefner, 1999). That is why most Cambodian parents believe that they *should* not be involved in their children's education. Although we know that exposure to the American school system has made some Cambodian parents aware of their expected role in their children's education, parents and community leaders identified many barriers to their successful involvement. Such obstacles are English language barriers in particular, illiteracy, and their experience in an educational system where parents were expected not to be involved.

In our quantitative analysis of our parent interviews, the main obstacle (see Table 5 for actual numbers and statistical analysis) was English language comfort. We speculate that parents who feel more comfortable speaking English across a variety of contexts can communicate more effectively with school personnel and learn what is expected of their involvement in their children's education in this culture and accordingly act more proactively. Additionally, community and educational leaders revealed that illiteracy, lack of experience with the American educational system, and the traumatic experiences with the Khmer Rouge resulting in distrust of all authority figures also make it difficult for Cambodian parents to be engaged in their children's schooling. The lack of involvement among Cambodian parents is not reflective of a lack of interest in their children's academic success or high valuing of education, but rather is a direct function of their complex life experiences which include conflicting cultural values, inability to communicate effectively with school personnel, and unfamiliarity with an educational system that expects their active involvement and which defines parent involvement in ways that are foreign to them.

A qualitative analysis of the parents' comments to open-ended questions reveals many of the conflicting feelings that Cambodian espouse given their high educational aspirations and their lack of know-how. Because these parents self-ascribe the label of "not educated," it becomes apparent that they perceive their involvement not only as unnecessary, but unhelpful. This attitude is reinforced by their unfamiliarity with the American educational school system. In fact, when parents are asked what kind of jobs they would like for their children, some will indicate doctor or lawyer as the desired profession.

However, when asked what level of education they hope their child will attain, most simply answer 4 years of college. This highlights their unfamiliarity with the required years of higher education that certain professions entail. Hence, these parents leave most school-related decisions (those mostly encompassing only homework at this point) up to their child's discretion, as their children are well versed not only in the English language (see Table 16) but in American mainstream culture as well. This creates an interesting paradox when considering that Cambodian parents not only desire but promote in their values system the attainment of higher education levels for their children, going so far as to correlate a good education with the development of high moral values. However, the parental involvement usually associated with successful academic achievement in our culture is often not present within this immigrant group. They actively seek to promote high moral values in their children, anticipating that in the United States as in Cambodia these values will encourage high academic achievement. But the organization, curriculum, and pedagogy of American public education will not, on the whole, reward this presumption.

Another factor contributing to the contradictory pattern between values and practices in parental involvement as suggested by the qualitative analyses of parents' comments may be the parents' comfort level with English as a spoken and written language. The parents' ability to grasp the American educational school system as a means for their own immediate survival is not necessary since they are not attending schools themselves, but the importance of a good education for their children is not only understood but desired. Therefore, their children become the sole mediators between their own parents' cultural traditions and those outside their own immediate social sphere. Hence, allowing their children almost complete autonomy in issues concerning homework levels of difficulty, amount of schoolwork, and student–teacher relationships becomes the norm in this population. Nonetheless, it is important to point out that most, if not all Cambodian parents, would have no quarrel, despite their comfort levels with the English language, in speaking with a teacher or school official whenever disciplinary or educational problems arise. Therefore, when a parent perceives that their child is having relatively little difficulty in school (whether or not this is the case, it can not be known) they allow their children educational autonomy.

The Cambodian family environment just described can be considered, in sociological terms, as environments for children's development, which put these children at risk for poor academic outcomes. Their relative cultural isolation and poverty are of great concern. However, these families have various attributes that are considered protective, including a predominance of two-parent families, high cultural socialization, and high educational aspirations and expectations for their children. So, how do their children fare?

⠣ Children's Cultural Attitudes and Identification

One of our main interests in this study was to elucidate the ways children of this developmental period construct, enact, and define their membership in their own ethnic group. For example, definition of and comfort with their ethnic identity, their attitudes toward their own ethnic group and others, and their perceptions of discrimination in interpersonal interactions are all processes that we wanted to understand better in this study. We were interested in these processes not only as a function of ethnic group, but also as a function of age and gender. Because much of the research in these topics has been conducted with adolescents and adults, we wanted to learn more about these processes in middle childhood, keeping in mind our understanding of community and family context.

⠣ Children's Ethnic Identities

As discussed in more detail in Chapter 3, ethnic identity has been conceptualized as one of the normative tasks of ethnic minority adolescents in the United States.[25] We know that children are aware of racial/ethnic categories, sometimes as early as 3 years of age.[26] We also know that other aspects of identity such as gender are also acquired much earlier.[27] Do we find evidence that children of Cambodian immigrants are forging an ethnic identity during middle childhood?

Cambodian children, when first interviewed in either first or fourth grade, showed awareness of their membership in a particular ethnic group as part of other aspects of their identity (see Akiba, Szalacha, & García Coll, 2004 for a more detailed analysis). In the current study, when asked to select all the labels that they felt applied to them from a variety of identity labels such as gender, role, and ethnicity (see Appendix B for list of labels used), children from both age cohorts selected a variety of labels that depicted multiple aspects of their identity. In terms of ethnicity, 95% of the younger cohort and 97% of the older cohort of Cambodian backgrounds chose "Cambodian" as one of the labels that applied to them (See Table 8). So as with adolescents (see, for example, Rumbaut, 1994b), children of immigrants during middle childhood tend to choose nationality labels as relevant to their identity.

With increasing age though, Cambodian children selected other labels that reflected both their increasing understanding of their own ethnicity and their process of acculturation to American culture. Older children chose a significantly greater number of labels than did the younger ones; the most frequent ones were "Khmer" (which denotes not only language but also the people and religion of Cambodia), "Cambodian-American," "Asian" and "Asian-American." In particular, the latter three reflect their learning process of socially constructed groupings that are relevant only in an American context; especially the last two, where people who have very little in common are perceived as homogenous categories (see Cooper et al., 2005 for a discussion of the origin of social categories).

Another dimension of ethnic attitudes and identification is how good the respondent feels about her/his identification with that label. This aspect has been referred to in the literature as ethnic satisfaction. Cambodian children show a mixed picture in this regard (see Table 9). When asked "Of all these words about you, which one makes you the happiest?" 40% of Cambodian children endorsed an ethnic label. When asked why this label makes you happy, children would say things like:

"I can speak to Mom in Cambodian"
"I don't really know [what] my life would be like if I wasn't"
"Because it shows who I am"

However, when asked if they would like to get rid of a label, 43.9% of Cambodian students indicated that they would. In addition, among those children who want to be rid of a label, a higher percentage of Cambodians chose ethnic minority–related labels to get rid of (78%) than Portuguese (28%) and Dominican (51%) students, indicating less satisfaction with their minority ethnic identity. Reasons given for wanting to get rid of an ethnic-minority label included "Because I want to be full American" and "I don't know what they're talking about when they talk Cambodian." So Cambodian children vary considerably in how they feel about their ethnicity, ranging from very happy with to wanting to get rid of ethnic-minority labels.

There are, however, interesting developmental differences. For the happiest label selected, a greater proportion of older students (52.5%) than younger students (32.1%) selected an ethnic-minority label as the one that makes them happiest (for the younger children, it was most often the gender label that most often made them happy). In addition, of those children who chose a hyphenated label (e.g., Cambodian-American), 65% of them were in the older cohort. When asked if they would like to get rid of a label, a smaller proportion of older students (33.9%) chose to get rid of a label than younger students (54.9%). By these two measures, older Cambodian students demonstrate a higher level of satisfaction with their ethnic identity than the younger students, perhaps showing that as they are exposed and have more contact with mainstream culture, they become bicultural (since they maintain ethnic activities at home) and more comfortable with their own ethnicity.

A similar developmental trajectory was found when we ascertained other aspects of children's ethnic identities. Among these are ethnic pride, centrality, saliency, and stability (see Appendix A for examples of the questions used to assess each of these constructs). Ethnic pride was measured by asking the child about how happy, proud, and good their ethnicity makes them feel. Centrality was measured by asking the child whether it was important (yes or no) for his or her classmates to know different aspects of his or her ethnicity. Salience refers to how important a particular identifying label is to a child and was measured by calculating how many times a particular label was chosen as the single most important label to the child over the 3 years of the study. Stability refers to how consistently a child identified with the exact same self-identifying labels over the three years (Portes & Rumbaut, 2001). On average, Cambodian children report being relatively proud of their ethnicity and for their ethnicity to be relatively salient and stable (see Table 9). However, in terms of comparisons to the other groups, Cambodians report relatively lower ethnic pride but higher salience than Portuguese children. These findings might reflect the pride of being part of an established and relatively successful ethnic enclave (Portuguese) at the same time that as children of many other white, European immigrants, ethnicity is less salient in their day-to-day life. They become more easily and rapidly part of the mainstream American culture. At the same time, older Cambodian students demonstrated more ethnic pride than younger ones, indicating a pattern of increasing comfort with their ethnic identity as they mature.

◼◼ In-Group and Out-Group Preferences

Both theory and research[28] suggest that another important aspect of childrens' perceptions of group membership is their evaluations such as preferences and discomforts with their own group and other groups. Referred to as in-group and out-group attitudes, these attitudes are widely studied within Social Psychology, primarily with adolescents and adults.[29] In order to ascertain these attitudes, we asked children to tell us how they would feel in hypothetical situations in which they would have to interact with children of other ethnicities (including white, black, Asian, and Latino) in their homes and schools in year two and three of the study (see Appendix A, for specific questions asked). Cambodian children have the lowest comfort with the out-group at home and in school (see Table 10 for actual values and statistical analysis), and they also have lower in-group comfort at home than Dominicans. In general, Cambodian children, as the other groups, show an in-group preference in that they feel most comfortable at home with children of their own ethnicity and least comfortable in any setting with children of other ethnicities. We interpret this finding as a reflection of Cambodians' relatively large cultural distance that separates them from mainstream American culture, as compared to Dominicans and Portuguese. Both Cambodian parents and children express discomfort in interacting with members of other ethnic groups: Parents were uncomfortable in speaking English with people outside their group and did not feel part of their ethnically mixed neighborhoods; children were uncomfortable interacting with others both at home and in school.

Developmental differences are present that suggest that the discomfort diminishes as children grow up. Our study showed cohort differences in that the older cohort shows more comfort with the in- and out-group at home in both years of the study. This is perhaps a function of having had more peer contact and therefore familiarity with children from both their same ethnicity as well as others. Importantly, for this group (as well as the Dominican and Portuguese groups), we found in a detailed analysis of these in-group and out-group preferences that children with greater amounts of in-group preference *also* were more likely to prefer spending time with out-group children. This finding is contrary to those presented in early in-group/out-group bias research assuming that a stronger sense of in-group preference also implies a greater amount of out-group prejudice. Further, for the Cambodians in particular, children who identified with nationality (i.e., Cambodian), multi- or shared nationality (e.g., Cambodian-American), and panethnic (e.g., Asian) labels were also more likely to have higher in-group social preferences (Marks, Szalacha, Boyd, & García Coll, 2007).

Another aspect of intergroup relations is perceptions of discrimination. As described in Chapter 3, research shows that perceptions of discrimination are reported as starting in middle childhood even though earlier we might see in-group and out-group preferences.[30] To assess perceptions of discrimination, we asked children to explain to us why in a hypothetical situation some children were excluded from participation in class, not invited to play, or called derogatory names (see Appendix A for samples of these questions). Only one third of Cambodian children perceived discrimination in the two years that they were asked. Not only did an absolutely small number of Cambodian children perceived discrimination, but they were also the ones that perceived the least discrimination of the three groups (see Table 11). They also perceived discrimination in fewer scenarios than the other groups. We can only speculate at this point of why Cambodian children would perceive less discrimination. Perhaps this is due to the fact that as they are considered Asian in their schools they are least discriminated against given their membership in a model minority.[31]

⠶ Children's Academic Outcomes

The other main developmental outcomes of interest in this study are several aspects of academic achievement. In addition to 3 years of grades, we included a series of attitudinal measures, broadly conceptualized under the construct of academic attitudes (see Appendix A for copies of the measures). These include attitudes toward school and teachers, actual practices like time spent on homework or watching TV and school absences, and expectations and aspirations about college. We also obtained official academic records during the 3 years of the study and teacher ratings of the student in the third year. The inclusion of a variety of academic outcomes, including self-reports of attitudes and behaviors, grades, and teacher ratings provided us with a rather comprehensive view of these processes during this developmental period.

Although some characteristics of Cambodian families would predict poorer academic outcomes for their children, this hypothesis was only partially supported in this study. From a human, social, and cultural capital perspective, the parents' lack of formal education, their linguistic and cultural isolation, and their lower occupational status and consequent poverty would predict that these children, both in absolute and in relative terms to the other two groups, would have less optimal academic outcomes. However, the prediction of lower academic outcomes based on their families' relative high-risk status was not overwhelmingly supported. We actually found evidence in support of the immigrant paradox—the phenomena in which less acculturated, poorer individuals have more optimal outcomes than those coming from families with more socioeconomic resources and higher acculturation in the academic outcomes of this ethnic group.

⁛ Academic Attitudes and Practices

Academic achievement is a multifaceted construct that includes not only "objective measures" such as grades but also children's attitudes toward school, their teachers, and academic achievement in general. One aspect of academic attitudes that has been found to be of significance in other populations is children's attitudes toward school and their teachers. In other words, children who espouse more positive attitudes toward school (i.e., they report being more engaged and to agree more with school values) and toward their teachers tend to also show better academic outcomes.[32] In our study, Cambodian children espoused generally positive attitudes (all means were above three on five point scales) toward school and their teachers (see Appendix A for a sample of these questions). But as predicted by their family's high-risk status, Cambodian children did show slightly less school engagement and less positive attitudes toward their teachers than the other two groups (see Table 12 for actual values and statistical tests). Thus in general, Cambodian children reported positive attitudes, even if slightly lower than their counterparts.[33] In addition, as Cambodian children get older, their school values and attitudes toward their teachers become more positive to where they are on par with the Dominican and Portuguese students. The initial more negative attitudes might be a function of cultural distance rather than actual lower academic engagement; in other words, as Cambodian children spend more time in school, they might feel more connected to the institution, its practices, and members. They might become more acculturated to schooling in the United States, a process they might experience on their own and largely independent from their families. Since they are also maintaining cultural routines at home, these children might be becoming bicultural.

Another important aspect of academic attitudes involves children's aspirations and expectations for the future.[34] In this respect, we asked children whether they wanted and expected to go to college and if others felt the same (see Appendix A for sample questions). Although Cambodians held very high aspirations to go to college, they had certainly lower expectations to do so (see Table 12), especially in comparison to Dominican children. However, in perceptions of teachers, school engagement, and values and desire to go to college, the older cohort has higher scores than the younger cohort, showing perhaps that with increasing age and exposure to school, Cambodian children feel more positive about schooling and their academic future.

Finally, in terms of actual daily practices that are relevant to academic outcomes, Cambodian spent on average 22 minutes doing homework each day and watch around two and a half hours of TV daily. These findings are in line with those from a nationwide survey reporting that most fourth graders spend half an hour or less on homework and watch two to three hours of TV daily (U.S. Department of Education, 1998). Cambodian children were absent from school an average of 7 days a year. In Rhode Island, most students (60%) miss fewer than 10 days a year (Annie E. Casey Foundation, 2005). Evidently, Cambodian children are within the average among children their age with regard to these self-reported behaviors. The only statistically significant difference between the Cambodian children and the children from the other two immigrant groups is in the time spent on homework, which is significantly lower (although not dramatically) than that reported by Dominicans. This is perhaps a reflection of the fact that more Dominican children attend parochial schools, which are reported to require more daily homework.

In sum, although Cambodian children espouse positive attitudes toward school, their teachers, and their future and have early positive behaviors, they scored significantly lower than the other groups in some respects. However, the differences observed are minimal given that most children score on the positive range of the distribution in most measures, and their scores are not as negative as expected from their families' high-risk status. Also, the older cohort espouses more positive attitudes, which indicates that with time Cambodian children might be showing more positive attitudes toward school, their teachers, and their future.

∷ School-Related Stress

Another way to look at children's adaptation to school is to assess their experiences of stress in response to various aspects of school such as peers, teachers, and academic demands (see Table 13 for actual values and statistical tests). On average, Cambodian children perceived little stress associated with school, just like the Dominican and Portuguese children. These differences were present in both cohorts (in second graders as well as fifth graders). Again, their slightly higher emotional manifestation of stress might be reflecting a more difficult adaptation process for Cambodian children to school, as a function of their families' cultural isolation and unfamiliarity with schooling in the United States. In general, examining the different sources of stress, Cambodian children report slightly more emotional and academic stress than other sources of stress. There is also a cohort effect, with older children experiencing slightly more academic stress than younger children. So even if Cambodian children are more comfortable with their ethnic identity and their attitudes about school are more positive in the older cohort, the older children worry slightly more about their academic performance.

So the picture that we obtain is one where Cambodian children have slightly lower, yet still mostly more positive academic attitudes than would be expected. Although they experience more emotional stress, the absolute numbers are not as negative as their families' high-risk status would predict.

∷ Grades and Teacher Reports

In spite of their families' high-risk characteristics and their slightly less positive attitudes toward school and their teachers and their experience in school of more emotional stress, Cambodian children have good grade point averages in school, and their teachers think of them as good students. So it seems that even if Cambodian children might feel less at ease at school, their academic performance as a group is not affected negatively, at least up through grade 6. These findings again suggest that their slightly less positive attitudes toward school, their teachers, and their future academic success and their slightly higher stress might be more a function of their relatively larger cultural distance with school culture rather than their actual disengagement with school.

Another way to examine academic success is by asking teachers to rate each individual child in comparison to his or her classmates in terms of behaviors (e.g., working hard, paying attention, etc.) and future development. Cambodians were rated by their teachers significantly higher than Dominicans and Portuguese (see Table 14 for actual values and statistical tests). Teachers rate Cambodian students in comparison to their other classmates as displaying greater effort, attention, carefulness, and enjoyment in their work as well as higher ranked social skills such as getting along better with other kids and behaving better in the classroom, than teachers of Dominican students and Portuguese. Teachers of Cambodian students were also more optimistic about the child's socioemotional development. From other research, we know that teacher expectations are important predictors of actual academic achievement,[35] and this seems to be the case in this study: Not only are Cambodian children rated as better students by their teachers, but a higher percentage of Cambodian children are in positive academic pathways (see below).

A final way that we examined academic achievement was to examine pathways in a more qualitative way (see Chapter 4 and Appendix A for a description of the methodology). We categorized the children's progression during the three years (based on grades and teacher ratings) as excelling, positive, mixed, negative, or abysmal. In this analysis, we find that in spite of their families' lower educational attainment, lower parental involvement and literacy practices and higher rates of poverty, and more cultural isolation, there is a group of 28 Cambodian children who are excelling in their academic pursuits. Twenty-one percent of Cambodian children are excelling (compared to only 10% of Dominicans and Portuguese). These children are providing evidence in support of the immigrant paradox in this study: They are getting excellent grades across the three years of the study, and their teachers attest to their excellence, all in spite of a relatively disadvantaged cultural and economic family profile. Sophal is one of them:

Sophal, an exemplary excelling Khmer kid, describes herself as "kind of smart, getting good grades, having a lot of responsibility, and playing and hanging out with friends." Two of the many labels she selected to describe herself were "girl" because her "ears are pierced" and "Khmer-American" because "I speak Khmer and I was born in America." She likes speaking both Khmer and English the same "because I can talk English with my friends a lot, and Khmer with my sisters a lot." She does prefer hanging out with Cambodians though, because she feels as if others "might make fun of me." Not only does Sophal watch Khmer videos, but she also listens to Khmer music daily with her family. Although she eats Khmer food every day, she also loves eating pizza and food from McDonalds. On a typical afternoon after school, she spends about 45 minutes completing her homework assignments, watches her two younger step-sisters, helps her mother with chores, and watches *Rugrats*, her favorite cartoon, with her sisters. Her parents have no rules about when she has to be home or who she is with, but she must do her homework before watching TV. She reads for pleasure a few times a month and thoroughly enjoys reading *Harry Potter*. Even though her family does not own a computer, Sophal has access to a computer at school. On the weekends, she spends time with her family at the movies, stores, and amusement parks. She loves singer/actor Will Smith and pop music. Art is her favorite subject in school "because we get to make mosaics." She enjoys school because of the projects, field trips, and parties. She believes it is very important to receive good grades "because I can learn more." Her list of priorities also includes staying out of trouble, doing her homework, and graduating from high school "so I'll go to college." She aspires to attend college and to be either a teacher so that she can "teach other kids to learn" or a nurse when she grows up. Attending every day of school is also very important to her "because my mom will be very happy" and "that's why I got the attendance award." While in 4th and 5th grades at B. J. Clanton-Mandela School, she was only absent once each year. During her 6th grade at Roger Williams School, she only missed three days of school.

Sophal's mother immigrated to the United States after seven years of schooling in Cambodia and has not traveled back to Cambodia to visit her family because of financial reasons. She works in a factory and her annual income is $15,000–19,999, while her daughter's step-father takes GED classes at the YMCA to improve his English. They have rented a house in a Dominican neighborhood where "no one been bother" for the past five years, and they have lived in three places in Providence since Sophal began school. She does not want her peers to know where she lives in Providence and also believes that others know that her family is from Cambodia based on "the way I look and sometimes the way I speak." Sophal's mother comfortably speaks English to neighbors and at work, yet mostly speaks Khmer at home. Her mother believes that school systems in this country succeed at educating children, and she hopes that her daughter at least graduates from college and "gets a good job." Either her

> step-father or mother checks her homework daily. Not only does her mom believe that her daughter is a good student because "her report card A-B, and she never make any trouble at school," but her teacher confirms this statement by describing Sophal as "very goal and task-oriented, willing to complete every assignment fully, and having a high academic standing."

What places these children on academic pathways that are so positive? We conducted statistical comparisons of Cambodian children who are excelling ($n = 27$) and those who show either abysmal or negative pathways ($n = 26$) to see which other characteristics differentiated these groups (see Table 15). Interestingly, and replicating the lack of association between family characteristic and the children's academic pathways in the whole group analysis, only one family characteristic differentiated the groups: The families of excelling and negative/abysmal kids are similar sociodemographically, but differ by year of immigration. Families of excelling children arrived in the United States on average three years later than the families of children who were on a negative or abysmal academic pathway. Academic pathways therefore are not related to any aspects of daily practices or family values such as cultural practices, educational values and practices, and literacy activities, but to the number of years that the family has been living in the United States. These findings are congruent with others that find that longer stay in the United States is associated with lower academic achievement (Suárez-Orozco & Suárez-Orozco, 1995).

However, Cambodian children who excel differ from those who are on negative/abysmal pathways in certain other important characteristics, but not always in expected ways. Excelling children experience less teacher-related stress and have less behavioral and physical manifestations of stress in the school setting (see Table 13 for actual values and statistical analysis). These findings contradict findings in other populations, where high achieving children experience more school-related stress.[36] In addition, as expected in terms of academic attitudes, children on excelling pathways show more positive attitudes toward school and teachers and higher engagement. Finally, the only behavioral difference between the groups is in terms of school absences: Children who are in negative/abysmal academic pathways are absent from school over three times more than those who are in excelling pathways. This is congruent with national findings that school absences contribute to academic failure.[37]

Another set of interesting distinctions refers to differences between Cambodian children who are in excelling versus negative/abysmal pathways in terms of ethnic identification and attitudes. Cambodian children who are in excelling pathways show more ethnic pride, more comfort with out-groups at home, and show English-language preference. In other words, they feel better about their own ethnicity and are comfortable with others. In sum, comparing Cambodian children who display very different academic pathways points to a single family characteristic (length of stay in the United States) and an array of attitudinal variables toward schooling and their own and other ethnicities as possible explanatory variables.

Arun is an example of a Cambodian youth on an abysmal pathway:

Arun is a fifth grader on an abysmal pathway. He describes himself as "small" and "not like his sister." He likes the music from *Titanic*, and he "does not like to read books or swear." He chooses the ethnic descriptors "Cambodian," "Khmer," and "Asian" and notes, "I want to be Cambodian." In school, he likes "doing handwriting and having free time" and does not like "doing math or getting suspended." He espouses positive school values and notes that he wants to graduate high school because he wants to drive a car and wants to go to school every day "to pass the grade." However, he indicates that he is often absent and does his homework only sometimes. He is also often bored at school and is not comfortable at school because "people were bothering me and checking in my desk." In addition, he reports that only a few of his teachers like him, believe that he can do well in school, or would be willing to help him if needed. Finally, he says that his classmates don't treat each other well "that they always swear, and they hate each other." Under this context, it is not surprising that Arun indicates he does not want his classmates to know about his home culture (e.g., what country he came from, what kind of food he eats at home, etc.); he does not spend time with friends outside of school, rather his time is spent with family members at home or at his cousins house.

On a typical day after school, Arun plays games until 4, does his homework, and then watches cartoons with his parents and some of his siblings. He spends only between 10 and 20 minutes a day on homework, usually in the living room where he has little privacy. While working, he is interrupted "all the time" by his brothers.

He does not have a computer in his home, and Arun's mother indicates that they do not own any books.

Arun's mom speaks solely Khmer, as does her husband, and her children regularly translate for her. Arun also prefers to speak Khmer but uses both languages when interacting with teachers and peers. Both Arun's parents and Arun eat Cambodian food daily, and they listen to Cambodian music and watch Cambodian TV a few times a week. They live in a rented apartment—the one of four residences they have had since Arun started school. In this apartment, Arun, his seven brothers and sister, and his parents live on a yearly income of between $10,000 and $14,999. Most of this money comes in the form of government aid, as neither parent is working or has worked since they came to the United States. Arun's mother wishes that they could move from their current neighborhood, which she views as unsafe (she notes that there was one person who was recently killed in a drug feud). The neighborhood is mostly Dominican, and she does not feel as though she belongs nor is it her community, but she feels she has no option to move to a better neighborhood "with so many children." Arun's mother does not believe that she should be involved in her child's education. But even if she did, she could not be involved, "Because I didn't know anything about school, I don't speak English." For these reasons, she does not meet with Arun's teacher nor does anyone check his homework. She believes that school, more specifically finishing college, is important for her son to get a job but worries that he will drop out before he reaches this goal. Unfortunately, by the third year of the study, Arun had dropped out of school after attending his sixth grade class for 3 days.

Unlike Sophal's family, who is English-proficient and incorporates both dominant and ethnic cultural routines into their daily life, Arun's family is far more culturally and linguistically isolated. Perhaps this isolation contributes to Arun's lack of strong peer support or positive teacher interactions. In addition, unlike Sophal, Arun who is one of eight children, is alone in his navigation of his own educational world—his parents are unable to check his homework, discuss school work, or give him specific advice on accomplishing his academic goals. It is interesting to note that both Arun's and Sophal's parents immigrated in the late 1970s despite the striking differences in acculturation levels of each family. This further highlights the importance of using multiple indicators (beyond year of immigration) when measuring acculturation.

⁘ Associations between Academic Outcomes and Ethnic Attitudes and Identification

Studying ethnic identification and attitudes in this study reflects two distinct purposes. One is to test the hypothesis that developmental processes underlying the "construction" of an ethnic identity are not only characteristic of adolescence but also of middle childhood. Our examination of the responses of the Cambodian children suggests that this is the case. Cambodian children choose ethnic/racial labels that they think apply to them and can talk about ethnic pride, centrality, and saliency. With age, these choices and explanations become more sophisticated.

The second purpose behind collecting this data is to test the associations between ethnic attitudes and identification and academic outcomes. From the work with adolescents from immigrant backgrounds and other ethnic minorities, we know that there are associations between these constructs during adolescence. In particular, ethnic minority adolescents and those from immigrant backgrounds who perceive more discrimination have worse academic outcomes.[38] There is evidence that some of these associations are beginning to emerge during middle childhood. For example, for these Cambodian youth, more ethnic pride and more in-group preference in school is associated with higher school engagement, more positive school values and perception of teachers, and higher college aspiration and expectations. Attitudes toward the out group at home and school also seem to be related to positive academic attitudes. Interestingly, no discernable pattern of association was seen with detection of discrimination. So even if children of this age start detecting discrimination, these perceptions are still not associated with academic attitudes.

⁘ Conclusions

For Cambodian youth, a striking cultural gap spans the area between home and school. These are the children of individuals who fled war and genocide, now living in a country they knew little about. Forced to navigate a competitive job market without substantial English skills or the safety net of a strong ethnic enclave, the majority of Cambodian parents continue to live below the poverty level and are socially isolated in their African-American and Hispanic communities and the larger American society. Many of these parents feel that they have little place, or ability, to help their children with homework and classes. Instead, these parents focus on the moral development of their children, central to which is learning and educational attainment, leaving concrete educational guidance to the schools.

Without the cultural continuity of an ethnic enclave (as our Dominican and Portuguese families experience) to back and bolster their home cultural experiences, Cambodian youth are left straddling two very distinct cultures. At home they speak Khmer and engage in many Cambodian cultural routines, while at school they are expected to use solely English and engage with teachers from the dominant American culture, and form relationships with peers from African-American and Hispanic immigrant backgrounds. These children therefore navigate their educational experience without help. This cultural divide between the home and school contexts places stress not only on children but on parents as well, who fear they will lose their sons and daughters to a peer culture they know little about.

Despite bridging these two worlds, many kids are making positive adaptations to the school environment obtaining good grades and eliciting approval from their teachers. Many of these children are described as models of good behavior and academic success for other youth, a perception that might in part contribute to their academic success. Both social and academic outcomes appear to improve over time, with ethnic label satisfaction, out-group preferences, school engagement, and perceptions of teachers are higher in the older cohort than in the younger. So, as Cambodian children adapt to school, they are not only becoming more comfortable with their own culture but they are more fully becoming members of a larger social network.

But the story is very different for some youth who, like Arun, may be more characterized by academic struggle and truancy. Individual associations between feelings toward school (i.e., higher levels of stress and more negative perceptions of teachers) and poor academic pathways point toward the stressors of cultural distance in school, perhaps a large part of the story for these youth. At the same time, higher ethnic pride and higher comfort with the out group are associated with positive academic pathways, showing the importance of positive ethnic identity and social development for this group. Development of a positive ethnic identity and positive out-group social attitudes may be further evidence of children overcoming this cultural isolation.

Despite analyses of associations between contextual and individual characteristics and outcomes presented above, the question remains: How do these predictors interact to predict the strikingly different pathways of excelling and abysmal pathway youth? Is recency of parent immigration a key predictor of outcomes? How important might this variable prove when entered into the model with ethnic pride?

6 ::

The Dominican Community: Recent, Growing, and Vibrant

The Dominican community in Providence has grown from a handful of families in the 1960s, to nearly 8,000 in the census of 1990, to over 15,000 in 2000 (U.S. Census Bureau, 1990a, 2000d). It is a vibrantly growing community with newcomers arriving regularly either directly from the Dominican Republic or from other northeastern cities, especially New York and New Jersey (see Bailey, 2000b; Itzigsohn, 2005). Many immigrants are driven by the perceptions of low cost of housing, good economic opportunities, and a safer environment for their children.

The character of the Dominican immigrant population has also changed dramatically over the years, from the 1960s with a primarily educated population of young adults originating from urban middle-class communities, to a much more economically, educationally, and regionally diverse population in the following decades. During the 1980s and 1990s, economic turmoil in the Dominican Republic lead to the migration of families from all spheres of society, including both skilled and unskilled workers, from both rural and urban locales. Family reunification and other sources of established community social capital provided resources for these new populations to immigrate. For many of the Dominican immigrants in our studies, their journey to the United States began with hopes and perceptions of great economic opportunities. Whether they came with previously well-paid occupational experiences or were seeking first-time employment, these visions of opportunity motivated their early adjustment to the United States, even through the realities of low job availability, limited Spanish-speaking opportunities, and relegation to the lowest paying jobs in our society.

Specifically, those with the most advanced educational skills (e.g., professional or college degrees) are hampered in their efforts by their limited English proficiency, while those with more limited educational backgrounds and English skills are in an even more precarious situation. Factory work, child care, cleaning positions, and maintenance jobs provide the entry level job to the U.S. job market for many Dominicans.

An important context for these migratory processes has been the 1965 Family Reunification Act, under which many Dominicans have come to the United States—making strong family networks a distinct characteristic of the Dominican migration process from its outset. The Dominican immigration context can be described as promoting a transnational community, creating a new U.S. community that does not shed its ties to the country of origin (Duany, 1998; Itzigsohn, 2005). Families, if they can afford it, send their children to the Dominican Republic for school vacations and summers to spend time with the extended family. Various U.S. commercial agencies (e.g., travel agencies, airlines) also facilitate the transnational movement of this mobile population. Further, if finances and immigration laws permit, relatives come to visit the United States for extended periods of time. Family members living in the United States can call upon their relatives abroad to attend birthdays, weddings, funerals, and respond to any family crisis, as many are in constant telephone communication with those back on the Island. There is also a proliferation of businesses that can be used to transfer money to the Dominican Republic in the local community— evidence, as well as the result, of this transnational phenomena. This constant back and forth contrasts with the Cambodian community's lack of ties or contact to the homeland or less frequent but still substantial communication between the Portuguese population and relatives in the Azores.

Dominican immigrants also often join well-established Latino communities, both locally and nationally (García Coll et al., 2002). The prominent news regarding the 2000 census in Providence and nationwide highlighted the significant growth of this broader Latino community (Suro & Passel, 2003). Locally, much of this growth was due specifically to the growth of the Dominican population. In Providence, Dominicans have joined a mostly secondary migration flow from New York City neighborhoods including Puerto Ricans, Central Americans, Mexicans, and South Americans. As is common in thriving immigrant communities, our community includes Spanish-language churches, businesses, sports leagues, restaurants, clubs, newspapers, television and radio stations, festivals, and community organizations serving Latinos. In addition to Latino organizations and businesses, there are more recently Dominican-owned and Dominican-identified establishments and organizations, such as food markets, travel agencies, radio stations, retail stores, and social-cultural organizations such as "Quisqueya en Accion" and "Club Juan Pablo Duarte." This population's entrepreneurship is not only seen in its ownership of numerous small businesses, but also in the successful election of Dominicans to seats in the state's House of Representatives and Senate.

In Providence, where our research takes place, Dominican families primarily live in the South Side of the city with African-Americans, as well as other recent immigrants from Latin America, the Caribbean, Southeast Asia, and Africa (Itzigsohn, 2005). However, as they can afford it, they also move to other nearby cities (e.g., Cranston) or neighborhoods looking for better schools and safer neighborhoods. In our sample, perhaps due to the concentration of Dominicans and other Latinos in their communities, Dominican parents report relatively high satisfaction with their neighborhoods (see Table 2). In particular, they feel a sense of belonging in their neighborhood, and report feeling that the neighborhood is their community. This is clearly in contrast to Cambodian parents, who feel the most negative about the neighborhoods they live in compared to the two other groups. The cultural continuity (e.g., shared language and tradition) within the Latino community may also be contributing to the positive connection that Dominicans feel to their neighborhoods. This cultural continuity may also help to promote positive feelings of ethnic pride and other emerging aspects of children's ethnic identities.

Nationwide and locally, Latinos tend to be younger than the population at large. This is evidenced very dramatically by their increase in the school census population (Chapa & De La Rosa, 2004). In the present study, Latinos represent about 48% of the elementary school students in the school district from which the Dominican samples were recruited (Information Works, 1999, 2000, 2001). Puerto Ricans and Guatemalans are the second- and third-largest Latino groups after Dominicans. Dominican children in our studies were the largest (if not one of the largest) ethnic groups in their schools (both public and independent). Thus, the Dominican children in this study were exposed to Latino cultural influences from multiple sources, including a significant population of Dominican peers in the school setting, an extensive network of Spanish-speaking adults in the community at-large and new waves of family immigrating to Providence from the Dominican Republic.

Although most children in the three immigrant groups from our study attend public schools, a greater number of Dominican children attend parochial or independent schools than the other two groups (See Table 3). This reflects in part the dissatisfaction expressed in the Dominican parents' focus group in which parents were critical of American public schools: too little homework, too little discipline. They saw parochial and independent schools as providing a more similar experience to their own schooling in the Dominican Republic, including more behavioral discipline, academic rigor, and demanding homework than public schools. In our sample, most of the parents completed their education in the Dominican Republic, and so they have a very different frame of reference of what formal education should be like. While in general, their knowledge of the American school system maybe limited due to lack of direct experience and contact with American educational institutions, the Dominican parents in our sample are very invested and involved in their children's education.

Despite parents' high academic aspirations for their children, the public schools the Dominican students attend oftentimes place them at risk for poor academic outcomes. Although 50% of the teachers have master degrees and the average teaching experience is ten years, there are significantly more teacher grievances in these particular schools than in the schools that Portuguese children attend (Information Works, 1999, 2000, 2001). Further, Dominican students' schools have four times the number of student suspensions than schools attended by our Portuguese children, and our Dominican children attend schools with a significantly larger proportion of students falling below the state's "Proficiency" mark in math and in writing (67% and 47% of Dominican students fell severely below proficiency in writing and math respectively, compared to 44% and 28% for Portuguese students). Dominican children also attend schools that are larger in student body size than Portuguese children, with a large proportion of racial minority students falling below the poverty line (student body characteristics oftentimes associated with fewer school resources; Orfield, 2001; Suárez-Orozco, 1987). Considering both the school characteristics and parents' concerns, the schools that the Dominican children are attending appear to put them at risk for lower performance and lower access to valuable educational resources. In many respects, the public schools that Dominicans and Cambodians attend are similar and for both groups less favorable than those which the Portuguese children attend; thus the school context of the Dominican and Cambodian groups places them at a larger risk of academic problems than the Portuguese.

⠇⠇ Dominican Families: Contexts for Children's Development

As with the Cambodian families, the Dominican families also provide a unique niche for their children's development, with both assets and vulnerabilities (see Table 4).

Family Immigration and Demographic Characteristics

As is representative of the national and local Dominican immigration, the Dominican families in our research arrived steadily throughout a 30-year period starting shortly after the immigration reform of 1965. Although their median year of immigration is the same as that of Cambodians (1984), their immigration spans a much longer period of time than the Cambodians. In these local communities, Dominican newcomers are still observed regularly, while the Cambodian migration stopped in the 1980s. Moreover, immigrants from other Caribbean, Central, and South American countries contribute to the constant renewal of the Latino culture and language in the local community, something also observed within the Portuguese community, but not in the Cambodian community. To a certain extent, Dominican parents' immigration patterns are more similar to the Portuguese, who are also "voluntary immigrants" (Ogbu & Simmons, 1998), than the Cambodians (who came in as refugees). So how might these vibrant communities represent both assets and vulnerabilities to the children's development?

Approximately half of the Dominican parents in our study migrated through other US ports of entry—many living at least briefly in New York and New Jersey—before finding their way to Providence. As the national trend of Dominican migration also reflects, many came because they had family members living in the Northeast, inclusive of Providence (Bailey, 2000b). This family migratory pattern is associated with a network of reciprocities and supports for the newcomer into the city that can contribute to successful adaptations (Portes & Rumbaut, 2001).

These family networks can also be supported by the ethnic enclave and provide sources of social capital for the whole family (Portes & Rumbaut, 2001; Zhou, 1997a), including the children. The presence of social networks is expected to contribute to more positive developmental outcomes (Portes, 1998).

Parents' age at migration is another important factor that shapes children's adaptations to the US. About half of the sample of Dominican parents came to the United States when they were adults, the other half when they were adolescents. Interestingly, age of arrival was not correlated with highest level of education which was almost universally completed in the Dominican Republic. However, these individual differences in age at arrival might have implications for acculturation to the host culture, inclusive of formal education. In our sample, how recent a parent arrives is correlated with their level of education and place of origin: More recent immigrants come more frequently from rural locations and have lower levels of education and less-skilled occupations. These socioeconomic characteristics differ dramatically from those of the initial wave of immigrants. In general, the pre- and postmigratory characteristics observed in our sample of Dominican parents agree with both national studies and our own ethnographic findings. We would expect that place of origin (e.g., rural) and level of formal education (e.g., low), which is correlated with more recent arrival, would contribute to less positive academic outcomes.

While their circumstances of migration are strikingly different, Dominican and Cambodian families share immigration characteristics. As with the Cambodian families, Dominican parents were, on average, in their mid-30s at the time of the study and they had been in this country on average since the mid-1980s. In addition, in both groups, most parents were born in the country of origin (there was very little, although some, marriage with other ethnic groups).

This pattern of migration is illustrated in the stories of our participants which emerged from the in-home interviews we conducted in Spanish. Below is a glimpse of one such story from a Dominican immigrant family in our study.

> Amelia and Daniel are immigrant parents who came from the Dominican Republic to the United States in 1981. They came directly to Providence, where Daniel's family was already established. These family connections, especially Daniel's sisters, helped the family to

get settled in the States and supported them through the transition. While having a family in the States was a tremendous facilitating factor in their immigration, the greatest motivation was, as Amelia puts it, the desire "for a good future." They share their home with Amelia's mother, Angela, who is 77 years of age, and their three children. Renata is a 15-year-old high school student, Julia is a 10-year-old elementary student, and their younger brother, Rafael, is 9 and attends elementary school as well.

In terms of assets or protective factors for their children's development, the Dominican families reported having the highest levels of education of all three groups with 67% of parents being high school graduates and 26% having some college education. In comparison to the Dominican population in Providence (U.S. Census Bureau, 2000e), our sample is more educated (only 46% of Dominicans living in Providence have a high school diploma and only 6% have a bachelor's degree). But for the Dominican sample in this study, the relatively higher parental educational attainments in their country of origin does not necessarily translate into other socioeconomic assets[1] that have been found advantageous for children's development. This can be seen when we take into consideration both the educational and the occupational level of our families.

Both Amelia and Daniel have earned a high school degree, which allowed Amelia to work as a secretary and Daniel as an accountant when still living in the Dominican Republic. However, Amelia, now 41, works as a babysitter, and Daniel, currently 44, works as a machine operator for a "fertilizer company." These occupations are lower in social standing than the ones they had in the Dominican Republic. These occupations allow them a combined income of about 20,000–29,999 dollars per annum.

It is of great concern that among our sample of Dominican families living in Providence, three quarters of the families live under the poverty line[2] and only a quarter own their own homes. This is in contrast to the figures observed for the larger Dominican population in Providence, where only 53% live below the poverty line and 9% own their home (U.S. Census Bureau, 2000d). The higher poverty level observed in our sample may be due to the fact that only 23% of the families have two parents employed (see Table 4),[3] and of these working parents, over 37% are unskilled labors. Moreover, the later the year of arrival, the higher the probability of being an unskilled worker and renting a house, perhaps reflecting the fact that more migrants are coming from rural areas recently than in earlier waves of Dominican migrants. One hundred percent of skilled workers in our study come from cities in the Dominican Republic. Coming from a rural area in the Dominican Republic is associated with having a parent not working. These high levels of poverty are of concern, since poverty has been consistently associated with negative developmental outcomes. Thus, it is an empirical question whether higher educational attainment of Dominican parents will be enough of an asset to their children's academic development to offset the obstacles created by the family's precarious socioeconomic status in this country.

In addition, almost half of the families in our research are single heads of households, a statistic that is reflective of both the Latino population at large in Rhode Island and congruent with the overall rates observed in the nation.[4] Several lines of research point out the negative effects of single parenting on children's development, inclusive of contributing to a higher incidence of families living in poverty.[5] So even if our sample of Dominican parents in Providence bring with them a relatively higher educational attainment (a protective factor) than Cambodians, they have similar sociodemographic risk factors.

There are two other characteristics of the Dominican families that are rather unique and might contribute to placing their children at further educational risk. One is family mobility, or the number of times that the family has moved since the child started school. Dominican families have moved almost twice as much as the other two groups of immigrant families. Household mobility has been identified as a potential disruption of the schooling process.[6] Another possible source of disruption for these children (but at the same time a source of ethnic enculturation—see discussion below in cultural practices) is the high percentage of families that do return to the Dominican Republic. Dominican families have the highest rates of travel to their country of the three groups: Close to 90% of the families have visited their country since they moved here. These families are part of a transnational community[7] that remits money to the native country and takes part in family life and rituals (e.g., weddings, baptisms, funerals, etc.) in both countries.

Amelia and Daniel have lived in their current house for the last four years; it is the third house they have lived in since their children began school. Amelia describes her immediate neighbors as being "good and normal," but she is not sure about those who live a bit further away. She notes that her neighborhood is composed mainly of "East Asians, Puerto Ricans, Guatemalans, and African-Americans." She likes where she lives because she has not had "any problems and everything is close by."

In keeping with the aforementioned data, Amelia maintains strong ties to the Dominican Republic, returning on average once per year to visit with her family. She usually stays there for at least 2–3 weeks. Amelia's children have been to the Dominican Republic twice before, for 2–3 month summer vacation, time usually spent at the beach and with extended family. The family also has other relatives in Connecticut and New York, whom they visit 2–3 times per year.

In sum, even if they migrate voluntarily to this country and they have a relatively higher level of education in comparison to the other two immigrant groups in this study, Dominican families do not present at this point in time the demographic profile of success seen in many voluntary migrant communities.[8] This socioeconomic disadvantage is congruent with other reports on these immigrants based on census statistics and other local and national research.[9] In comparison to the Dominican population that this sample was drawn from (Dominicans living in the city of Providence), our sample is more educated (67% have high school diplomas compared to 46% for larger Providence population) but poorer (78% of our families live below the poverty line compared to 53% in the larger population). This might reflect the relative recency of arrival of our sample, as we required that at least one parent was born in the Dominican Republic. However, they were comparable in household size and proportion working. In our sample, the high rates of poverty, single-headed households, and mobility are especially worrisome aspects of the developmental niches of these children.

Cultural Socialization

Dominican families display a rich cultural heritage that is supported by the maintenance of cultural routines at home, by participation in a thriving local Latino community, and by having frequent contacts with their country of origin.

As do the Cambodians, Dominicans report a relatively low comfort with English and a relatively high usage of their own native language with their children in comparison to Portuguese parents.[10] Ninety-five percent of parents completed their interviews in Spanish. This is comparable with the language use of the population (U.S. Census Bureau, 2000a) where over 91% of Dominican families in Providence report using primarily Spanish at home. These practices are even stronger for more recent Dominican immigrants.

These high rates of Spanish use and concomitant discomfort in English might be in part due to the prevalence of the use of Spanish in the community[11] and thus knowledge of English is not necessary to manage many aspects of daily life. Not only are there many local businesses and enterprises where Spanish is the dominant language, but many mainstream institutions have hired interpreters and/or bilingual workers who can handle the increasingly larger Spanish-speaking population. Let us consider Amelia's own account of her and her family's language preference and comfort:

> Amelia feels comfortable speaking in English in most circumstances, such as speaking to her neighbors, coworkers, and strangers on the phone or encountered during daily routines. However, she does not prefer English and feels most comfortable speaking in Spanish, the language she speaks at home to her husband, children, and mother. As a reflection of this preference, she chose to conduct the interview for this study in Spanish. She reports that her children on the contrary speak both languages equally.

Dominican families report the highest frequency of ethnic-group cultural activities (see Table 5), as compared to the Cambodian and Portuguese families. Dominican children also report the highest frequency of cultural activities themselves, reflecting how their own daily practices mirror their participation in a larger family and vibrant local community cultural life. The Dominican community as described earlier has infused the established Latino community with new communication outlets, restaurants, retail shops, and cultural festivities (including the annual Dominican festival and quinceaneros), where Spanish-American[12] foods, traditional customs, and Spanish language are the norm. Interestingly, individual differences are observed within this sample which are associated with immigration characteristics: Those who immigrated as adults maintain a higher number of cultural routines.

All of these cultural practices are reflected in the daily routines in which Amelia's and Daniel's family take part:

> The family's routine usually consists of eating Dominican food every day, except on Sundays, when they enjoy either American or Chinese food. They also attend church every Sunday, and the service is conducted in Spanish. Both parents watch Latino videos, TV, listen and sing to Spanish music, and read Spanish newspapers and magazines. Additionally, they are members of the Club "Juan Pablo Duarte," a sports and cultural club. Their children engage in the same activities as their parents, reading Spanish materials and listening to Spanish music slightly less often. In addition, the family celebrates Dominican Independence Day.

Returns to the native country, although possible sources of disruption to the schooling process, represent a complementary way for Dominican families to maintain a rich cultural life that their children are continuously part of within and outside the family. In comparison to Cambodian and Portuguese parents, Dominican parents report the highest rates of travel to their home country and the lowest rates of having plans of staying permanently in the United States. Dominican children describe vividly in their interviews their many visits to relatives in Dominican Republic, especially during school vacations and for family tradition (74% of Dominican children in our sample had traveled to the Dominican Republic).They also refer to their bilingualism as an asset, when queried by our interviewers, explaining that it allows them to communicate with their family "back home" in Spanish and function in their local communities in both languages. One Dominican child explained why the label "Dominican-American" made him the happiest because "If I am Dominican I can speak Spanish and if I am American I can speak English" or as another child noted, "I can speak both languages and ... it makes me feel special." In contrast to the relative cultural isolation of Cambodian families and their children, Dominican children experience many continuities and reinforcement to their family culture in the local community and in their visits abroad.

Thus, Dominican children are not only part of households and a larger local community that keeps the Spanish language and Latin-American culture alive, but they also have direct experiences with their parent's native country. We would predict that the strong continuity between family, local Latino community and country of origin, should contribute not only to stronger children's cultural daily practices, but also to stronger ethnic attitudes and identification. In fact, almost three quarters of Dominican parents report encouraging their children to feel good about their ethnicity.

The maintenance of Spanish by Dominican adolescents in Providence has been found to be a critical cultural practice associated with an ethnic identification of Dominican or Dominican-American (Bailey, 2002). Since 85% of Dominicans have African ancestry, these adolescents speak Spanish language as a way of distinguishing themselves from African-Americans and other African migrants (Bailey, 2001b). As such, the maintenance and reinforcement of the Spanish language by family members, newcomers, extended family in the Dominican Republic, and the Latino community at large in Providence support the second generation's "choices"[13] of identity.

Of course, these strong family cultural practices, participation in a local Latino community, and strong ties to the country of origin may indicate (although not necessarily[14]) low acculturation to the mainstream culture. Distinctive linguistic practices might, for instance, be associated with other differences from mainstream culture such as parenting practices. In an earlier publication (García Coll & Magnuson, 2000), we reported that higher comfort speaking the English language is associated with higher overall traditionally defined parental involvement in children's education, such as requesting a meeting with the teacher or checking daily homework(for more information, see section below). We have also seen how in the Cambodian sample, the relative linguistic and cultural isolation of Cambodian parents are associated with a larger cultural distance not only for parents but also for their children.

Thus, Dominican families, even if they have spent an average of 15 years in this country, do not feel as comfortable with their English skills as some immigrants, like our Portuguese families. This is reflected in their use of the Spanish language with their children. They speak mostly Spanish to their children, again reinforcing their original cultures but perhaps placing their children at risk if they come into school with limited English proficiency. In addition, we can speculate that the parents' lack of comfort with English contributes to their families' lower socioeconomic status given their relatively higher schooling and even employment status in the Dominican Republic.

Thus we are expecting the strong cultural practices observed in our Dominican families to be associated with children's strong ethnic identification, pride, and in-group social preferences. We are curious about the association of these strong cultural and linguistic practices with children's social identities and peer relationships. Is language use and preference a main dimension of identity in this age period as Bailey (2002) found for adolescents? Do Dominican children become bicultural, or do they remain strongly attached to the culture of origin and not assimilated to mainstream culture? What are the costs and benefits of cultural practices, inclusive of language use, for educational outcomes?

Educational Values and Practices

A major motivation of our Dominican parents' migration to the United States is to be able to have a better quality of life for their families. Many Dominican parents reported in their interviews and in the focus groups that their move to this country was primarily motivated by the pursuit of better educational opportunities for their children and occupational opportunities for themselves. As such, a majority of Dominican parents express high educational and occupational aspirations for their children. Ninety-eight percent of Dominican parents reported that they wanted their children to complete a college education. Eighty-five percent of these parents described professional occupations (physicians, attorneys, engineers, etc.) as their aspirations for their children's future—a reflection of their common goals and values for their children's educations.

Congruent with these goals, Dominican parents show a high belief in the importance of parental involvement in their children's education (see Table 6). It is interesting to note that the longer the time the parent has spent in this country, the stronger their belief in the importance of parental involvement in their children's education. This could be because earlier waves of immigration were more educated or alternatively, more contact with the educational system here has led to adherence to this value system that is espoused by the American Education System.

Dominicans have the highest percentage of parents who have met with (and meet most frequently with) their children's teachers. They also have the highest levels of all groups in terms of home-based rules (e.g., a time the child has to be home every night), a finding that is congruent with the view of Latino parents as stricter than white Americans.[15] In addition, an overwhelming majority of Dominican parents report that they regularly check their children's homework and provide material support in the form of space in the home and access to a computer for academic activities, both activities much higher than the Cambodian parents. Parents in the focus group, though, reported that their early efforts to be highly involved in their children's school diminished by fourth and fifth grade as language became more of a barrier. In accordance with this observation, there was a significant difference in family literacy activities between the younger and older cohorts, with parents of older children reading less often to their children than parents of the younger cohort. In general, the beliefs and practices of Dominican parents' involvement in their children's education was most similar to the Portuguese parents. This is in spite of their more recent migration and lower socioeconomic status than the Portuguese parents. Moreover, coming from a city in the Dominican Republic is associated with having met their child's teacher, having a computer, having a place for doing homework, and having a place for books than coming from a town or a rural location. Living in a city might make you more familiar with urban educational systems and their expectations from parents. This confirms how preimmigration contexts are important characteristics when analyzing both group and individual differences in parenting practices.

Dominican parents also report higher levels of various family literacy activities than Cambodian and Portuguese, such as parents more frequently reading for pleasure and parent and child more frequently reading to each other (see Table 7). Perhaps Dominican parents' motivation to migrate to this country for better educational opportunities for their children and their own experience with formal education might contribute to a higher level of parental involvement, academic resources, and literacy practices than the Cambodians. In sum, despite their similar socioeconomic disadvantage, Dominican parents look more similar to Portuguese parents than to Cambodian parents in terms of parental involvement, educational resources, and literacy practices in support of their children's education.

As far as Amelia's children's education is concerned, she believes that parents should be highly involved. She aspires for her children to obtain a professional degree, be it a master's or a doctorate. However, when asked how many years of schooling are required in order for her child to obtain this, she mentions that only 4–5 years of higher education are necessary after graduating from high school. In any case, she believes that the only thing that will get in the way of her child's education is her own child. Amelia states that "it is really up to her [Julia]; we will give her all the support she needs." Amelia shows her support by consistently attending Parent/Teacher nights. Additionally, she states that if she ran into any problems with a teacher, such as finding her child's homework too easy or miscommunications between parent and teacher or teacher and child, Amelia would have no trouble speaking to her child's teacher's superior.

Amelia believes school can help her child become a good person "by giving her a good education," and therefore, "she can be 'someone' in the future." As a result, Amelia does her best to help Julia with her homework or "whatever she needs [they] try for." This includes equipping Julia's room with a desk so that she may have a place to study quietly. A computer at home also allows all of their children to use the Internet for school-related activities. In addition to this, Amelia reads to her children a couple of times per week, mostly in Spanish, and conversely, her children read to her as well, usually letters from school that are written in English. In fact, her children read library books every day.

So far, the demographics profile for the most part places Dominican children at educational risk while their parents' educational values and practices could provide a buffer. Will the parents' educational values and practices buffer the children's educational outcomes against the risks inherent in their demographic profile or in the characteristics of their schools? Will a subgroup of Dominican children, as in the Cambodian group, surpass the low educational attainment expected from their families' sociodemographic high-risk status? It is interesting to note though that given the relatively higher literacy practices reported by Dominican parents, Dominican children reported the lowest level of reading for pleasure of the three groups. Since reading outside the classroom and home assignments are related to higher academic achievement,[16] this particular finding is worrisome.

Children's Cultural Attitudes and Identification

The recognition of the strong cultural contexts that Dominican families provide to their children, through their own daily routines, their participation in a local Latino community, and their ongoing connection with their country of origin support the prediction of strong ethnic identification, pride, and in-group preference for Dominican children. How did these expectations fare?

Children's Ethnic Identities

One of the ways that we measured ethnic identifications was by asking children during the 3 years of the study about which labels (specific examples of ethnic, role, and gender labels were offered to the children among which they were free to choose as many as applied) fit them (see Table 8). Although the total number of labels did not differ among the groups, the types of label chosen did (see Marks et al., 2007). Among Dominican children, just as with Cambodian children, the most commonly chosen ethnic label was a label depicting their parents' national origin, "Dominican." This label was chosen by 87% of the younger cohort and 95% of the older cohort, representing a significant increase with age. The second most frequently chosen label was "Spanish" [17] (85% of the younger and 89% of the older), which denotes how important the language is to these children's identity, in accordance with the findings by Bailey in Dominican adolescents.[18] Finally, hyphenated labels were the third most frequent label chosen, a choice that increases also with age. Bailey, too, found that "Dominican" and "Spanish" were two of the labels that Dominican adolescents chose to identify with most frequently (2001b). Comparing the three ethnic groups, Dominican children used hyphenated labels (i.e., Dominican-American) more frequently than Portuguese, and panethnic labels (i.e., Latino) and ethnolinguistic labels (i.e., Spanish) more frequently than both Cambodian and Portuguese.

In sum, Dominicans do not look very different than the other group in terms of nationality labels; like the Cambodian children, they selected higher proportions of panethnic, ethno linguistic and hyphenated labels. Also similar to their ethnic minority Cambodian peers, Dominican children chose racial and American labels with less relative frequency (on average, once in 3 years). So this provides evidence that children in middle childhood can identify themselves with ethnic labels, showing some exploration of ethnic identity. It is important to note that children at this age displayed a very high degree of accuracy in selecting labels: fewer than 3% of labels selected by the children were incorrect (e.g., a Cambodian child saying that he or she was Portuguese).

We also measured other aspects of identity: contrary to expectations, they do not reflect any particular strength or outstanding pattern for Dominican children as expected from their strong cultural context. Dominican children show relatively high values for pride and centrality, but their scores typically fall between the other two immigrant groups (see Table 2). In terms of salience and stability, Dominicans are significantly different than the Portuguese: they show higher salience but lower stability than Portuguese children, reflecting the fact that Dominican children changed their specific selection of labels more often across the three years than Portuguese children. Their scores on ethnic label satisfaction show that most children are satisfied with their ethnic identification, but only about one third of the children select an ethnic minority label as the one that makes them happiest. In addition, one third would like to get rid of a label and close to a third would change the color of their skin if they had the choice. So the picture that emerges is one of intense pride, but also some inconsistency.

To further illustrate this point, let us call once more on Amelia's family, this time focusing on her daughter Julia.

Julia is a 10-year-old Catholic fifth-grader whose favorite color is yellow and favorite animals are dogs and penguins. She is an A and B student who sees herself as a "Dominican-American" who is "smart" and "not selfish." Additionally, Julia believes that race is a nonqualifying factor for determining the importance of a group of children. She believes that "all kids are the same, and kids are different from color." This is a response she gave after being asked who she believed was the most important group of kids in school. Furthermore, when asked how she felt about her own skin color she stated, "good." When asked to elaborate on her response, she answered that "it doesn't really matter what color of skin it is."

Julia uses both Spanish and English to navigate through her day—speaking primarily English at school and Spanish at home. Her after-school activities include going home with her parents and grandmother, doing her homework, and then playing with her brother and sister. During the weekends, the activities that she participates in include going to the mall, church, and "stores in general." These are activities that are repeated most weekends with her family. Weekends, however, are not solely devoted to family members; she also spends time with her friends, who are composed mainly of Asian and Latino children, and her cousins. They (her friends and cousins) usually play Nintendo, computer games, basketball, or cards. She has also been to the Dominican Republic twice before, and this time was spent visiting her extended family and on the beach. Going to the DR is something that Julia enjoys; "You are more free," she notes. "There are no cars and they [parents] let you go out alone more."

In-Group and Out-Group Preferences

In contrast, we find some evidence that Dominicans typically show in-group social preferences (see Table 10). In general, in both years of measurement and in both contexts (home and school) Dominicans display more in-group preference than the other groups. Interestingly, Dominican children also tended to show relatively positive attitudes toward the out-groups both at home and school, supporting the theoretical distinction made between these two constructs. In other words,[19] having a strong preference for one's own ethnic group does not necessarily translate to having prejudice attitudes against other groups. In a recent in-depth analysis of ethnic identity and in group and out-group social preferences (Marks et al., 2007), we observed a negative correlation between identification with racial labels and in-group social preferences among Dominicans. For these children, identifying with being black, which was not prevalent across the three years, was in opposition to feeling a sense of in-group social preference for other Latino children. Though the negative association between racial identification and in-group social preference is mild it may be an early reflection of greater difficulties observed among Dominican teenagers in this community. Bailey's ethnographic work (Bailey, 2002) pinpointed a strong conflict between ethnic and racial identities, as one of the most difficult and troubling aspects of teenage life for these Dominican youth. According to this work, Dominican adolescents face identity crises in which they must reconcile being considered "black" by others (which carries negative stereotypes), and being Dominican.

Table 11 shows the children's levels of perceived discrimination. Half (first year of interviews) to a third (second year of interviews) of Dominican children detected discrimination in one of the hypothetical scenarios. Only in the first year is this rate significantly higher than the other groups; we see a drop in the rate of detection of discrimination in the Dominican group in the following years. These relatively small rates are surprising given the social construction of blackness in the United Sates. It was expected that since Dominicans in the United States are considered racially black (Bailey, 2002), they might be more subject to discrimination than the other two groups. We did not find any support for this assertion, reflecting perhaps the lack of perceptions of discrimination at this age or the successful integration of this group into its immediate social environments.

⠃⠃ Children's Academic Outcomes

Academic Attitudes and Practices

Dominican parents value educational attainment; many have migrated to this country in order to provide their children opportunities for a better life and they understand that this is accomplished through obtaining higher education. Their ecological niche is, however, one of poverty, high mobility, and other educational risk factors. How do the children fare?

Dominican children display relatively positive academic attitudes (see Table 12); these include positive perceptions toward their teachers, high school engagement, and positive school values. A majority of the Dominican sample wants and expects to go to college and they perceive teachers, parents and peers as agreeable with these values. They report spending 33 minutes a day on homework and watching almost three hours of TV, both figures are in line with the national averages for fourth graders (U.S. Department of Education, 1998). All of these academic attitudes and academic behaviors are positive attributes of the Dominican children that correspond to their parents' high interest and positive values around education.

Julia's own experience is of value to help illustrate the arguments made above.

Julia usually completes her homework after arriving home from school. Whenever her mother cannot aid her with school work, her older sister, 15-year-old Renata, will help her. Renata usually helps Julia by bringing her to the library, so that she may understand the bigger school projects she is assigned. Both enjoy reading library books every day. What Julia enjoys most about school is her friends, gym, and math class. She enjoys gym because she likes baseball and math because she finds it easier than most subjects (especially addition). She feels content in her school environment, viewing it as an enjoyable place to be because of the "fun activities" and nice teacher. Not only does she view school as a fun place, but an important one too. Julia aspires to get good grades so that she can "get to a good college." This demonstrates that Julia not merely hopes to go to college, but that she wants to go to a *good* college very much "because [she] want[s] to get a good job and be able to succeed." She hopes to become a "teacher because [she] likes to work with kids." This is

> an aspiration she shares with her parents who help her work hard in school. She states that they "say that anything I want to do I can do if I try."

As with the ethnic identity and group preference data, Dominican children's scores fall between the other two groups and were only significantly different in having higher perceptions of teachers in comparison to both Cambodians and Dominicans, and in reporting higher expectations of going to college and more time spent on homework than Cambodians. Based on previous research, we would expect that these positive academic attitudes would be correlated with positive academic outcomes. A surprising finding is that many of these attitudes improve with age since we find a difference in cohorts on this measure; for example, older children have even more positive attitudes toward teachers, higher school engagement, more positive school values and express more desire to go to college. This is contrary to past findings which show that children start middle childhood with positive attitudes and high engagement in school but these attitudes decline as they progress through elementary school (Anderson & Maehr, 1994; Eccles, 1999; Midgley, Feldlaufer, & Eccles, 1989).

However, there is a finding in this area that is worrisome. This is the number of school absences. Table 12 shows the three-year average of school absences obtained from the children's school records. Dominican children have the highest number of absences, significantly higher than both Cambodian and Portuguese children. Their average is also higher than most students in Rhode Island, as most students (60%) in Rhode Island miss fewer than 10 days of school a year (Annie E. Casey Foundation, 2005). Since school absences have been associated with negative academic outcomes,[20] this finding places Dominican children at educational risk.

It might be very important to figure out why Dominican children miss school much more than the children of the other two groups and the average student in Rhode Island. One possibility is the nature of the immigrant community that Dominican families belong to, a transnational community with constant back-and-forth between the Island and the mainland. This finding would be congruent with our knowledge of the migration pattern of the Dominican community in the United States and our knowledge of the local community. As the only transnational immigrant community represented in this study, we would expect that Dominican families would travel to their country of origin more often. This practice might translate to missing more days in school (i.e., spending Christmas in the Dominican Republic might mean more time than the one allotted by the school system; attending a family funeral or wedding might take more time than a local affair). Thus, a family practice that characterizes the immigration pattern of this particular population and that might contribute positively to the children's sense of belonging to an ethnic community might otherwise have negative consequences for academic outcomes. Another possibility is that as children grow older, they are expected to contribute to the household more seriously. Both families and teacher have reported anecdotally that older kids might stay home with a sick younger sibling so parents do not miss a day of work. Another anecdotal explanation that has been offered is that based on a hot–cold theory of disease (for a description of this phenomenon): Some parents do not want their kids to go out on cold days, especially if they have any type of respiratory illness or sequelae. Translating that practice from a tropical climate to a New England climate would make many winter days "stay home days," contributing to even more absences to school. Finally, the high number of absences could reflect real disengagement from school. Regardless of the factors associated with school absences, missing a high number of school days contributes to lower academic achievement.

School-Related Stress

Dominican children scored relatively low in all measures of school-related stress and they did not differ significantly in any school stress-related dimension from the other two immigrant groups. (see Table 13). The Dominican children seem to be in-line with the trends for the other groups. Their highest level of stress is academic stress, and there is only one cohort effect, whereby older students report more academic self-concept stress. In sum, Dominican children for the most part espouse positive attitudes and practices and experience very little stress in regard to their education and schooling. So, the only worrisome practice is their high number of school absences.

Grades and Teachers' Reports

How do Dominican children do in school outcomes? Table 14 shows the group averages in grades, teacher ratings, and the distribution of academic pathways. The three-year average GPA shows that for the most part Dominican children have a B average, which reflects a good academic standing. The GPAs, however, show an age effect whereby younger children have higher GPAs than older children. Their teachers also rate them positively, although Cambodian children are rated significantly higher than Dominican children. Thus, as a group, Dominican children seem to be doing well on average, although younger children might be contributing mostly to that effect.

Julia attends a public school in Providence where she is very well, receiving A's in most of her core classes. Her teacher describes her as a student who is "self-motivated and stays on task"; moreover, she states that "Julia works very hard and enjoys an academic challenge." Her only particular weakness, according to her teacher, is that she is "a little shy." Nonetheless, Julia's teacher's long-term expectations are that she will "stay focused and go on to college."

But a finer-grain analysis of the individual academic pathways (see Chapter 4 and Appendix A for a description of this methodology) shows more individual variability in academic outcomes that the findings of three-year average GPA suggest. Although 43% of Dominican children are considered to be in excelling/positive academic pathways (a rate on par with the Portuguese children), these percentages are less than those observed in Cambodian children, where 56% of children are in positive pathways. Moreover, 32% of Dominican children are in negative/abysmal pathways (only observed in 20% of the Cambodian sample). Thus, no evidence of the immigrant paradox (as was found for Cambodians) was observed in the Dominican sample. Actually, comparisons of students with excelling versus abysmal pathways show that parents of students who have abysmal pathways are more recent arrivals (average year of mother immigration was 1983) than parents of students who are in excelling pathways (average year was 1972; see Table 15), which is contradictory to the immigrant paradox findings of more recent immigrants having more optimal outcomes. Perhaps the differences in the migratory waves of Dominicans (earlier migrants being more educated and of higher social class than later immigrants) partly explain these findings. Other discriminating characteristics between Dominican students with excelling and abysmal academic pathways are that students who have abysmal pathways less often have both parents working, have more school absences, and experience more school-related stress. In addition, Dominican students who have abysmal academic pathways score higher on ethnic identity centrality, a finding that is not expected from either theory nor past research on ethnic identity and will require some further explanation.

Associations between Academic Outcomes and Ethnic Attitudes and Identification

We examined correlations between academic attitudes and various aspects of ethnic identities. Several interesting correlations emerged. Children who wanted to change the color of their skin (to lighter or darker) also espoused higher school engagement but lower school values. Higher ethnic pride was related to more positive school values and higher college aspirations and expectations. Language use, and by inference acculturation, is also related to academic attitudes among Dominicans. English language preference is related to more positive attitudes toward teachers, while both English language preference and preference for bilingualism (rather than preference for Spanish) are related to higher school engagement scores (although bilingualism was also associated with lower college expectations). So as in other groups, we are finding some associations between indicators of ethnic identity and academic attitudes in this developmental period. However, some of the findings are puzzling. Unlike in other groups were the immigrant paradox evidences itself, more acculturation in Dominicans (as indicated by preference for English or bilingualism) is related in most instances with more optimal outcomes.

⠶ Conclusions

Dominican children and their parents are part of a transnational community. Many of these youth have a strong connection to the Dominican Republic, grow up in neighborhoods with many other Spanish-speaking individuals, and attend schools where bilingual classes and students are common. It is perhaps not surprising in this context that the Dominican children (and their parents) have the highest levels of cultural practices of all the groups. While culturally rich, most of these children live in environments characterized by poverty. Despite their parents having the highest level of education of the three groups, 77% are living below the poverty line and less than a third are skilled workers. In addition, Dominican families had the highest level of residential mobility of the three groups. Our Dominican youth are living in some of the poorest sectors of Providence and, like the Cambodian children, are attending schools with high levels of suspensions, failing test scores, and high numbers of teacher grievances.

Not surprisingly, descriptive analyses suggest that for these children economic and school conditions are a major part of their educational narrative. For example, children whose parents had more recently immigrated (and thus were less financially secure) and children with a lower proportion of working parents were more likely to be in the abysmal pathway group. In addition, school stress and higher levels of absences also characterized academically failing youth, perhaps evidencing the consequences of a chaotic school environment.

However, it is clear that cultural identification and attitudes are significant parts of their narrative as well. For example, we saw that ethnic pride contributed to higher school values and college aspirations, while ethnic centrality was associated with academic failure. In addition, wanting to change the color of one's skin was related to higher school engagement, and a greater preference for English was related to positive attitudes toward teachers. From these associations, it is clear that the relation between cultural attitudes and identifications and academic attitudes for Dominican youth is complicated and at times seemingly contradictory. One is left to wonder how high ethnic pride might bolster positive academic attitudes while high centrality predicts an abysmal academic pathway? Are family and school contexts marked by poverty the strongest correlate to academic failure? Or is the way one reconciles an ethno-linguistic identity and stigmatized racial identity with one's student identity the strongest predictor of outcomes? We will look to the final models in Chapter 8 to find out.

7 ⠿

The Portuguese Community: Steady, Long Established, and Partially Integrated

The Portuguese immigrants and their children in this study represent the tail-end and the slowing down of a long migrant stream that spans several centuries (see Bailey, 2000b, for a comprehensive view of this community). As part of massive migrations into the United Sates, there was a large-scale Portuguese migration during the 1880–1920 period and then another period of significant migration from 1960[1] to 1980. Overall, immigration from Portugal to the United States during the early 1990s was less than one-fourth of its late-1960s peak, and the local community reflects this in terms of its relative integration with English speakers and the non-Portuguese community. In contrast to other western European countries, a much larger percentage of Portuguese immigrants entered into this country post-1957; yet in contrast to other post-1965 newcomers who are considered people of color, their racial features (e.g., skin color) are white.[2]

A majority of the families in our study are actually from the Azores, where half of the Portuguese population in the Rhode Island and southern Massachusetts region originated. Newcomers from the Azores were first attracted by the whaling industries in the 1800s and later on by the developing textiles industries in the area. Testimonials from the families in our study talk about family members and acquaintances from their towns of origins that were living here as providing major incentives to migrate into this area.

Escaping poverty has been the main historical reason for migration, many being subsistence farmers or landless peasantry. According to local informants, the quality of life has improved in the Azores and the manufacturing jobs have decreased in New England, so only the poorest, less educated individuals are said to be migrating more recently. Others from higher economic and educational levels are not.

Even if they are newcomers, more recent Portuguese immigrants can benefit from a relatively established local Portuguese community which maintains a local economy, language, foods, and other traditions. The Portuguese community's long history of immigration has resulted in the existence of Portuguese institutions such as churches and Holy Ghost societies or "halls" that remain focal points for the community and serve as arenas for operation of a local political machine, which is Portuguese-American dominated. Several clubs (e.g., Portuguese Sporting Club and Holy Ghost) and churches are the central institutions in Providence and East Providence. Many of these institutions have been here since the big migration of the first part of the twentieth century and have been invigorated and renewed by large waves of more recent newcomers.

The clubs have hundreds of members, and given the proximity to one another, they become the focus for recent immigrants. The abundance of Portuguese-owned businesses, inclusive of groceries, bakeries, travel agencies, restaurants, beauty parlors, insurance agencies, and funeral homes in relatively adjacent areas, create an easy access to all these ethnic institutions. In Providence, there are various Portuguese sections with such a concentration, but these are smaller and highly integrated. As a consequence, the Portuguese immigrants seem to have more choices than do Cambodians and Dominicans: They can be part of a "Portuguese community" or instead blend into the dominant culture rather easily after acquiring English skills.

Moreover, while the Providence Dominican and Cambodian communities are linked in many ways to large but more distant communities in New York City and Lowell (northeast Massachusetts), respectively, the Providence and East Providence Portuguese community is contiguous with a much larger southeastern Massachusetts Portuguese community. Providence is really the western-most part of a larger community with Portuguese media, population, and businesses. Communication is strong between communities that share primarily, but not exclusively, media—newspapers, radio and TV stations—and family members can be dispersed over a rather large territory. Differences between the East Providence and the Providence Portuguese communities include their size, concentration, and surrounding communities. Although the nearby city of Providence has several small Portuguese enclaves, including one in South Providence, these areas have been gentrified as housing prices have increased dramatically, making it unaffordable for recent immigrant families.

The successful establishment of the Portuguese community is attested by its political accomplishments. There is evidence of a significant penetration of Portuguese/Portuguese-Americans into positions of power in the East Providence city-police, elected officials, and school committees. This must give the Portuguese a stronger voice than our Dominican and Cambodian communities have in Providence. Thus, as far as navigating the unfamiliar institutional systems in this country, Portuguese families may very likely be tied into ethnic politics, networks, and solidarity, using these ties as a way of ensuring access to social and cultural capital.

Providence and East Providence provide a different locality for immigrant families. Families of Portuguese ancestry constitute a larger percentage of the population in East Providence (total population: 48,688, Portuguese population: 15,066 than in Providence (total population: 173,618; Portuguese population: 7,002; U.S. Census Bureau, 2000g, 2000h). This translates into a feeling of being the dominant ethnic group in one locality and part of an ethnic enclave in the other. A slightly larger percentage of the population (about 1/3 of the population) is foreign born in East Providence compared to only about 20% in Providence. The Providence Portuguese population tends to be younger (the median age for Providence is 30 vs. 37 for East Providence) and poorer ($ 29,505 vs. $ 38,902, median household incomes) even if they have the same educational attainment (41% vs. 50%, high school graduates or higher; U.S. Census Bureau, 2000g, 2000h). It seems that the more established, prosperous East Providence community represents a zone of emergence, whereby more established families move after making their initial migration to Providence from the Azores.

As a reflection of the Portuguese community's relative concentration and absolute numbers, Portuguese children are the dominant and almost exclusive ethnic group in the schools from which a majority of the children in this study were recruited. Even if 75% of the Portuguese students in our sample lived in East Providence and 25% in Providence, the schools they attended were ethnically and racially very similar. They attended schools in which there were significantly higher numbers of white students, 70% (as compared to black, Hispanic, or Asian), and thus they attended schools and lived in neighborhoods in which they are members of the most prevalent ethnic and racial group. Although all the schools from which the samples of children in this study were recruited were in need of improvement in writing and math (see Table 3 for exact figures) as indicated by the yearly assessments of the Rhode Island State Department of Education (see Information Works, 1999, 2000, 2001), the Portuguese children are attending "better" schools comparatively. This is evidenced by a series of indicators that are associated with higher educational achievement in other samples. In comparison to Cambodians and Dominicans, the Portuguese students attended schools that were higher achieving in math and writing, had higher income families, better student attendance, smaller classes, fewer suspensions, higher teacher education, and fewer teacher grievances (due to weapons, conflict, or other reasons).

❖ Portuguese Families: Contexts for Children's Development

As with any immigrant group and as already observed in the other two groups, the Portuguese families provide unique niches for their children's development, partly as a function of their immigrant status. As previously described, the family characteristics in this study can be conceptualized within the broad categories of family immigration and demographic characteristics and cultural and educational values and practices.

Family Immigration and Demographic Characteristics

How representative is our sample of the immigration pattern described above? Given the fact that they had to have a child in first or fourth grade, our sample is truncated and we would not expect to project population parameters to the Providence and East Providence immigrant populations. But still, it is important to know which characteristics remain in our sample. As expected, most of the families in our sample live in East Providence and 93% migrated from the Azores. They arrived within a period of 30 years (1964–1999), with 1979 representing the mean and 1975 representing the median. Reflecting this particular group's migration pattern, their window of migration is larger than that of both the Cambodians and the Dominicans. Of importance to know is that Portuguese parents had in average five more years in the United States which could allow them to acculturate more than parents in the other groups and that their cultural practices and attitudes might reflect their acculturation (see related findings below). Many of the families in East Providence had initially settled in Providence, reflecting a traditional migration pattern into the city, and then when it can be afforded, into a more affluent, yet ethnic area. Also reflecting their long-term migration, about one in ten for both mothers and fathers had spouses who were American born, typically Portuguese by ethnic identification.

Age at immigration is another important dimension. Roughly half of our sample arrived in the United States at age 15 or younger and half were older than this. This might have implications for observing individual differences in acculturation in our sample, since the younger the immigrant is at the time of migration, the higher the probability of acculturation. It also has implications for their educational attainment, since those who arrive at age 15 or younger have 4 more years of education than those who arrive at older ages. Not only do the older immigrants end up with lower educational attainment, but we could expect that they would have less familiarity with the educational system here.

As observed in this population's migration pattern, there is a shift over time from a predominance of city immigrants toward an increase from villages and the countryside. Moreover, half of the current Providence sample families are from villages or the countryside compared to nearly half of the East Providence families which come from city backgrounds. We would expect that more recent, older immigrants from the countryside would espouse more traditional Portuguese values and practices than those who migrated younger from the city and have been here longer.

The Portuguese families present a rather interesting demographic profile which very much reflects the migratory pattern of this group (see Table 4 for actual numbers and statistical comparisons with the other two groups).

In terms of human capital, Portuguese families present many assets for their children's development in relative and absolute terms. They have a preponderance of two-parent households, in which often both parents are working (see Table 4). A majority own their homes and provide relative stability of residence. Very few live below the federal poverty line. A majority continues to have contacts/visits with their country of origin (which might contribute to biculturalism) but plan to remain in the United Sates permanently. Thus, in comparison to Cambodian and Dominican families, these families present a relatively large number of protective factors, including stability and resources.

Despite these assets, the level of parental education does place these children at risk. Most parents do not have a high school diploma (44% of the Portuguese sample had completed only elementary education; 36% had completed high school, and 19% had completed high school and some college); they actually have significantly fewer years of education than Dominican parents (see Table 4). An interesting and relevant finding was provided by our focus group of members of the Portuguese community. During the focus group, recent immigrant parents and their children were mentioned as a "problem" for the Portuguese community. The focus group expressed their concerns that these children were not being well served by the educational system in East Providence P.137 *served well?*. Similar findings were reported by Bailey (2000b) based on his ethnographic study of this community, where historical explanations for lack of an orientation toward education were indicated. Thus the lack of interest in pursuing an education was traced back to agrarian communities where the traditional emphasis was on few students going beyond the early grades, emphasis on working early on the family plot or as a wage earner and observing in others a lack of social mobility as a function of higher levels of education. In short, immigrant families were perceived by "older" more established migrants as multiproblem, poor, uneducated, with limited English skills, and in need of many services to help them integrate into the community at large. This perception contrasts with these families' advantaged position relative to the other two immigrant groups in this study but reminds us that this relative advantage is only to other immigrant groups, and not in absolute terms.

Paloma and Miguel are immigrant parents who were both born in the Azores Islands. Paloma's family came to the United States in the 1960s for the "better opportunities" and jobs. They were able to move with the help of her brother and grandmother, who set the family up with jobs and a house in Providence. Miguel arrived as a young adult nearly 20 years later in 1984.

Paloma and Miguel both hold steady jobs that bring in an annual household income that ranges from $40,000 to $49,999 dollars. Paloma, 36, works as a cashier for Dunkin Donuts; she had hoped to be a teacher, a dream that she now holds for her daughter Izabel. Miguel, 38, owns an auto-body shop and restaurant; between the two working a minimum of 6 days a week. In all of the years that they have both been here since arriving from Portugal, they have held a steady job. Paloma and Miguel have lived in their current home for six years, in a residential neighborhood that is mostly composed of Portuguese and Hispanic residents. Paloma likes the neighborhood although she notes that it is "getting worse."

Paloma and Miguel live with their three children, Vanessa (17), Izabel (10), and Cathy (4), as well as Paloma's 57-year-old mother, Azuzena, who, having completed 6 years of public schooling, now contributes to the household income by doing domestic work. In addition, she helps by taking care of the children when Paloma and Miguel are at work. Vanessa, the oldest of the children, works as well; like her mother she holds a cashier position at Dunkin Donuts.

Cultural Socialization

As expected from their earlier date of immigration to the United States, Portuguese families, on average, report cultural practices that reflect more acculturation to this country and relatively less maintenance of their culture of origin (see Table 5 for actual values and statistical tests), although individual differences are observed as a function of age of immigration, recency of migration, and urbanicity in the country of origin. Many of the Portuguese parents feel comfortable speaking English across a variety of situations and use more English with their children than the other two groups. This a very different usage of language than that observed in the Cambodian and Dominican parents, where their native language predominates both their interaction with others and their children. Probably, the existence of a very established, highly acculturated and partly integrated Portuguese-American community facilitates their learning and usage of English. They have also been in this country on average five more years than the other two groups, perhaps enough time to be more comfortable in the English language. However, individual differences in language comfort are related to immigration processes. If a parent was born in the United States, or arrived to this country before the age of 16 and was born in a city, they tended to feel more comfortable speaking English.

In terms of cultural routines, Portuguese families still maintain practices that are tied to their culture of origin, including cooking native Portuguese dishes, listening to Portuguese music and attending church services. Of the three immigrant groups, Portuguese families had the lowest frequency of cultural practices, but these practices were still very evident in weekly routines. Parents reported participating in each cultural practice an average of twice a week, while children reported participating slightly less frequently (see Table 5). This perhaps reflects the existence of a very well established cultural community with constant new immigrants who can support such practices such as the annual celebrations of the Holy Ghost. Being born in the Azores, having spent less time in the United States, being older at the time of migration, and having origins in villages or the countryside are all associated with practicing more cultural routines.

It is interesting, however, that in contrast their children have the lowest levels of cultural practices of all groups. These children seem to be the most acculturated of all groups. This is in spite of the fact that 94% of them report that they speak Portuguese (but most prefer English for communicating with others: 99% of the children, in comparison to 59% of the parents, preferred to be interviewed in English rather than in Portuguese). It seems that speaking the language, following culturally defined practices, or espousing an ethnic identity is a "choice" for these children, and they can choose one aspect over the others.

Paloma feels very comfortable speaking in both Portuguese, which she uses when speaking to her family, and English, which she uses at work and occasionally with the children. Paloma is a confident English speaker and has never needed assistance from her children with translating letters or bill or with interpreting in the school, work, or neighborhood context.

Paloma maintains many ties to Portugal and its culture, both in her own home and through contact with relatives abroad. Paloma and Miguel cook Portuguese dishes daily, listen to Portuguese music on the radio (although no one in the family reads Portuguese material nor watches Portuguese media), and the entire family attends church services twice a month, which are often given in Portuguese. They also celebrate traditional Portuguese holidays, which Paloma describes as "feasts." Getting together with extended family is something that is not only possible but a common occurrence for Paloma's family. Many of her relatives are in close by New York, Massachusettes, and Providence. Paloma also keeps in constant contact with her many relatives and friends in Portugal; she calls or writes 2 to 3 times per month and visits the country one to two times per year for periods of 1–2 weeks. The children have also visited Portugal, although not nearly as frequently. In addition, they are able to see Portuguese relatives living in Florida and Canada, usually once per year. Paloma and Miguel's family plans to stay in the United States permanently; Paloma, at least, has known this since she first migrated here.

Educational Values and Practices

Although Portuguese parents themselves do not have high level of educational attainment and various key informants from the community attested to their low educational aspirations, we know that many immigrant groups do have high educational aspirations for their children although they might not believe in the value of their own involvement in their children's education. Our sample of Portuguese families presents a mixed portrait of these important dimensions for their kid's education. On the positive side, in a previous analyses of their responses to the education involvement questions (see García Coll et al., 2002 for details of the analyses), we found that 85% of Portuguese parents said they wanted their kids to complete a college education, and 93% mentioned professional occupations as their aspirations for their children. So even if many of them do not have a high school degree, they have high aspirations for their children. This is in sharp contrast with the focus group and ethnographic findings that categorized recent Portuguese immigrants as not interested in educational pursuits. Perhaps parents who volunteered for our study represented those most invested on their kid's education or our informants were generalizing from a minority of problem families.

In addition, Portuguese parents' conception of parental involvement resembles most closely that espoused by middle-class families in the United States and in the academic literature. In other words, parents who believe that parents should be involved in their children's education, report behaving like parents who are considered highly involved in American culture: They check homework frequently, they meet their children's teacher, and they provide all sorts of resources. Not only do their belief systems and practices seem to be coherent, but in comparison to the other two immigrant groups, Portuguese parents had higher levels of involvement and provided more educational resources (see Table 6 for actual values and statistical analysis). A majority of parents have met with their children's teacher, although significantly fewer times than the Dominican parents.[3] Ninety-six percent of Portuguese parents report that someone checks their children's homework on a daily basis. Reflecting perhaps their more affluent economic conditions, an overwhelming majority of Portuguese parents also report having a place for their child to do their homework and a place where books are kept. Over half of Portuguese families own a home computer.

Some variability is observed in attitudes and behaviors as a function of individual differences in immigration history. Parents who were older than 15 at the time of migration or came from a rural setting think that parents should be less involved in their children's education in comparison to parents who immigrated at younger ages or came from cities. Similarly, parents who were older at immigration have met less frequently with their children's teachers. In contrast, parents who have been in the United States longer think that they should be more involved in their children's education, perhaps reflecting assimilation to American culture's value placed in parents' involvement in their children's education.

An even more mixed picture emerges when we examine indices of family literacy activities (see Table 7 for actual values and statistical analysis). In Portuguese families, on average, the parents read for pleasure only a few times a month, while their children do so a little more often. Accordingly, there are slightly more children books in the household (on average over 10) than other kinds of books (less than 10). Although a majority of Portuguese parents read to their children in the past, only 38% of parents now read to their children. Given the high values on educational attainment and their coherent belief in parental involvement in their children's education, it is surprising that they do not portray a consistent pattern of high family literacy practices. This might be due to the fact that even if they are more comfortable speaking English than the other two immigrant groups, their reading skills in English are not as well developed. In the Portuguese sample, 59% of parents completed their interviews in English, showing that a significant number of them, even if they can converse in English, might prefer Portuguese. It might also reflect lower literary skills in their own language related to immigration history. Parents who migrated after 15 years of age or who were originally from the countryside, read less often for pleasure.

Paloma believes that parents should be highly involved in their child's education. Her belief in the value of parental involvement is readily apparent in her participation in Izabel's education. Paloma checks Izabel's homework every day and has met with Izabel's teacher two times in the past year—meetings that she, herself, requested. She feels "fine" about communicating with teachers or school officials if ever a situation necessitates it. When asked what she would do if she found her child's school work too easy, she states that "I'd go up to school and let them know that she's way ahead of that".

Paloma believes that what makes an adult a good person consists of an "an education [and] getting along with all kinds of nationalities". She sees school as an institution that can help her children become this type of person "by teaching them right." Paloma hopes that Izabel will become a teacher, something that she believes Izabel will be able to achieve through "a lot of learning." However, when asked how many years of schooling is necessary for Izabel to achieve this goal, she simply states that she needs to have "college."

While Paloma reads for pleasure only "a few times a year," she notes that her children read every day. Paloma no longer reads to Izabel, but from time to time, Izabel reads aloud to her mother; usually stories that she herself writes in English. In the house are more than 50 children's books plus 50 more or so of other types. They also have a computer, although Paloma notes that she has "never touched it" and her children rarely use it.

In sum, the Portuguese families present a mixed environment, full of protective factors, indicated by demographic characteristics associated with positive developmental outcomes (e.g., two-parent families and higher incomes) but also some high-risk factors (low parent education and low literacy practices) for low educational attainment. In terms of ethnicity, both community and families maintain traditional cultural practices and yet are connected to the larger mainstream community, creating the possibility of biculturalism for the children.

Children's Cultural Attitudes and Identification

We were particularly interested in the Portuguese children's ethnic attitudes and identification because of their unique migration pattern and racial features (white), as well as their families' and their own cultural practices. These children are very close to the prototype of the earlier European migration that within one generation "becomes white."[4] Thus, although the three groups of children of immigrants in this study—Cambodian, Dominicans, and Portuguese—have in common that at least one parent (and for a majority of children, two parents) was born in the country of origin, the children differ strikingly in their racial features (e.g., skin and hair color, eye shape, and facial features). The way that others might think of them in terms of ethnicity/race differs because of these strikingly different racial features. The children also differ in family and immigration contexts. How do these factors translate into specific ethnic identifications and attitudes for Portuguese children?

Children's Ethnic Identities

One of the main research questions of this study was to find out whether children of immigrant backgrounds at this age—middle childhood—can choose ethnic identifiers amongst other identity labels (e.g., gender, student, daughter) as adolescents and adults typically do. In other words, are children of immigrants aware of their membership in ethnic groups? Are these memberships salient aspects of their identity? Does being considered white and having parents who have been in this country for a longer period of time create a different context for ethnic identity?

Table 8 shows the data on the children's selections of labels that apply to them across three years of assessments. All Portuguese children chose a gender and a nationality (i.e., Portuguese) label at each time of assessment. Thus, in this study, all children irrespective of their nationality and age can identify with some aspects of ethnicity as early as first grade, indicating that during middle childhood we can find evidence of ethnic identity formation.[5] In addition, as in the other two groups, nationality was the most frequent label chosen by Portuguese children: chosen by 87% of the younger and 99% of the older group, showing that with age, nationality becomes an even more salient identifier. It is interesting to note than even if most of the families were from the Azores, the most frequently chosen label was "Portuguese" (and not "Azorean"), which clearly identifies them with their language and their culture and not the place of birth.[6] The label "Portuguese" also refers to the way that the local community is referred to by the larger community, so it reflects some knowledge of the local community use of social categories.[7] In contrast, Portuguese children did not identify with hyphenated (i.e., Portuguese-American) nor panethnic labels (i.e., European-American) as often as the other two groups, labels which are really not used in the daily contexts that they are part of. However, older children more often chose hyphenated labels (i.e., Portuguese-American)[8] showing increasing biculturalism with age, as expected (see Table 8).

After nationality labels, Portuguese children chose significantly more racial labels than the other two groups and older children did this more often than younger ones. This confirms our expectation that these children would be identifying themselves increasingly with being white, reflecting the acculturation patterns of this particular ethnic group and other European immigrants who become "white" by the second generation. They also chose "American" significantly more often than the other two groups, again attesting to their biculturalism, as being both Portuguese and white Americans.

Table 9 shows the values and statistical tests of other aspects of children's ethnic identities measured in this study, which primarily reflect feelings and attitudes associated with their identity. We expected that perhaps because of their race, the established ethnic community, and the longer time spent in the United States by their families, Portuguese children would show positive feelings and attitudes toward their own ethnicity, even if they were more acculturated. This would reflect the fact that even if their families and communities are espousing traditional cultural practices, they would be more quickly acculturating and identifying with the dominant white middle-class culture. Confirming our expectations, we find that Portuguese children report high ethnic pride (significantly higher than Cambodians) and average centrality (not significantly different from the other two groups). They also show high stability (significantly higher than Dominicans and girls even higher than boys), and older children show even higher ethnic pride than younger ones. These positive feelings associated with being Portuguese might reflect the strength of the community and the fact that their families do maintain some cultural routines, and thus even if both the families and their children are more acculturated, the children can derive meaning and pleasure out of these ethnic identifications.

At the same time, Portuguese children report lower salience (significantly lower than both Cambodian and Portuguese), and less than a quarter of them select an ethnic label as the label that makes them the happiest. Gender (28%) and family role (21%) were chosen as the labels that made Portuguese children the happiest. Thus, Portuguese children feel proud about who they are as a dominant ethnic group but this aspect of their identity is not as salient as expected. Ethnicity is just one of many other positive identities that these children espouse;

because they are part of a majority group, ethnic identity is not the most salient aspect of their identity; gender and family roles might be more salient in their day–to-day lives.

In-Group and Out-Group Preferences

Ethnic identification, and all its dimensions (pride, centrality, stability, etc.), is just one aspect of the social processes associated with one's ethnicities; other aspects refer to one's attitudes toward our own group or other ethnic groups.[9] These attitudes are measured as preferences: how comfortable the child feels at home and at school with their own group (in-group preference) and with other ethnic groups (out-group preferences). Table 10 shows the values and statistical comparisons of the children's in-group and out-group preferences. In absolute terms, Portuguese children showed their highest preference toward their own group at home in both second and third years of the study, although they were lower than Dominican in this respect. So they felt the most comfortable with other Portuguese children at home. But older Portuguese children showed more preferences toward the out-group than younger Portuguese children. In relative terms, Portuguese children were in most instances in between the other two immigrant groups, except for out-group preferences in the school setting in the third year of the study, where they show stronger out-group preferences than both Cambodians and Dominicans.

Another aspect of intergroup relations is indicated by perceptions (or lack thereof) of discrimination (see Table 11 for values and statistical analysis). The results here are puzzling, as we had predicted that because of the strong Portuguese community and the resemblance of Portuguese children to white children (the dominant group), that Portuguese children would show the lowest rates of perception of discrimination. Although the percentage of Portuguese children detecting discrimination (less than half) and the rate of detection (in less than 1/3 of the scenarios) were in absolute terms rather small, the Portuguese children did not stand out from the other groups in terms of lower perceptions of discrimination. Actually, the rate of detection was significantly higher for Portuguese children than for Cambodians in the second and third years. Again, the hypothetical advantages ascribed to this group by its racial resemblance to the dominant white middle class did not translate into perceiving less discrimination in this group in this study. We had to wonder if the perceptions of discrimination came more from being a newcomer (a recent immigrant) than from their being Portuguese, and given the age of the subjects, if they can make that distinction. A community informant mentioned that many of the white, non-Portuguese students consider themselves Irish and tease the Portuguese, especially the newcomers in the school setting.

In terms of children's ethnic attitudes and identifications, we can see how the context of immigration provides a background for its development and expression. Portuguese children during middle childhood are aware of their membership in a particular ethnic group that is defined by being Portuguese, white, and American. This reflects the significance of an established ethnic enclave and the easier possibility of assimilation into mainstream American culture shown by their predecessors (both Portuguese and other European groups). These inclinations grow with age, which shows the increasing adoption by the children of prevalent views of the community espoused by the community and others. In general, these children espouse positive attitudes and feelings toward themselves and others except for perceptions of discrimination. Perhaps these children are also feeling judgment by more established members of the community who see them as part of problematic families.

Children's Academic Outcomes

From a demographic perspective, the Portuguese families present both assets and vulnerabilities for their children's educational attainment. In some respects, they have several advantages: They are mostly two-parent families, and they have relatively high incomes (according to the 2000 census data, while the average median household income was $26,867 for the total population of Providence, it was $29,505 for Portuguese residents; 39,108 for total East Providence population, $38,902 for Portuguese residents; U.S. Census Bureau, 2000g, 2000h) As so many households have two parents working, they also provide residential stability, a factor that has been identified as associated with higher educational achievement.[10] These families also exhibit educational practices that are associated with better educational outcomes. They have high aspirations for their children's educational attainment; they believe in and are involved in their children's education.

But there are also risk factors. Demographically, the parents, although they have high aspirations for their children, have relatively low educational attainment themselves. In terms of educational practices, although they report being involved in their children's' education, they have relatively low literacy practices. Finally, since acculturation has been associated in other populations with lower educational attainment,[11] we wondered whether the higher acculturation rates observed in both parents (e.g., longer time in the United States; more English comfort) and children (e.g., few cultural activities; English language preference) place them further at risk. So how do Portuguese children fare in academics both in absolute terms and in comparison to the other two groups?

Academic Attitudes

In general terms, Portuguese children espouse rather positive attitudes about teachers and schools and their desires and prospects for attending college (see Table 12). In addition, in four out of five measures, older children scored higher than younger children, providing evidence that their attitudes are getting even more positive as the children age. Portuguese children have also significantly higher perceptions of their teacher in comparison to the other two groups and higher school engagement than Cambodians. We wonder if the more positive attitudes toward teachers are a reflection of the better match between students' self-ethnic identification and the ethnic characteristics of the teachers (most of them self-identify as white).

In terms of actual practices, Portuguese children's practices tend to agree with typical national and/or state averages. They are absent from school for an average of 7 days (most students in Rhode Island are absent for less then 10 days); they report on average almost half hour of homework and 2 hours of TV a day, which correspond to the national averages. In comparison to the other groups, they are very similar, except in that they have fewer absences than Dominicans.

School-Related Stress

Another way of examining children's academic attitudes is to have them talk about sources of stress in school. Table 13 shows the actual values and statistical analyses of the children's school based stress-related experiences. In general, Portuguese children report low levels of stress in school. Their highest values are associated with academic self-concept and physical manifestations of stress, but these values are higher in younger children than in older children, suggesting a possible decrease of stress as the children spend more time in school. The only difference with the other groups is that Portuguese children report less emotional manifestations of stress than Cambodians. Thus, in general, Portuguese children confirm their positive experiences at school, by experiencing relatively low levels of stress which is expected given their school's relative positive characteristics.

Grades and Teacher Reports

One of the main questions for the Portuguese sample was given their mixed profile of attributes (both positive and negative family and child risk factors) where were they going to end in terms of grades and teacher reports (see Table 14).

Portuguese children had a B average, similar to the Cambodian and Dominican children. As observed in other samples, younger children had higher GPAs than older ones (similarly to the other two groups). Thus, even if their community and families' characteristics were rather different, no statistical group differences were found in the 3-year average GPA. Thus, the demographic (two-parent household, higher incomes, and residential stability) and parental involvement advantages observed in the Portuguese group as a function of their relative and absolute family and community characteristics do not translate into better school grades. Perhaps their risk factors—low parental education, low literacy practices, and higher acculturation—might lead to a more average performance than that expected from other demographic characteristics. Similar findings are evident when we examine teacher ratings. Portuguese children are rated for the most part at the positive end of the scale (girls more frequently than boys), but they are not better than the other groups as expected from their community and family attributes. Actually, they are rated lower than Cambodians.

In terms of academic pathways, which is a qualitative analyses of both grades and teacher reports over the 3 years (see Chapter 4 for a description of the methodology), again Portuguese children do not capitalize on their community and family advantages. They look very similar to Dominicans and have much smaller numbers of excelling and positive children than Cambodians. In other words, the initial advantages of the Portuguese families and communities are perhaps trumped by child and family literacy and perhaps acculturation processes that undermine their academic achievement.

Another way to examine variability in academic performance is to look at only excelling and abysmal students and see which variables differentiate these groups. No family attributes differentiated the groups. In general, kids who showed an abysmal pathway reported more stress in teacher interactions, academic self-concept, and in physical manifestations (see Table 15). They also showed more absences (mean absences for the excelling group was three, for the abysmal group it was ten). Given the nature of the variables, it is unclear if children are reporting more stress and absences because they are doing poorly in school or vice versa.

Let us consider the case of Izabel:

Izabel, Paloma and Miguel's middle child, is in fifth grade, has average grades, likes R&B music, and describes herself as "not mean." Izabel chooses, among others, the labels "girl," "Catholic," "white," "English," "American," and "Portuguese" to describe who she is, explaining that she is Catholic because she "goes to church," English because "I talk in English," white "because that is the color of my skin," and "Portuguese" because "that's where my parents are from." None of these labels, however, is her favorite label; her favorite is "daughter," although she is not sure why.

Izabel prefers to speak, and be spoken to, in Portuguese; however, when it comes to watching movies, TV shows, and hearing stories, she prefers that they be in English. She eats Portuguese meals with her family every night, listens to Portuguese radio programming, and goes to church every week with her family. Izabel's three best friends are all Portuguese. When asked how she would feel if Portuguese children came to her house and to what extent she would want to befriend Portuguese children, she states "very comfortable" and "very much" which she feels is true for Hispanic children as well. For Asian or African-American children, her answers are more complicated. While she is fairly ambivalent toward making Asian friends, she notes that she would feel very comfortable having Asian children over to her house. The situation reverses itself in the case of African-American children, who she is eager to make friends with but feels neither comfortable nor uncomfortable having them at her house.

Izabel, for the most part, enjoys school and reports high levels of engagement and school values. For example, she believes that getting good grades and doing your homework in school is very important since it allows you to learn. Izabel consistently reports liking her teachers and thinks that they like her as well; in fact, having good teachers is something that makes her proud of her school. Despite these positive interactions, school is not always completely comfortable for her. She notes that students in her class do not get along well, because "a lot of people bully a lot of other people," and that she feels a little left out while at school and that some kids in her class do not like her "for no reason." Nonetheless, she reports that she goes to school every day "because I like school."

When Izabel arrives home from school she usually starts her homework, which takes her anywhere from 60 to 90 minutes to complete. Although it is her least favorite part of school, she always does her homework "because it helps me get good grades." Other times, she first stops at her aunt's salon, where she spends time with her two cousins. Once she is finished with her homework, she likes to watch "Nickelodeon and [the] Disney channel" or to play videogames. During the weekends, she spends time with her family at her father's restaurant or hangs out with her friends and cousins in "Walmart and Walgreen's." During school breaks such as summer vacations, Izabel usually goes to Florida with her "mom, dad, and sisters," so that they may "go to beaches [and] to in [the] pool."

Izabel believes that graduating from high school is very important since it will allow her to "get a job." She would like to become a teacher because "[she] like[s] kids." Although Izabel believes that both her parents and teacher think it very likely that she will go to college, she only believes that any possibility of her going to college is "kind of" true. Nevertheless, she does have a desire to go to college, and if teaching does not work out, she plans to "[work] at the bank."

Associations between Academic Outcomes and Ethnic Attitudes and Identification

The final set of analyses was done in order to ascertain whether there were any patterns of associations between academic outcomes (inclusive of attitudes and grades) and aspects of ethnic attitudes and identifications.[12] As mentioned previously, several lines of research have shown that ethnic identity and attitudes toward others is related to academic outcomes during adolescence.[13] Do we find evidence of these associations in Portuguese children in this age period? We do for three aspects of ethnic identification and attitudes. Wishing to have a darker/lighter color was associated with lower overall school engagement, overall school values, and overall perception of teachers. Higher ethnic pride is also associated with higher school values. In addition, higher out-group preference both at home and at school was also related with higher overall school engagement, overall school values, and overall perception of teachers. Thus, we find evidence that in this developmental period, ethnic-based attitudes about the self and others are starting to be associated with school engagement and values. Noteworthy again is the fact that perceptions of discrimination are not associated at this age with school outcomes.

Conclusions

The Portuguese children in our sample are growing up within a large and resilient ethnic enclave; one that has given rise to, and supports, Portuguese political leaders, organizations, religious institutions, and media. Unlike many ethnic enclaves, the Providence Portuguese community is largely integrated into the larger culture, and there is consistent evidence of such integration in our findings within the Portuguese sample.

For example, the majority of our Portuguese youth are growing up in relatively financially secure, two-parent households. Many of their parents own their homes and are gainfully employed. Most parents are very comfortable in English and have a good working knowledge of the U.S. educational system. In addition to endorsing high expectations and aspirations for the educational progress of their children, they are highly involved in the process. Their children are attending academically and financially stable schools, with peers and teachers who share a common racial/ethnic heritage.

Like the Dominican group, many Portuguese parents maintain a strong connection with their native countries and consistently engage in cultural practices; Portuguese children, however, report the lowest levels of cultural routines among the three groups. These children consistently identified with the Portuguese label and saw it as a strong source of pride. But for these children, this label is far less salient and less likely to be chosen as the label that makes them the happiest than for children of the other groups. In addition, these children are more likely to identify with a racial label than the other groups—another indicator of greater acculturation to a dominant American culture.

For the most part, Portuguese youth were making average grades and eliciting positive reviews from teachers. They showed positive academic values and the highest perceptions of teachers among the three groups. While similar to Dominican youth in academic pathway distributions, the correlates to such success or failure proved to be very different between the groups. School absences and stress were the only variables associated with academic pathways for Portuguese youth, with no family context or cultural attitudes/identification variable appearing as a major influence on outcomes. Perhaps the ethnic and racial similarity between these youth and their school/neighborhood communities, as well as their low ethnic identity salience and high ethnic identity stability suggest a more "symbolic ethnic identity"[14] for these youth, one that provides them with a great sense of pride but is perhaps less salient in the daily negotiation of educational and social environments. In the final model, such an assumption might be further tested; when considering all contextual and individual variables, will Cultural Identification and Attitudes prove insignificant in determining the outcomes of these youth? We will also be interested to see if any of the immigration context indicators emerge in the final model as there was a clear divide between recent and well-established, earlier arrival Portuguese families.

8 ::

Modeling Children of Immigrants' Academic Achievement

Interviewer: *Why did you select "student" as the word you like best [to describe yourself]?*

Because I get to learn.

> —*Fifth grade, Cambodian girl*

So that I can get a good education and a good job.

> —*Fifth grade, Dominican boy*

Because most of my brothers haven't finished school yet, and I give them a good example.

> —*Fifth grade, Portuguese girl*

For each of the children in our studies, school is a central part of life. After all, it is in the school context that the daily negotiations of peer and teacher relationships, as well as the development of ethnic identities, take place alongside children's academic growth. For many families, regardless of ethnicity, a child's education represents hope for the family's future—a direct path to the better life sought by so many immigrant parents. In our studies (as detailed in the past three chapters), we saw many instances of academic achievement and high academic aspirations among children whose family economic circumstances (e.g., low parental education or family income) might predict otherwise. Nearly half (47%) of the children in our studies received A's and B's in school across the 3 years. But not all children were succeeding in school. Even at these early ages, we observed a few instances of child school dropout, academic failure (6.7% in the abysmal pathway), and academic disengagement for some students over time. The varieties in children's academic attitudes and skill development are richly captured by the comments of their teachers. One abysmal pathway student (Portuguese fifth grader) was described by her teacher as: "poor self-esteem, not serious about her work, performs poorly academically, an 'I don't care' attitude, complains about being sick all the time." In contrast, an excelling student (Cambodian second grader) was described by his teacher as: "hard worker, eager, polite, motivated, goes beyond average effort of many other students. Always listening, attentive, participates often in class. Never misses a homework assignment—confident and competent, his hard work is an example to others. I often see him laugh and smile." So how do these differences in academic attitudes and outcomes arise? How do characteristics of family and school settings combine to explain the academic outcomes of children of immigrants? Which aspects of children's academic attitudes, cultural attitudes, and ethnic identities can be combined to explain their academic achievement?

Up to this point in our discussion of children's academic pathways, we have focused our attention on describing children's academic attitudes and success. We have also begun to examine these academic processes with respect to contexts—aspects of children's families, schools, and the immigrant context that may be related to academic attitudes and achievement. However, we have not yet combined all of these contexts and academic processes into one empirical (i.e., statistical) model. Simultaneously examining the family, school, and immigration context factors that are associated with children's academic attitudes and achievement under one empirical model has some notable advantages. First, it allows us to present a parsimonious picture of contextual correlates of children's academic processes by asking, "what are the *strongest* correlates of academic attitudes and achievement?" Second, it allows us to control for some effects outside of our contexts of interest that are also known to influence the child's academic processes, such as child's age and gender, thereby giving us more accurate estimates of the associations between contexts and academic processes. Third, the particular approach we have selected for modeling our data—Structural Equation Modeling (SEM)—is well suited to building a theory-driven empirical model. This approach enables us to build a parsimonious model for each of our immigrant groups that is linked to our theoretical perspectives, providing us with a framework for interpreting our results with respect to our extant theories. All of these advantages provide us with a powerful opportunity to hone in on a core story for each group and advance our current understanding of the roles of family, school, and immigration contexts in promoting the academic success of children of immigrants.

In this chapter, we will revisit our theoretical model from Chapter 4 to build our own empirical models of second-generation children's academic achievement. Based on the data from our research, we built our models guided by theories (reviewed previously throughout this book) that children's academic achievement can be understood in part by children's academic attitudes, in part by resources and cultural practices in the family setting, and in part by school setting characteristics such as teaching experience and pedagogies, and school economic resources. Each of these domains—academic attitudes, cultural attitudes and identities, family and school settings—combines in unique ways to explain the variability (or differences) we observe in each immigrant group's childhood academic achievement. Figure 8.1 represents our guiding theoretical model.

This theoretical framework proposes an empirical *causal model*; it suggests a direction of "effects" flowing from school and family characteristics on the left, to child-level processes on the right, testing causal links between constructs.[1] This model is also a hierarchical one: Family and School settings may have effects on any of the child-level processes, but not vice versa. For child processes, we propose that both Cultural Attitudes and Identification and Academic Attitudes will have independent, direct effects on the child's Academic Achievement.

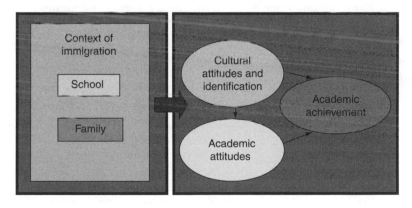

FIGURE 8.1.
Theoretical model used for empirical model building.

In addition, we propose that children's cultural attitudes and identities may also shape or modify their academic attitudes. For instance, a Cambodian boy who identifies strongly with his family's cultural identity may also have higher academic aspirations that are linked to this aspect of his identity. Both his ethnic identity and his academic aspirations may, in turn, be directly related to his high academic achievement.

This series of proposed associations serve as the structural basis for building our empirical models. Note that there are several "alternate" models that may be considered here as well. In our example, the Cambodian boy's ethnic identity may be so highly related to his academic aspirations that the proposed association between academic attitudes and achievement does not reach statistical significance. In other words, the boy's academic aspirations mediate the originally observed association between his cultural identity and his academic achievement. As we built our models, we used a process of elimination, considering such "alternate" models, to hone in on the final model that provided the best statistical fit to our collected data.[2]

Importantly, given the rich, detailed differences in the immigration contexts of our Cambodian, Dominican, and Portuguese communities, our empirical models were built separately for each immigrant group. Following a parallel design approach, construction of each model was carried out in exactly the same manner for each immigrant group using SEM.[3] This parallel design approach (Cooper, 1999; Marks & García Coll, 2007) is a research technique applied in cross-cultural research that allows the investigator to document both similarities and differences in patterns of psychological processes across different cultural groups. For example, although we measure the same constructs of family context across groups, the flexibility of parallel design allows differences in the way distinct measures within the family context associated with child academic attitudes and achievement for each immigrant group. In other words, while family context is important to academic outcomes for all three immigrant groups, specific measures of the family context (e.g., parent year of immigration or employment) may capture academic variability better for one immigrant group than another. By building models with the same "ingredients," but allowing those ingredients to interact with one another differently *within each immigrant group*, we do not assume where similarities or differences should exist between cultural groups. We can then make theoretically based comparisons between groups by examining each group's final model with respect to one another. Given the same modeling "ingredients," how does each group's final model differ from the others? How are they similar? Do the same markers of family and school context explain academic achievement among Dominican children, as for Portuguese children? These important nuances of our analytical approach reflect an increasing awareness in the field of developmental psychology that not all manifestations of a particular psychological process will appear (or be measured) in the same way in different cultural contexts. An example of this is found (below) in our own study's measurement of Academic Attitudes. As we will see, there are powerful messages that can be derived by understanding development across cultural groups and examining both similarities and differences in psychological processes across groups.

⠒⠒ Model Building Procedures and Latent Variables

So how did we go about building each of our Dominican, Cambodian, and Portuguese empirical models? An overview of the model-building process is as follows:

1. Build Latent Variables[4] (i.e , measurement models) for proposed latent constructs: Academic Achievement, Academic Attitudes, and Cultural Attitudes and Identification
2. Examine structural fit for proposed child-level associations, considering alternate models
3. Consider effects of Family characteristics on child-level variables, documenting improvement in model fit
4. Consider effects of School characteristics on child-level variables, documenting improvement in model fit

Below, we begin by providing detailed information about building our latent variables for each immigrant group and end the chapter with a presentation of each immigrant group's final empirical model.

First, a measurement model (or "latent variable") was fit for each group to represent *Academic Achievement*. This "Academic Achievement" analysis resulted in the same latent variable for each group: a combination of children's grade point averages (GPAs) for each of the 3 years, as well as teacher ratings of child academic success in the third year. In the previous three chapters, we observed different distributions of academic success by immigrant group: Cambodian children were proportionally on a higher percentage of "Excelling" and "Positive" academic pathways than the other two groups, while Dominican children were on a proportionately higher number of "Negative" and "Abysmal" pathways. This chapter extends our understanding to look more deeply into each group and ask, "Which child-level psychological processes, and school/family characteristics, are associated with children's academic performance?"

In addition to some of these between-group academic differences, we observed that teachers gave more favorable ratings to girls than to boys in all the three immigrant groups. For this reason, gender is included in our model building as a covariate. Further, as children's grades tended to decrease slightly over time, we controlled for effects of child age on Academic Achievement as well. These two control variables allow us to build models in which our estimates of children's Cultural Attitudes and Identification, Family and School variable effects are free from the influence of the small variations in achievement by gender or age.

In Figure 8.2, the Academic Achievement latent variable is represented by an oval shape; latent variables are used to measure concepts that are indirectly observed, with several *indicator variables* that serve as its measures (these are "observed variables," directly measured in the study and represented by rectangles in an SEM model). Note that there

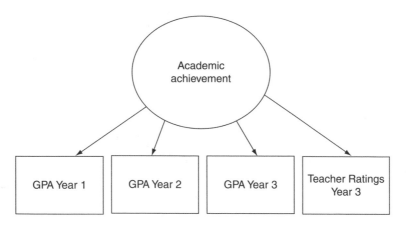

FIGURE 8.2.
Academic Achievement latent variable for all three groups. (*Notes*: Fit statistics for models by immigrant group: Cambodian [X^2/df=0.05, p=.82, NFI=1.00, RMSEA = 0 001], Dominican [X^2/df=0.93, p=.32, NFI=.99, RMSEA=.001], and Portuguese [X^2/df = 0.005, p = .94, NFI = 1.00, RMSEA = .001]).

is an arrow—or a path—drawn from the latent variable to each indicator variable. In SEM, paths are represented as arrows with direction and estimates of the strength of association between the two constructs are presented as a path coefficient with a corresponding p-value to indicate significance ($p < .05$). These path coefficients can be interpreted similarly to regression weights generated from traditional linear regression modeling. In our studies, we oftentimes present the *standardized path coefficient* (range of possible values -1 to 1) so that the magnitude of effects for individual paths may be compared to one another within each model. A note of caution is warranted here: standardized coefficients may not be compared across models (e.g., Cambodian vs. Portuguese).

Oftentimes in an SEM model, information about indicator variables and the measurement model statistics are not presented in favor of providing only the final model fit statistics. However, we believe that—particularly in the context of a parallel analysis with multiple cultural groups—it is very important to consider multiple levels of the model building process. In keeping with common practice, however, we do not display the indicator variables in our representation of the final models presented later in the chapter (although they *are* mathematically included in the actual model, including them in the final drawing can be cumbersome!).

The next step in our modeling procedure was to build latent variables to represent *Academic Attitudes* of each immigrant group. Figure 8.3 presents the possible indicator variables considered in building the Academic Attitudes latent variables. Please note that detailed information about all our indicator variables and measures can be found in the Appendix A.

Unlike Academic Achievement, Academic Attitude latent variables varied slightly by immigrant group. For all three groups, Academic

School engagement

Academic aspirations

Academic expectations

Perceptions of teachers

School values

School-related stress

FIGURE 8.3.
Variables considered in building Academic Attitude latent variables.

Engagement and Aspirations were necessary for measuring Academic Attitudes. In addition, academic expectations for going to college were included in our measure of Attitudes for the Cambodians. In the Dominican model, expectations and children's perceptions of teachers were necessary for providing the best measurement model fit. For the Portuguese, perceptions of teachers and students' school values provided the best measurement model along with engagement and aspirations. School-related stress scales did not provide a good fit with other indicators of Academic Attitudes for any of the groups and were dropped from all analyses. Table 8.1 below summarizes the differences in measurement models for Academic Attitudes and presents the final measurement model fit statistics for each group.

This is an excellent example of the utility of a parallel design approach—if we had combined all three groups under one measurement model, we would likely not have observed these subtle and meaningful differences in measuring Academic Attitudes. For example, it is interesting that for Portuguese children, Expectations for College did not combine well with other indicators of Attitudes. Instead, traditional School Values (the moral should-do's related to school) provided a better measurement solution. This makes sense given our

TABLE 8.1 Characteristics of measurement models for Academic Attitudes

	Standardized Path Coefficient		
	Cambodian	Dominican	Portuguese
Indicator Variable			
School Engagement	.79	.52	.63
Academic Aspirations	.80	.84	.33
Expectations for College	.80	.91	ns
Perceptions of Teachers	ns	.40	.65
School Values	ns	ns	.54
School-related Stress	ns	ns	ns
Measurement Model Fit			
χ^2/df, p value	.058, .94	1.36, .23	1.87, .10
NFI	1.00	.99	.99
RMSEA	.01	.04	.03

Notes: All indicator variable regression weights significant at $p < .001$; ns = not significant; not-significant indicator variables dropped from final measurement models; df = degrees of freedom; NFI = normed fit index; RMSEA = root mean square residual; χ^2 statistic is presented as a function of the model degrees of freedom, along with corresponding p value ($p \geq .05$ indicates adequate model fit).

observations that this group is more acculturated than the other two groups. Because schools are an American institution, Portuguese families (who have been here longer) have more experience with U.S. schools. In turn, their children may be more inclined to adopt traditional American School Values. For the other two groups—Cambodians and Dominicans—Expectations for College are an important part of measuring overall Academic Attitudes. This likely is a reflection of children's strong desires to attain higher educational levels (echoed by their parents) that we observed throughout our interviews. As one Dominican second grader noted, "I want to pass all my grades and go to the university and to get a job." Of final note, as seen in the Table 8.1, we obtained adequate fit statistics for measuring Academic Attitudes for each of the three groups for a variety of fit indices (see endnote for typically acceptable ranges for these fit statistics).[5]

As a next step in our modeling, we attempted to fit a latent variable for each group representing children's *Cultural Attitudes and Identification*. Because of the measurement benefits of using latent variables, we attempted to fit what might be broadly considered a latent variable capturing psychological processes associated with ethnicity and acculturation. Interestingly, in keeping with a strong base of empirical literature documenting the many nuances within and between these constructs (see Figure 8.4), we were unable to fit such a latent variable to our data for any of the three immigrant groups. Therefore, we proceeded by testing each of the scales noted below individually, as its own construct, in building the structural model.

These psychological processes have been, to a certain extent, found to be independent from each other in other populations (e.g., Cameron

Ethnic pride
Ethnic identity salience
Ethnic identity centrality
Child cultural practices
Child language preferences
In-group social preferences
Out-group social preferences

FIGURE 8.4.
Variables considered in building Cultural Attitudes and Identification latent variables.

et al., 2001). However, given the many nuances in cultural attitudes and early ethnic identities within immigrant groups (detailed throughout the previous three chapters), it is not surprising that one singular latent variable did not adequately represent our data for the variety of processes encompassed by this part of our theoretical model. It is also important to note here that it is quite possible that in other age ranges, other samples, or data sets, such a latent variable may fit. This is both the drawback and the strength of building a structural equation model: For any given model—any given latent variable—there are alternate datasets and alternate theories that may or may not fit as well as ours. It is therefore extremely important to remember precisely what our models represent: the adequacy of a fit between our theory and our own observed data!

To proceed with model building, we next began *fitting our structural models*. The very first step was to confirm that for each of the three groups, there was a significant direct effect of Academic Attitudes on Academic Achievement. This was true for all three immigrant groups (again, model fit statistics indicated that our models were fitting our observed data). Next, we needed to determine which of the Cultural Attitudes and Identification variables might have an effect on (1) Academic Achievement and (2) Academic Attitudes. Here, we were looking for significant main effects of individual Cultural Attitudes and Identification variables on either of our two Academic latent variables. Keeping only those variables whose path coefficients were significant and improved model fit, we moved onto documenting which Family setting variables had main effects on the two Academic latent variables and finally considered our School setting variables in the same manner. A summary of the original list of variables considered for the Family and School settings are presented in Figure 8.5.

Each of these indicators of the Family and School contexts were initially included because of their relevance for describing family immigration contexts and children's education-related settings (described in the previous chapters). We have already observed numerous differences in demographic factors associated with family economic resources (e.g., income, parent education, parent employment), with the Cambodian and Dominican families having fewer resources than the Portuguese families. But which, if any, of these demographic factors is important to explain child academic outcomes after all other child-level processes are taken into account? Of much importance, the family's year of immigration serves as a marker of the immigration context: both for

Family:
- Living below poverty level
- Proportion of parent employment
- Parents' education
- Parent–child book reading
- Home educational resources
- Family cultural socialization

School:
- School racial composition (% white)
- School economic marker (% of students receiving free or subsidized lunch program)
- School proficiency in math and writing (% of students below or severely below proficiency in these subjects)
- Teacher number of years' experience
- Teacher pedagogy: family socioeconomic status (SES) matters in education
- Teacher pedagogy: ethnicity matters in education

FIGURE 8.5.
Family and School setting variables considered as having a direct effect on child-level processes.

the characteristics of parents when they migrated to the United States and for the economic and social resources of the receiving community when they arrived.[6] For which group(s) might this marker of immigration context be associated with child academic achievement after all other child-level processes are taken into account? In the School context, we observed different resources available for our three groups: Portuguese children attend schools where they are in the ethnic and racial majority, with greater economic resources. Will these school characteristics be related to their academic achievement, after considering the children's other psychological processes (e.g., ethnic identity pride and centrality)?

After we completed our first-pass at examining main effects of Cultural Attitudes and Identification, Family and School setting variables on Academic Achievement and Academic Attitudes, it was time to create our final models for each group (presented below). As we layered-in our variables—first child-level Cultural Attitudes and Identification, then Family, then School—we kept track of several characteristics of the model. These included monitoring several model fit statistics to ensure an adequate structural fit to the data. We also were careful to watch the effect of entering new variables on associations already included in the model—such effects (e.g., mediating) are important nuances to observe in any linear modeling approach (Baron & Kenny, 1986). When we came to our "final" proposed model, we explored at least three alternate models (one of which always included constraining the path between Academic Attitudes and Academic Achievement to be equal to zero) to ensure the fit of our theoretical model to our data was indeed the most optimal.

⠅ Cambodian Final Model

As noted previously, all structural models began with a strong positive association between Academic Attitudes and Academic Achievement: The better children's academic attitudes are, the better their academic achievement is. This core association holds here in the Cambodian model, despite a large number of other indicator variables that help to explain Academic Achievement.

Let's first consider children's Cultural Attitudes and Identification (Figure 8.4). It is very interesting to note that different aspects of children's ethnic identities were directly associated with either Academic Attitudes or Achievement (but not both). Cambodian children who ranked their ethnic identities over the years as most important to them (instead of gender, family role, or even the label "student") also had higher academic achievement. In addition, Cambodian children's ethnic pride and in-group peer preferences, two constructs related to *feelings* about ethnicity, were associated with better academic attitudes. It is clear from this model that Cambodian children's developing ethnic identities play important, multidimensional roles in promoting academic success—both directly through grades and through attitudes.

If we now turn our attention to the variables presented in light gray in Figure 8.6—the Family and School setting indicators—we see evidence of the *immigrant paradox*.[7] Considering mothers' Year of Immigration, we see that children from *less* acculturated families, who tend to have fewer economic resources, are performing *better* in school. Why might this be? For some children, the desire to have better jobs than their parents or to help secure financial stability for themselves and their families is a powerful motivating factor for succeeding in school. For example, one Cambodian fifth grader told us that a college education is a way "to do better, get a good job, help my parents." Or as another fifth grader explained, "I want to be a teacher. I want to use my brain,

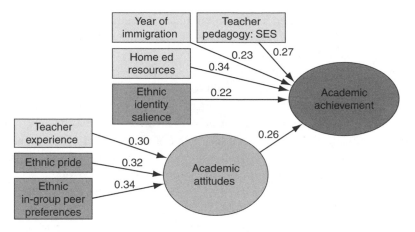

FIGURE 8.6.
Final Cambodian structural equation model: child's Cultural Attitudes, Family, and School effects on Academic Achievement and Academic Attitudes. (*Notes*: model fit statistics: $X^2/df = 1.31$, $p = .05$; normed fit index $= .97$; comparative fit index $= .99$, root mean square residual $= .04$; path coefficients are standardized, and are significant at $p < .05$. Model controls for child gender and age on Achievement.)

not hands." For this largely economically disadvantaged group, having just a few extra resources in the home for education also is strongly associated with children's higher academic achievement. Extra educational resources in the home may be a reflection of a family context where academic development is supported and stressed. Many teachers of excelling Cambodian children mentioned the influence of parental educational support for promoting academic development, stating: "[he is] extremely motivated to learn. Education [is] a priority in his life. Self-disciplined and well organized. Family is supportive and communicates frequently with his teacher." Or of another excelling second grader, "enjoys school and life in general. His family is very supportive of his education and gets help and direction at home from his parents as well as his older brother."

In addition, two markers of the School setting, Teacher Experience and Teacher Pedagogy, also were important to explaining child academic attitudes and achievement. Cambodian children in classrooms with more experienced teachers had more positive attitudes toward their educations. For children in classrooms with teachers who do not believe SES is a factor in children's educational outcomes, academic achievement was higher. These remarkable associations highlight the importance of the *quality* of the classroom environment on promoting education (and supporting positive ethnic identity development) for Cambodian children. Note that—despite attending some of the lowest-performing, economically challenged schools in our area—we observed no significant associations between negative characteristics of schools on Cambodian children's academic achievement. In other words, teachers can make a difference in children's lives, independent of the level of achievement of the school. To summarize, Cambodian children's academic achievement and positive school attitudes can be explained in our final model by a combination of positive developing ethnic identities and positive teacher qualities in the classroom—both promoting resilience despite few family economic resources, more recent family immigration, and attending low-performing schools.

⠓ Dominican Final Model

As in the Cambodian model, Cultural Attitudes and Identification were an important part of explaining Academic Attitudes and Academic Achievement in the final Dominican model. However, the qualities of the associations (and types of variables) observed are very different for the two immigrant groups. Ethnic identity centrality is *negatively* associated with Academic Achievement for our Dominican group. In other words, children who reported wanting other children to know they are Dominican, who placed a strong personal importance on being Dominican, had lower academic achievement. In addition, children who reported having stronger preference to play with other children who were *not* Dominican had better Academic Attitudes. Of utmost importance here is that these associations were observed for a specific school context: students attending schools with a higher percentage of white peers. It may be, then, that this observed disengagement from "being Dominican" is an adaptation to a racially white majority school environment. This shift away from a specific ethnic identity to achieve a positive academic outcome is reminiscent of work by Fordham and Ogbu (1986) exploring the conflict between an ethnic identity and school identity in African-American children. They note that for African-American youth adopting the identity of a diligent student was perceived as "acting white" and disassociating from one's ethnic identity by their peers. Further supporting our suggestion that a similar process may

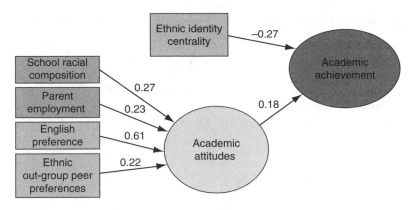

FIGURE 8.7.
Final Dominical structural equation model: Child's Cultural Attitudes, Family, and School effects on Academic Achievement and Academic Attitudes. (*Notes*: Model fit statistics: $X^2/\text{df} = 1.40$, $p = .04$; NFI $= .98$; CFI $= .99$, RMSEA $= .05$; path coefficients are standardized, and are significant at $p < .05$. Model controls for child gender and age on Achievement.)

be occurring among our Dominican youth is the finding that attending a school with a larger white student population was associated with more favorable academic attitudes; in such an environment, Dominican youth may find it easier to adopt a school identity (instead of an ethnic one) to avoid the risk of rejection by peers. In contrast to the Cambodian group, for whom more recent migration and strong ethnic identity predicted academic success, preferring to speak English (over Spanish) was associated with better Academic Attitudes. In Figure 8.7, note that the strength of association between English preference and Academic Attitudes (standardized path coefficient 0.61) is nearly 3 times as high as the association between Parent Employment (0.23), or Ethnic Out-group Peer Preferences (0.22), and Academic Attitudes. Preferring to speak English is oftentimes considered a marker of psychological acculturation—unlike the Cambodian group, it appears that more highly acculturated Dominican youth are espousing better Academic Attitudes, and thereby achieving greater Academic Success.

The importance of developing a strong ethnic identity for family connectedness was evident during our interviews with the Dominican children; of one Dominican girl a teacher notes, "Her Dominican heritage is very important to her and her family but it is also very important to my other Dominican students." However, as the above model indicates, for some students high ethnic centrality comes at the price of a strong student identity. Several struggling youth noted that while "Dominican" was their favorite label for reasons such as, "because it's so much fun" or "because that is my language, my mom's Dominican and my family," "student" on the other hand was the label that they wanted to get rid of because "I don't like going to school."

The importance of positive attitudes toward in and out-group peers in maintaining a positive academic identity was revealed in the interviews as well. When asked how much she would like to be friends with black children, one excelling Dominican girl notes, "their color doesn't matter, the only thing that matters is that they are my friends." Or, as another excelling youth states, he would want to be friends with children who are from a different ethnic background because "I want to have Dominican and American friends." It appears, therefore, among some Dominican youth that a distancing from forming a singular Dominican ethnic identity (i.e., lower Centrality) may be a positive adaptation to the school environment which creates opportunities for student identities and interethnic group peer preferences to develop.

❖ Portuguese Final Model

On first glance, perhaps the most notable characteristic of the final Portuguese model is the lack of child Cultural Attitudes and Identification or School setting variables included (see Figure 8.8). Aside from a strong effect of child age on Achievement (older children had worse grades), only Family setting characteristics related to the immigration context provided the best fit for our data. This makes sense given our understanding of the Portuguese community and children. As we explored in Chapter 7, there exist important differences in immigration context between the more recent Portuguese immigrant community and more established, earlier immigrants. For more recent arrivals, less education in the United States and less financial stability translate into lower educational involvement. We see this connection mirrored in the parent interviews as well; many of the parents who noted that they did not meet with their child's teacher pointed to a lack of English comfort as a major obstacle to involvement. For example, one mother explains "I don't speak English, I don't understand them." It is therefore not surprising that parent's year of immigration was the strongest family context correlate of child academic achievement, as it was also our most powerful marker for a variety of other acculturation measures,

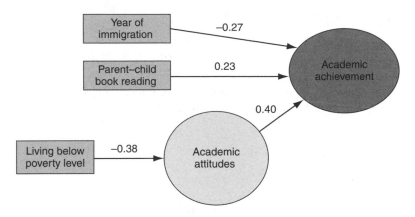

Figure 8.8.
Final Portuguese structural equation model: Family Effects on Academic Achievement and Academic Attitudes. (*Notes*: Model fit statistics: $X^2/\mathrm{df} = 1.31$, $p = .05$; NFI $= .97$; CFI $= .99$, RMSEA $= .04$; path coefficients are standardized, and are significant at $p < .05$. Model controls for child gender and age on Achievement.)

including parents' levels of comfort speaking English in several settings including work, their children's schools, and conversations with neighbors (r's $> .40$).

In addition, prominence of parents' year of immigration over child's Cultural Attitudes and Identification and School variables may well reflect the type of community these children are growing up in. The Portuguese children in our sample are, for the most part, raised in highly acculturated and integrated communities. In addition, they are attending schools where they are racially and ethnically similar to their peers and teachers. Although Portuguese children reported high levels of pride in their ethnicity, this pride (and the other aspects of Child Cultural Attitudes and Identification such as language use) was not related to children's academic attitudes or achievement when Family variables were taken into account. Instead, we observe the importance of the immigration context in explaining child academic outcomes.

We understand from Chapter 7 that more recently immigrated Portuguese families are of rural origins, with less formal education and fewer economic resources. Accordingly, mothers' year of immigration is negatively associated with Academic Achievement such that the more recently the family has immigrated, the lower the child's academic achievement. In addition, living below the poverty level is associated with lower child academic attitudes. However, for parents, a greater number of hours spent reading with their children was directly associated with higher child academic achievement. It thus appears that despite the risk for poor academic outcomes among children from recent immigrant families, parent–child book reading can provide benefits in promoting academic achievement in this population.

▓ Summary

The use of theoretically driven model building *within immigrant group* provided us with valuable models explaining academic achievement for each of our immigrant groups. Examining the similarities in "academic achievement" stories within immigrant group, we see that there are a greater number of similarities between the Cambodian and Dominican groups and fewer similarities with the Portuguese group. The similarities for our two ethnic minority groups highlight the importance of early ethnic identity characteristics such as pride and centrality in explaining academic achievement. However, the *ways* in which ethnic identity characteristics relate to academic achievement and the *contexts* that are associated with academic achievement varied greatly between the two minority groups. Among the Cambodians, who exemplify the "immigrant paradox," supportive and experienced teacher characteristics—along with greater ethnic pride—explained the success of academic achievers. For Dominicans, academic achievement was observed in the context of predominantly white classrooms in which Dominican students had lower ethnic identity centrality and less preference for speaking Spanish. Both groups are finding ways to promote their academic achievement but are doing so in different social and classroom environments. Given the academic and social benefits of building healthy identities both as ethnic group members and as students, we might pause and consider the differences in these academic contexts. For Dominican children, who in our studies are disproportionately in lower-achieving academic pathways, finding ways to bring their feelings about their ethnic identities and student identities into harmony with one another might help improve academic attitudes (and thereby achievement)—particularly among the students attending low-achieving schools with a higher proportion of racial minority peers. In the next and final chapter, as we reflect on these models and all of the details we have observed regarding developmental processes and immigration contexts for second-generation children, we remind ourselves of (1) the importance of understanding immigration, school, and family contexts for explaining child development among immigrant groups and (2) the growing need to apply these findings in our communities where educational and economic disparities between immigrant groups persist.

9 ⊞

Final Reflections

This student is a success story waiting to happen.
    —Teacher comment about a Portuguese second-grader

The purpose of this study was to increase our understanding of developmental processes during middle childhood in children of immigrants. The lack of knowledge on normative processes in these growing populations makes it imperative to conduct studies like ours. We need relevant data that will inform practice and policies to target the unique needs and challenges faced by these populations. We need to identify both universal and community-specific processes that will contribute not only to our understanding of these phenomena but also to the provision of the necessary conditions to ensure successful developmental outcomes in this quickly growing segment of the population.

The groups that we studied—Cambodians, Dominicans, and Portuguese—represent a large part of the spectrum of contemporary immigrant stories. Some are refugees, while others are considered "voluntary" immigrants; some hail from urban, others from rural environments; some are of Asian ancestry, others of Latino or European-American descent, and while some became part of an established U.S. ethnic enclave or are closely tied to the country of origin others exist in cultural isolation; we observed many dimensions in which immigration contexts differ. Through ethnographic work and parental interviews, we obtained a rich description of the cultural/psychological adaptations of these groups as they are incorporated into the urban fabric of Providence and East Providence. We see a Cambodian community that is relatively culturally isolated by language and refugee history and lack a plethora of brokers and institutions that could provide means of financial incorporation and social adaptation to the mainstream for both parents and children. We see a Portuguese community as one of the many established European immigrant groups that have contributed to this region's unique history. Finally, there is the more recent and still growing Dominican diaspora, an entrepreneurial and transnational community that is quickly making its mark not only in the local Latino community but in the larger Providence community as well.

Examination of the universal processes of migration, of adaptation, and of acculturation as a function of both the conditions of the sending community and the receiving community reveals a more nuanced reality of child and parent psychological adjustment below the surface. The precipitating conditions in the country of origin not only provide the initial impetus for migrating (i.e., war, poverty) but are the base for many of the immigrant's current behaviors and his or her relationship with that country. Whether they came from a city or a rural environment, the level of education that they obtained before migrating, and their cultural constructions of parental involvement in their children's education, all of these pre-immigration conditions make a difference in their adaptations and those of their children in this country. In addition, the history and the current status of the relations between their native countries and the United States determine the flow of newcomers who may help maintain their practice of the original language and culture, as well as their level of contact with relatives and friends afar. Not only are the ethnic enclaves renewed by an influx of new immigrants, but families are supported in maintaining cultural routines including ethnic holidays (e.g., Cambodian New Year, Feast of the Holy Ghost) and cultural childrearing practices. Depending on the characteristics of the community—transnational or refugee—it might permit (or deter) visits to the country of origin, something that was vividly described by Dominican children as significant events in their lives. Where each immigrant community falls along these dimensions contributes to the developmental niche where the child will be brought up. In this respect, it is clear that the family environment of these three immigrant groups has as many things in common (e.g., importance of parents) as different (e.g., how involved are parents in the children's education).

But other macro forces in the receiving community also contribute to that childrearing niche. Availability of affordable housing, jobs that can be done with minimal English skills, safe neighborhoods, and thriving schools creates living conditions that become part of the daily life of children. The parents' access to well-paid job opportunities determines many of the child's immediate conditions, and as manufacturing and other low skills jobs disappear in this geographic area, providing a supportive context for the child's development becomes an increasingly difficult task for immigrant parents. Our sense is that these parents' daily struggles are not only a function of the acculturation process at the individual or family level but of the economic, historical, and current conditions of each immigrant group and the population at large.

Schools, in particular, have the potential for becoming great equalizers—institutions that increasingly open or close the doors of chance for personal and group advancement in the social stratification system of our country. Unfortunately, many of the schools that immigrant children attend in this country are poorly performing schools, as is the case for the majority of children in this study. Many immigrant parents have faith in the education system in this country, without knowing the drawbacks and limitations of their children's particular schools. Yet it is critical that children learn the academic and social skills necessary to succeed in this country, becoming culturally competent and financially secure. Whose responsibility is that?

As was shown in this study, all immigrant parents recognize the importance of their children succeeding academically, even if they differ in profound ways in *how* they relate to their children's school and teachers. Schools in turn create new definitions of children's success and failure, requiring new daily routines that are supported (or unsupported) by family in the child's daily life. This daily life can become increasingly foreign to the parents as the child progresses through school, creating a source of anxiety for many parents who are afraid to lose their children to the perceived dangers of American life (drugs, gangs, early pregnancy, etc). The dilemma of immigrant parents, then, is to equip their children with the tools that permit them to be successful in the dominant culture but not lose sight of them in the process—a fear that was expressed by many parents. For example, many Dominican parents complained that the schools did not impart enough discipline; some Cambodian parents expressed their fears that their children, especially boys, would become American and join the "Asian" gangs; Portuguese parents complained that Americans are too lenient, and thus children are too disrespectful of their elders. A sense of fear, potential loss, and inevitability was expressed by many. Clearer and closer communication between parents and teachers would assist in this process. Some parents in our study had access to bilingual/bicultural personnel in the schools, creating a united front on behalf of the child. Practices such as home visits, especially at the beginning of the year, and use of interpreter in open houses or any other school activity that involves performance by the children were especially welcomed.

So how are the children of immigrants doing during middle childhood? We meet our children in this study in either first grade or fourth grade, at the beginning or in the midst of middle childhood. This is a period of child development that psychologists have studied relatively little, compared with early development and adolescence. But, in fact, a great deal happens in middle childhood. During this period, school becomes a focus of children's lives, and teachers and peers grow in significance. For immigrant families, this is the time when children should be acquiring many of the skills needed to achieve the American dream. Children need to learn the basics of how to read, how to read to learn, how to write, and how to complete math operations at levels that sometimes exceed their family members' current abilities. As children's skills develop, they will oftentimes be asked to serve as resources for their families (e.g., language brokering). It has been documented in the literature that these children will assist in a broad range of daily activities from translating at doctor's visits, to preparing family financial documents, to helping parents with job or government aid applications (Orellana, 2003). Sometimes these competencies lead to new roles and responsibilities for the child, placing them in a position as language brokers for their families.

But individual schools differ in quality as indicated by their yearly report cards. Many of the schools that the children in this study attend are considered in need of improvement: A significant percentage of the children in those schools are failing to demonstrate the acquisition of basic skills in reading, math, and science. Other reports attest to deficiencies in school climate, where both teachers' and students' behavior reflect their discontent with the system. Given these indicators, it is questionable whether the children of immigrants in this study are receiving the quality of education they critically need. This is particularly the case for the schools that the Cambodian and Dominican children attend—which were overwhelmingly low-performing schools with low-SES student populations, large class sizes, high levels of suspensions, and low levels of teacher satisfaction. One of the purposes of this study was to ascertain in terms of attitudes, grades, and teacher assessments how these are children fairing in these schools. The answer is, it depends on the group. Within the Cambodian sample, we see evidence for the immigrant paradox: with many children excelling in spite of their parents' low human, social, and cultural capital. A larger percentage of Dominicans and Portuguese are showing academic pathways that are placing them at risk for future academic failure. The contributors to academic pathways also differ by group, making it impossible to make swift generalizations about the academic outcomes of children of immigrants as a whole.

In addition, in these schools and in their daily interactions with other outlets of mainstream culture (i.e., media), children of immigrants also learn about the meaning of social categories inclusive of those of their own, ascribed ethnicity and race. We know that children as early as 3 years of age can identify the social valence of race (e.g., know that a white doll is more desirable than a black doll) and the social valence of ethnicity by 7 years (Bernal et al., 1990). But what happens in middle childhood? Current theories point to adolescence as the time when identity processes are most salient and actively engaged. Does that mean that identity exploration is not taking place in middle childhood, even if these categories might be identifiable? How about social attitudes toward both in-groups and out-groups? Are they related to ethnic identity? And do children in this stage of development perceive discrimination? And finally, are these processes related to academic outcomes as they are in some older populations?

Ultimately, the pathway to success for these children—to make their parents' migration and sacrifices worthwhile—is to do well in school. Therefore, in this study, we also measured academic outcomes in these children. Because positive attitudes toward teachers, studying, and school are necessary ingredients for academic success, we measured a range of academic attitudes. In addition, good grades become the ticket to higher education, financial aid, and other resources necessary to move out of poverty. The value of an education is clearly reflected in the average income by the degree attained: $20, 431 yearly for a high school diploma; $37,782 yearly for a college degree (U.S. Census Bureau, 2003). While in previous generations, immigrant families could open stores or other small businesses without a college education to create financial stability, in the current economy of giant discount goods and restaurant chains, this is becoming less and less of a possibility for the new generation of immigrant youth. As manufacturing and other low-skill jobs continue to decline in availability, a college education may be the only ticket to financial stability for these second-generation youth and their future families. Making it through school is imperative to escape their poverty and become socially mobile. Having positive evaluations from teachers contributes to these favorable outcomes, as they reflect these children's successful adaptations. Thus our main questions were how do the children of the immigrant groups in this study fare in terms of school attitudes, teacher evaluations, and grades? And what aspects of family, school, and cultural attitudes and identifications relate to grades during the 3 years of the study?

⠶ Children's Cultural Attitudes and Identification

In this study, we found evidence that all children are actively identifying/constructing identity and other racial/ethnic categories. Every child identified with an ethnic label; most of them chose nationality as one of their most important label over the 3 years of the study regardless of their age. Moreover, most children in this study showed signs of healthy identity development: They choose "accurate" ethnic/racial labels, have logical explanations for why these labels apply to them, and are proud of their membership in these groups. Moreover, most children did not perceive discrimination related to race or ethnicity, did not show strong social biases against other ethnic groups, and would like their skin color to remain as is. These are good developmental outcomes to observe in this population otherwise perceived as high risk and impoverished.

So what are the implications of these findings for policy, practice, and research? In terms of policy, personnel who work with diverse children in this age group should be made aware of the importance of these developmental tasks for these children. Fostering, promoting, and maintaining these positive early starts to ethnic identity and interethnic group social relations is of the utmost importance given numerous studies which document consequences of decline in adolescence. In other words, in older populations, declines in ethnic/racial self-esteem and/or dissatisfactions with their own color and ascribed ethnicity is associated with disengagement in school and with other risky behaviors. A good foundation for ethnic/racial development in middle childhood might prevent such declines and negative outcomes. A school policy of color blindness therefore might not provide the necessary support for these children's continued development of healthy ethnic/racial attitudes and identification, as society outside the classroom for the most part is not color blind and it has constructed a social stratification system based on class and race/ethnicity. Pretending that these categories are not operative is a disservice to these children. Moreover, recognizing the power of social categories in the world and learning tools to fight stereotypes while at the same time acknowledging our commonalities and uniqueness can be a great opportunity to exercise critical thinking, reading, and writing skills. Looking at demographic shifts can also be used to practice mathematical skills.

In addition to color blind policies and practices, one size fits all approach will not work either. This approach might treat all immigrants or all people of color the same. Being white is more important for Portuguese children than the corresponding racial terms are for Dominicans and Cambodians. So talking about racial identity would be heard differently by kids from each group. In addition, as seen in our final statistical analyses, different aspects of cultural attitudes and identification are related to academic success in each of the immigrant groups in different ways. For Cambodians, a more salient (e.g., selecting as their "most important" label across the 3 years) ethnic identity was associated with better academic outcomes. In contrast, for Dominicans, a more central (e.g., wanting others to know that they are Dominican) ethnic identity was associated with lower academic achievement. For the Portuguese, ethnic identity was not associated with academic outcomes in the final model. For this group, the conditions of migration and the characteristics of life in their new communities create unique niches in which they form their early identities, niches with different contexts, and psychological processes, than the Dominican and Cambodian children experience. The acknowledgment of the universality of these processes and the simultaneous individual pathways created depending on immigration context is needed. For example, a historical analysis of how these racial and ethnic terms have evolved could be used to provide insights into the historical processes of immigration into this country, giving insight into the evolving categories of "us" and "others" throughout American history.

Thus, teacher preparation programs should be integrating into their curriculums and supervised practices the extant knowledge on the development of cultural attitudes and identification in middle childhood and beyond. In this way, teachers would be sensitive to emergent identities and be able to identify any negative feelings or associated consequences (e.g., poor academic outcomes or school disengagement) that might arise. Curriculum in schools should take into account the populations they serve in their book choices for history/social science and literature so children feel affirmed. Relegating the exploration of this knowledge to special dates only (e.g., Martin Luther King Day, Columbus Day) reinforces the marginalization of these populations rather than their integration into a more diverse mainstream. Finally, communities can explore social and cultural programs in their own businesses, churches, schools and community centers, using these social science perspectives. Our studies' results may be used to compliment standard community practices to encourage and reinforce the saliency and meaningfulness of children's developing racial and ethnic identities.

In addition, teachers and other school personnel need to get to know their particular communities and the children's own knowledge and understanding of racial/ethnic categories. For example, instead of imposing preconceived categories, categories should be elicited from children. In our own research, "Spanish" was deployed by students to describe Latino/Hispanic students, while the "Latino" and "Hispanic" labels were used infrequently. In contrast, we found that most of the teachers and administrators in our sample schools did not know what country their "Asian" students are from, when nationality (Cambodian) is these students' category of choice for self-identification and "Asian" is deployed only by older students. Basically, adults need to understand how these ethnic labels are deployed, contested, and adopted by the children themselves (Thorne, 2005). School personnel need to get to know diverse children more profoundly in order to be supportive of the important task of ethnic/racial identity development.

At the same time that we find ample evidence of positive developmental outcomes in cultural attitudes and identifications in these three groups, there was a small group of children in the Cambodian and Dominican groups that reported conflicts or negative cultural attitudes and identifications. Some of these differences correspond closely to their own immigrant community's incorporation (or lack thereof) to mainstream culture in the United States and their knowledge of the valence of their ascribed race/ethnicity in the mainstream community. To us, some of these differences seem normative and actually adaptive, while others might place the kids at risk. For example, the groups differed in their identification with racial labels: Portuguese chose more often what we considered a racial term, "white" (and a more cultural one, "American"), portraying the typical assimilation process of other European groups that become American and white, part of the mainstream, in one generation. The other two groups, if racially identified in this country, would be categorized as "black" or "African-American" for Dominican and "Asian" for the Cambodian. They would be considered nonwhite, and as observed in other populations of nonwhite individuals (Waters, 1994), the children in this study "choose" to identify with their ethnicity and nationality, (e.g., Dominican and Cambodian), respectively, rather than their race (e.g., black and white). In this way, they distance themselves from belonging to the groups that are associated with lower social status in their daily context (e.g., African-Americans, people of color; Bailey, 2001a).

This dissociation is also reflected by their responses to the question of whether they would like to change their skin color. About 33% of Cambodian and Dominican children responded that they would like to change their skin color as opposed to only 14% of the Portuguese children. This is taken as evidence that the children in this study have knowledge of the negative stigma associated with darker skin (and the positive valence of white skin) in this country and that some children in the two groups "of color" would rather be lighter skinned. They are not comfortable "in their own skin."

The groups differed in ethnic label satisfaction as well, indicating that some children feel dissatisfaction not only with their ascribed race but also with their ethnicity. Forty-four percent of Cambodians and 35% of Dominicans would get rid of one ethnic label, as opposed to 27% of Portuguese. Again, the two "groups of color" reflect some negative feelings about their ethnicity. All of these findings suggest that a relatively small but significant group of children express negative cultural attitudes and identifications at this age. Most of these opinions refer to attitudes toward the self—ethnicity, race, skin color—and not attitudes toward others. However, we also find evidence that the Cambodian children not only have less preference for the in-group but they show consistently less preference for children in the out-group, especially at home. Again, this might reflect the relative social isolation that the Cambodian community experiences.

Not only do Cambodian children express this isolation, but their parents do as well. In addition, this social isolation is also evident in the analysis of the community done as part of the ethnographic work of this study. Cambodian parents more often report that they do not belong in their neighborhood, that they do not feel like their neighborhood is their community, and that they do not belong to any particular community than the Dominican or Portuguese parents. In the ethnographic analysis of the Cambodian community, there is an evident lack of the ethnic institutions (e.g., media) that contribute to the cohesion and sense of community in the Dominican and Portuguese communities. In addition, not only are Cambodians isolated from other Cambodians, but also these families have very little connections with mainstream institutions and individuals. Their children's school is the main context of mainstream American culture, and given the sense of isolation and lack of interaction that these families and children report, it would be good for schools to take a more proactive role in bridging the gap. Perhaps, having parents' nights with translators, house-calls/visits that urge parents individually to come in, or translated newsletters with tips on effective ways to help their children might lure parents into a closer relationship with schools. As in other population (Delgado-Gaitán, 1991), these approaches not only would break the social isolation, but would facilitate their parents' involvement in their children's education.

Finally, the most intriguing finding of the study in terms of cultural attitudes and identifications is the negative association between ethnic identity centrality and academic outcomes in Dominican children. This is the opposite of what has been found in other populations, including the Cambodian population in the current study. In other words, in many samples, a positive ethnic identity is associated with better academic outcomes (Fuligni, Witkow, & García, 2005; Marks, Powell, & García Coll, In Press; Phinney, Horenczyk, Liebkind, & Vedder, 2001). In the Dominican sample in this study, the negative association between centrality and achievement is accompanied by two other indicators that suggest a different adaptation is enacted by these children to attain better academic attitudes. Children who prefer English over Spanish, express preferences of peers of other ethnicities, and want to get rid of their skin color have better academic attitudes which in turn are associated with better academic outcomes. So Dominican children who are (and want to be) more acculturated have better academic outcomes in this study. It is important to note that these behaviors occur in school contexts where there are more white peers and a higher percentage of parents are employed. What is interesting about this finding is that it resembles the findings from ethnographic studies conducted by Ogbu (2004) where African-American adolescents report that being involved in academics is perceived as "acting white." The Dominican-American children in our studies are wrestling with their racial identities in the

school context in a similar process of dissociation from "being black"—
a process that appears to facilitate Dominican children's academic
achievement. It is also interesting to note here that the construction
of "race" in the Dominican Republic is such that anyone who is *not*
of Haitian ethnicity is considered white. This is the opposite of the
one drop rule in the United States where anyone with black ancestry
is considered black; rather, in the Dominican Republic, anybody with
some white ancestor can claim to be white. Many Dominican parents of
the children in our study therefore do not consider themselves black,
but rather white. It is not until children encounter new socially constructed ideas of race in the United States that Dominican-American
families come to realize that they will be ascribed as black by other
members of the community. While their white identification in contexts
where there are more whites is also accompanied with better grades
and teacher ratings, in minority peer contexts, this identification may
carry social costs, as these children may be *accused* by peers of "acting
white." As with Cambodians, the subtleties of their ethnic/racial identifications and the relations with academic outcomes make one size fits
all approaches untenable.

These findings as a whole raise many questions. We do not know
how stable these ethnic/racial attitudes are. (Will they still feel this way
in early adolescence?) We do not know the consequences for other developmental outcomes (e.g., health and behavior). However, we do know
that negative feelings about identifications are related to poorer academic outcomes (Marks et al., 2007). So the adults (i.e., parents, teachers)
around these children need to ascertain any negative feelings that children have in order to provide them with experiences that will affirm
rather than undermine the development of positive feelings toward
their own ethnicity/race and that of others. School personnel need to
get to know the history of local groups in order to identify children
who potentially feel more isolated and negative toward themselves and
other groups. Curriculum can affirm the value of multiculturalism and
diversity as societal values, can confront racism and negative valences
associated with membership in certain groups, and can provide cross-
racial/ethnic experiences outside the classroom that reinforce the value
of these categories. It is especially important to help children associate
their own ethnicity/race with success in school: They need role models and mentors in their communities who can provide such knowledge
when their families cannot.

The implications for research are many. We need to study the development of these cultural attitudes and identifications longitudinally and as a function of different school and community settings (that differ in the number of groups present and majority/minority ratio). We also need to ascertain the role of adults in school and out of school interventions especially for children who show more negative attitudes and identifications.

Children's Academic Outcomes

Given current conceptualizations of child development, academic outcomes are not only seen as an individual's achievement but also one that reflects as well the strengths and weaknesses of the environments that these children navigate—families, communities, and schools. The children in this study are part of environments that have both protective and high-risk factors that are considered critical for academic outcomes. Each immigrant group differs in the kind of protective (e.g., two parents present in Cambodian families, home ownership in Portuguese) and risk (e.g., low educational attainment for Cambodian, high mobility for the Dominican) factors that their children are exposed to. Some are inherent parts of being an immigrant to this country (e.g., low English comfort); some are part of living in poverty (e.g., residential mobility).

As we mentioned before, most parents in this study report high aspirations for their children, educationally and occupationally, even if they might differ in their involvement in their children's education. In turn, the children uniformly reported positive academic attitudes and practices that get even more positive over time. The children in this study overwhelmingly are engaged in school, they like their teachers, and they have adopted positive school values. They want to go to college and expect to do so. They spend typical amounts of time (given their ages) in homework and TV viewing. They seem even more positive and engaged in school than other groups. Previous research has shown a decline in attitudes through middle childhood in native-born samples (Alexander et al., 1997; Eccles, Midgley, & Adler, 1984). This is not observed in any of our groups. Actually in many of the academic attitudes measured, we see a cohort effect where older children show more positive attitudes than younger children, indicating the possibility that these positive attitudes increase as children go through elementary school.

For parents and schools (and society at large if these attitudes remain positive and translate into high level of academic work), this is wonderful news. These children want to do well now and in the future. They recognize that doing well in school is important and that it is their "job" to do well. Both parents and schools need to be aware of these attitudes and values and come up with ways that can reinforce them especially since many students in similar urban schools report not being as engaged or caring. Children of immigrants in this study do not fit the stereotype of the disengaged urban student; they reflect more on their older counterparts (immigrant adolescents and their positive attitudes toward school) than on their peers. We need to learn from these children how they develop these attitudes and how they remain optimistic over time. Research examining the positive attitudes of immigrant and second-generation youth generally suggests that cultural values and family dynamics are largely at play. Fuligni has linked the high expectations of these youth with the belief, shared by children and parents, that education will lead to upward economic mobility as well as with cultural values that stress educational attainment as a way to give back to the family (Fuligni, 2001b). Knowing more about family processes that support these positive school attitudes might help us intervene with other students who are not doing as well.

In contrast, it is interesting that we find more variability in academic performance and teacher reports than what we observed above in children's attitudes and practices. There are several interesting findings in this regard. The first is that even if the three immigrant groups differ tremendously in their immediate cultural and socioeconomic context, few differences in academic performance are observed between the groups. Moreover, in spite of their relative poverty and other risk factors, many children are doing well, they have B's and A's as 3-year grade point averages (56% of Cambodians, 44% of Dominicans and Portuguese). These findings agree with other reports that have documented children of immigrant families outperforming their native peers (Fuligni, 1997; Kao & Tienda, 1995; Portes & Rumbaut, 2001).

However, there are two immigrant group differences in the study that provide some intriguing evidence that Cambodian children are excelling beyond all expectations in spite of difficult family (e.g., low parent educational attainment, high poverty, large families, low parental involvement in education) and community (e.g., isolated community with no strong ethnic enclave and very few contact with the mainstream) contexts. More Cambodian children have higher teacher ratings and are more often considered to be excelling students (based on both grades and teacher reports) than in the other two groups. Glowing teacher reports were common for these children; of a Cambodian fifth grader one teacher writes, "He is a very motivated student. Excels in all areas and is always helping his peers. Student was winner of elementary level spelling bee for Providence." Similar findings were reported by Portes and Rumbaut, (2001), who found that Cambodian adolescents showed better academic outcomes than their sociodemographic profiles would predict.

These findings are the opposite of what theories of human and social capital would predict which are based on deficit models of family influences. In other words, these models do not examine assets at the same time that they measure risk. It is true that Cambodian parents are poor, uneducated, and do not have the tools to involve themselves in their children's schooling, but they have high aspirations and expectations for their children's future and doing well in school is expected from their children. In addition, the children are kept very close by their families; they do not venture out of the households after school, or on weekends or school vacations. In some ways, the fear of the outside expressed by these families and children, accompanied with valuing education, might keep these children on the right pathway. More must be learned about these resilient children. Portes and Rumbaut (2001) suggest that the advantage of being a refugee group that was helped to incorporate to this country reveals itself in higher achievement in their children. But we do not see in our sample any benefits of all the early refugee programs, as many families are still poor, with low levels of education, and poorly acculturated.

Yet although a significant percentage of children are doing well, not all children are succeeding. A percentage of each immigrant group of children is experiencing academic difficulties and disengagement with school. If we examine the academic pathways, 32% of Cambodians, 41% of Dominican, and 32% of Portuguese have negative or abysmal academic pathways. Why do some children succeed and others do not in school? In Chapter 8, we considered all the factors simultaneously which could contribute to academic outcomes in these children. We considered school, family, cultural attitudes and identification, and academic attitudes. There were several interesting findings that emerged from this set of analyses. First, very different factors, or similar factors with different directions, are associated with positive academic outcomes in each immigrant group. Even if aspects of schools (i.e., teacher's pedagogy), families (year of migration), cultural attitudes and identification (salience of ethnicity), and academic attitudes (engagement) are related to academic outcomes in more than one group, the nature or direction of the association differs from one group to the other. The only exception was academic attitudes. As expected, academic attitudes and practices are related to academic outcomes in all groups: Children who have more positive attitudes toward school and teachers have higher academic achievement. As expressed before, this is great news, especially the fact that we see that these attitudes improve over time for all three immigrant groups.

But what explanatory factors differ, in their relation to each other and to the academic outcomes examined, from one group to the next? Looking at the models in Chapter 8, we see that for the Cambodian sample having a more salient ethnic identity, having teachers who do not believe SES is a determining factor in educational outcomes, and having parents with recent immigration journeys (evidence of the immigrant paradox) are associated with better academic outcomes, while having greater ethnic pride and higher in-group peer preferences are associated with better academic attitudes. However, for the Dominicans, a strikingly different pattern emerges. For these youth, having a more central ethnic identity is actually associated with *lower* academic achievement. In addition, for Dominican youth in schools with more white-identified students and in families with higher educational backgrounds, having a higher preference English and a higher preference for out-group peers (both possible indicators of higher acculturation) are associated with higher academic attitudes. Finally, for the Portuguese, only family variables are related to academic attitudes and achievement. For these youth having parents who immigrated earlier and who display higher levels of literacy practices (as indicated by parent–child recreational reading) are associated with higher academic achievement, while growing up in a financially stable home is associated with more optimal academic attitudes.

These findings support the notion that academic outcomes are not solely individually determined outcomes. We are not saying that individual cognitive and socioemotional characteristics are not important, nor that agency is irrelevant; rather we are affirming that children and families operate within contexts that are larger than the individuals and that these forces need to be acknowledged in working with both individuals and groups of children of immigrants. The complexity of such processes is clearly enhanced when we consider different cultural groups. Parents' year of migration makes a difference, but it can have the opposite effects depending on the characteristics of the cohort migrating and the differing effects of acculturation. Aspects of the child's ethnic identity (centrality, salience, pride) and in-group/out-group preferences as indicators of cultural attitudes and identifications of the child are also related to academic outcomes, but the direction of effects is a function of the ethnic/racial background of the school and the socioeconomic status of the family. Finally, schools and teachers matter more for some groups than others, processes that are indicated by the racial/ethnic composition of the school or the pedagogical philosophy and experience of teachers. What is clear is that both proximal and distal factors associated with schools, families, and the child work synergistically to produce academic outcomes. Theoretically, this was expected, but these findings question the wisdom of many educational reform efforts that concentrate on individuals and disregard the other systems such as family and schools.

So what are the implications of these findings for policy and practice? The main implications are that interventions that are aimed at enhancing academic outcomes in children of immigrants will be most effective as more developmental factors are considered. It is not implied that interventions aimed at children or families or schools by themselves will not be effective, but that the magnitude of the effects will be smaller than more comprehensive ones. It also implies that mechanisms of positive change that work in some populations cannot be assumed to be generalizable to all other populations. Deep understandings of communities and their assets are necessary in order to be able to enhance academic outcomes in ways that are congruent to other aspects of the children's development.

Implications for Current Immigration Debate

Over the course of this study, overt national attitudes toward immigrants have dramatically changed. During the initial 3 years of data collection, we conducted periodic systematic scans of major national, regional, and local newspapers (1999–2002) for write-ups on immigration and particularly on schooling and academics in these populations. The majority of the newspaper articles documented the demographic changes in the United States, how immigration was contributing to those changes, and lamenting the lack or cuts of funding for ESL, bilingual, or adult literacy programs. In addition, the occasional valedictorian was noted whose family had just recently arrived in the United States. However, increasingly voices in the distance that were questioning bilingual education in California, Massachusetts, and Texas were being heard.

Although not as systematic, we have continued to monitor the media coverage of news that involved immigrants or national immigration policy since finishing data collection in 2002. The national zeitgeist has completely changed. The events of 9/11/2001 have contributed to a fear of "others," and many policies at the national and local level have been enacted to make our borders more secure, to impede the entrance of "nondesirable individuals"—from suspected terrorists to undocumented workers—and to send those who are illegally in the United States back to their country of origin. The news now focuses on raids occurring nationwide, on illegal families living in fear, on their children who are American citizens by birth been left behind. p. 188.

In the midst of these debates, groups who have come legally into this country, as we assume the majority of the families in this study have done, have been affected by these policies. As we understand, Cambodian families came as refugees and Portuguese and Dominicans as the product of family reunification programs that followed the 1965 immigration reforms. Many of these families and the services that were instituted to support the successful integration of legal immigrants into the United States have been swept in the controversy over illegal immigration. People who look "immigrant" or speak another language are being stopped and asked for their social security card to secure employment or to complete a purchase.

In addition, many families are been split over their legal status. Family members who are illegally here, sometimes because of bureaucratic red tape in processing their status, are being turned in and deported to their country of origins. Raids and deportation of illegal immigrants have left their children, citizens of the United States, without the benefit of a caring family. Even if all the family members are legally here, immigrants are afraid to interact with officials of any kind—schools, police, fire—because they might be questioned and something might be found wrong that will get them into problems with the authorities. Many live in fear.

This is not the first time that this has occurred in the history of this country. It is clear that the United States has historically had mixed feelings about immigrants and that the ensuing immigration policies have reflected those changes (see Perea & García Coll, 2008, for similar changes in attitudes and laws about bilingual education). Perceptions of abundance and/or safety are accompanied by more lenient, even receptive attitude toward immigrants. But now at a time when the United States has to grapple with economic and political security of the world, rather than adopting comprehensive immigration reform—something that thousands clamored for in street demonstrations last year—we are building a wall in our Southern border. We never thought that we would see in our lives a wall demolished (Berlin) and one new one erected (between Mexico and the United States)!

But are immigrants really a threat? When researchers have addressed this question, they find that, in fact, immigrants who are living in the United Sates as a whole are less likely to commit crimes, want to learn English, and appreciate the value of formal education (Rumbaut & Ewing, 2007; Suárez-Orozco, Suárez-Orozco & Todorova, 2008). Many have two jobs, live modestly, and invest any extra resources in their kid's education (i.e., sending them to parochial schools). So in spite of living in poverty, not knowing English, and having low levels of education, these immigrant parents not only embrace American ideals, such as the American dream, but they *enact* those ideals through their high aspirations, hard work, and identification with education as the path to upward mobility.

These attitudes and work ethics are also found amongst their children. This study is among the first to document that these positive attitudes are also associated with more positive school outcomes during middle childhood. These positive attitudes and their association with more positive academic outcomes have been observed repeatedly in older populations. So in spite of all odds, the potential of positive attitudes and the hard work necessary for success is there for children of immigrants.

So where does the fear that immigrants are a threat to the United States come from? Several recent articles have identified an "assimilationist threat." The perception that immigrants will fail to adopt the cultural norms and lifestyles of the United States (Paxton & Mughan, 2006) is a current source of fear among some U.S. citizens. On the other hand, some U.S. citizens hold a cosmopolitan worldview, embracing proimmigration perspectives and rejecting ethnocentrism. These individuals are typically highly educated and employed in white-collar professions and have lived or traveled abroad (Haubert & Fussell, 2006). Popular differences in fears and opinions can perhaps be attributed to life experiences which have allowed individuals to learn about different cultural practices. Thus, policies can be enacted that promote travel abroad and life experiences that will open the horizons of all U.S. citizens so attitudes toward "others" are not founded in fear and misinformation. It is our hope that studies like ours will be able to inform public opinion and perhaps dispel some of the unfounded public fears concerning this quickly growing population.

Which leaves us with the final question, what will inform public policy and practice? We would hope that studies such as ours will be used to inform policy, particularly when research helps to understand or even correct popular opinions and fears regarding immigration. As the fastest growing population of American youth, it is of great importance that it becomes a priority for us to support these kids to become the "success stories" they are striving to be. The development of positive cultural attitudes and identifications must not be treated as a "cultural threat" to American society but a tool which will allow these youth to be productive and vibrant contributors to adult society. Understanding each group and family system will enable society and its institutions to be truly informed and not act out of fear or speculation. Only then will we be able to support the development of policies that will help in the incorporation of these growing populations successfully—something that will no doubt benefit us all.

TABLES ⠗

TABLE 1 Distribution of Sample by Ethnic Group, Sex, and Age

	Sex				Age Cohort			
	Girls		Boys		Younger		Older	
	n	%	n	%	n	%	n	%
Cambodian	73	51.4	69	48.6	70	49.3	72	50.7
Dominican	75	53.6	65	46.4	70	50	70	50
Portuguese	58	47.5	64	52.5	56	45.9	66	54.1

TABLE 2 Neighborhood Characteristics and Perceptions of Neighborhoods

	Cambodian		Dominican		Portuguese		Statistical Test
	n	%	n	%	n	%	
Like the neighborhood they live in	116	77.6	91	82.4	94	87.2	ns
Feel they belong in the neighborhood they live in	110	67.3	88	86.4	92	88.0	$\chi^2(2,290)$ $= 16.85^{***}$
Feel their neighborhood is their community	109	33.0	89	82.0	93	75.3	$\chi^2(2,291)$ $= 60.61^{***}$
Feel they belong to a particular community	111	9.0	90	42.7	93	30.1	$\chi^2(2,293)$ $= 30.41^{***}$
Participate in clubs and/or organizations	113	11.5	92	14.1	92	25.0	$\chi^2(2,297)$ $= 7.25^{*}$

Note: $^{*}p < .05$, $^{**}p < .01$, $^{***}p < .001$.

TABLE 3 School Context and Teacher Characteristics Stratified by Immigrant Group

	Cambodian $n = 125$	Dominican $n = 90$	Portuguese $n = 101$	Statistical Test
Teacher Characteristics	M (SD)	M (SD)	M (SD)	
Education (percent of teachers with MA or above)	76.2	50	44	$\chi^2(2,250) = 19.98$***
Experience (years at current school)	5.21 (7.03)	4.89 (6.04)	6.39 (5.61)	ns
Teaching experience (yrs)	15.67 (11.8)[a]	10.16 (9.78)	13.71 (9.85)	$F(2,250) = 5.90$***
Percent white	82	76	97	$F(2,344) = 482.97$***
Teacher grievances	5.39 (5.83)	4.57 (5.17)	1.28 (3.7)[c]	$F(2,344) = 20.80$***
School Characteristics	M (SD)	M (SD)	M (SD)	
Type of school (percent attending public school)	94.4	76.3	86.1	$\chi^2(2,344) = 18.722$***
School size (number of students)	563.37[b]	633.97[b]	379.72[b]	$F(2,344) = 53.491$*
Average class size	24.01	23.64	21.08[c]	$F(2,315) = 92.46$***
Student attendance	91.52[b]	90.70[b]	97[b]	$F(2,344) = 96.35$***
Total number of suspensions in school	88.28 (109.45)	123.50 (132.30)	35.26 (101.75)[c]	$F(2,344) = 15.81$***
Percent of students enrolled in ESL	22.97[a]	18.86	21.24	$F(2,344) = 3.63$*
Percent of students eligible for free/reduced price meals	93.56	91.81	56.52[c]	$F(2,344) = 373.18$
Percent of students in school who are black	20.29	21.12	17.58[c]	$F(2,344) = 12.362$
Percent of students in school who are white	12.9	16.28	70.54[c]	$F(2,344) = 482.97$*
Percent of students in school who are Hispanic	47.88	48.32	9[c]	$F(2,344) = 331.94$*
Percent of students in school who are Asian	18.40[b]	13.51[b]	2.65[b]	$F(2,344) = 117.69$*
Percent of students severely below proficiency in math	46.59	46.54	28.38[c]	$F(2,341) = 91.85$*
Percent of students below proficiency in math	30.61	31.02	33.62[c]	$F(2,344) = 7.691$*
Percent of students severely below proficiency in writing	65.62	66.61	43.62[c]	$F(2,344) = 146.38$*
Percent of student below proficiency in writing	30.29	29.36	46.66[c]	$F(2,344) = 126.64$*

Note: * $p < .05$, ** $p < .01$, *** $p < .001$, ns not significant.
[a] Cambodians and Dominicans significantly different from one another.
[b] All groups significantly different from one another.
[c] Portuguese significantly different from other two groups.

TABLE 4 Parental and Household Characteristics Stratified by Immigrant Group

	Cambodian $n = 127$	Dominican $n = 101$	Portuguese $n = 99$	Statistical Test
Parental Characteristics	M (SD)	M (SD)	M (SD)	
Age (years)	37 (7.95)	36 (5.95)	37 (5.47)	ns
Education (years)	4.27[a] (4.5)	11.10 (3.2)	9.88 (3.73)	$F_{(2,300)} = 92.85$***
Year of immigration	1984 (3.4)	1984 (10.0)	1979[c] (10.2)	$F_{(2,287)} = 10.97$***
	%	%	%	
Immigrant mother	100	94.9	86.9	$\chi^2_{(2,321)} = 18.0$***
Immigrant father	100	96.9	90.8	$\chi^2_{(2,320)} = 13.0$**
Household Characteristics	M (SD)	M (SD)	M (SD)	
Size	5.4[a] (1.61)	4.3 (1.11)	4.5 (1.2)	$F_{(2,325)} = 20.99$***
Mobility (number of addresses since child started school)	1.74[g] (.87)	2.26[g] (1.34)	1.33[g] (.61)	$F_{(2,335)} = 21.18$***
Percent of families with two working parents	26.2	23.2	60	$\chi^2_{(2,269)} = 11.57$***
	%	%	%	
Own home	25.9	23.9	70.2	$\chi^2_{(2,302)} = 55.68$***
Skilled workers	15.7	26.8	42.0	$\chi^2_{(2,176)} = 10.08$**
Single-parent homes	26	48.5	12.1	$\chi^2_{(4,325)} = 36.83$***
Income (below 1999 poverty line)	67.6	76.9	21.8	$\chi^2_{(2,261)} = 56.80$***
Parents have visited country of origin	12.9	88.5	71.3	$\chi^2_{(2,290)} = 130.48$***
Parents plan to stay in the United States permanently	82.5	69.0	94.6	$\chi^2_{(2,305)} = 20.12$***

Note: * $p < .05$, ** $p < .01$, *** $p < .001$, ns, not significant.
[a] Cambodians significantly different from other groups.
[b] Dominicans significantly different from other groups.
[c] Portuguese significantly different from other groups.
[d] Cambodians and Dominicans significantly different from one another.
[e] Portuguese and Dominicans significantly different from one another.
[f] Cambodians and Portuguese significantly different from one another.
[g] All three groups significantly different.

TABLE 5 Family Cultural Practices

	Cambodian $n = 127$ M (SD)	Dominican $n = 101$ M (SD)	Portuguese $n = 99$ M (SD)	Statistical Test
Comfort with English language (0 = Doesn't speak English, 3 = Very comfortable)	1.12 (.90)	1.40 (.92)	2.25[c] (1.0)	$F(2, 323) = 41.2$***
Degree of English spoken to child (1 = no English, 3 = English and other language, 5 = English only)	2.06 (.79)	2.09 (.75)	2.84[c] (1.08)	$F(2, 306) = 25.1$***
Frequency of parental cultural routines	2.24 (1.07)	3.24 (1.32)[b]	2.13 (1.53)	$F(2, 325) = 21.25$***
Frequency of child cultural routines	1.98 (1.01) %	2.09 (1.23) %	1.39[c] (1.11) %	$F(2, 325) = 12.06$***
Parent encourages child to feel good about ethnicity	75.6	72.7	56.1	$\chi^2(2, 320) = 10.7$**
Parent thinks child has been treated badly because of ethnicity	2.4	8.3	7.1	ns

Note: * $p < .05$, ** $p < .01$, *** $p < .001$.
[a] Cambodians significantly different from both the Portuguese and Dominican families.
[b] Dominicans significantly different from both the Portuguese and Cambodian families.
[c] Portuguese significantly different from both the Dominican and Cambodian families.
[d] Dominicans significantly different from the Cambodian families.
[e] Portuguese significantly different from only the Dominican families.
[f] All three groups significantly different from one another.

TABLE 6 Educational Values and Practices

	Cambodian $n = 127$ M (SD)	Dominican $n = 101$ M (SD)	Portuguese $n = 99$ M (SD)	Statistical Test
Belief in parental involvement (0 = Not at all, 7 = Very much)	2.48^a (1.57)	6.18 (1.30)	6.11 (1.42)	$F(2,322) = 244.89^{***}$
Number of times met with teacher this year	2.11 (1.61)	3.49^b (4.42)	2.19 (1.21)	$F(2,219) = 5.78^{**}$
Rules for the child[†] (0–2)	$.26^g$ $(.36)$	$.85^g$ $(.28)$	$.62^g$ $(.39)$	$F(2,323) = 82.32^{***}$
	%	%	%	
Someone checks child's homework	58.4	92.5	95.9	$\chi^2(2,316) = 61.16^{***}$
Parents have met with child's teacher	68.3	81.8	78.4	$\chi^2(2,322) = 6.13^*$
Child has a place to do homework	42.7	74.7	91.8	$\chi^2(2,321) = 63.58^{***}$
Child has access to a computer	78.4	96.8	88.7	$\chi^2(2,315) = 16.25^{***}$
Family owns a computer	29.1	43.4	58.2	$\chi^2(2,324) = 19.18^{***}$
Family has a place in their home where books are kept	52.4	84.4	87.2	$\chi^2(2,308) = 31.66^{***}$

Note: $^* p < .05, ^{**} p < .01, ^{***} p < .001$.
[a] Cambodians significantly different from other groups.
[b] Dominicans significantly different from other groups.
[g] All three groups significantly different.
[†] Sum if two items: parents have rules for when the child has to be home, who the child can spend time with. Correlation $R = .473$.

TABLE 7 Family Literacy Activities

	Cambodian $n = 127$ M (SD)		Dominican $n = 101$ M (SD)		Portuguese $n = 99$ M (SD)		Statistical Test
How often parent reads for pleasure (0 = never, 3 = few times a month, 5 = every day)	2.88[a] (1.85)		3.62 (1.38)		3.18 (1.70)		$F(2,295) = 23.2^{***}$
How often child reads for pleasure (0 = never, 3 = few times a month, 5 = every day)	4.14 (1.05)		3.74[e] (1.79)		4.28[e] (1.01)		$F(2,313) = 4.41^{*}$
Children's books in the home (1 = 0 books, 2 = <10, 3 = 10–50, 4 = >50)	1.82 (.73)		2.73 (.64)		3.11 (.73)		$F(2,305) = 97.3^{***}$
Other books in the home (1 = 0 books, 2 = <10, 3 = 10–50, 4 = >50)	1.78[a] (.76)		2.77 (.87)		2.56 (1.0)		$F(2,291) = 37.5^{***}$
	n	%	n	%	n	%	
Child reads to parent	121	31.4	94	88.3	97	78.4	$\chi^2(2,312) = 87.57^{***}$
Parent reads to the child presently	107	22.4	61	70.5	72	37.5	$\chi^2(2,240) = 37.79^{***}$
Parent read to the child in the past	105	22.9	51	70.6	86	62.8	$\chi^2(2,242) = 44.56^{***}$

Note: * $p < .05$, ** $p < .01$, *** $p < .001$.
[a] Cambodians significantly different from both the Portuguese and Dominican families.
[e] Portuguese significantly different from only the Dominican families.

TABLE 8 Labels[†]

	Cambodian n = 82 M (SD)		Dominican n = 82 M (SD)		Portuguese n = 81 M (SD)	
	Younger	Older	Younger	Older	Younger	Older
Nationality	2.82 (.55)	2.97 (.15)	2.76 (.58)*	3.40 (1.87)	2.86 (.72)***	3.47 (.89)
Hyphenated	3.25 (2.45)***	5.50 (2.70)	3.56 (2.47)***	6.44 (2.70)	2.11 (1.23)***	3.31 (1.64)
Panethnic	.88 (.96)***	3.47 (.99)	1.43 (1.25)***	4.47 (1.44)	.10 (.23)*	.31 (.63)
American	.77 (.86)	1.00 (.91)	1.38 (1.01)	1.63 (1.00)	2.05 (1.06)	2.47 (1.01)
Racial	.95 (1.10)*	.43 (.74)	1.41 (1.23)	1.37 (1.58)	2.75 (.80)***	3.06 (.80)
Ethno-linguistic	3.93 (1.30)	3.71 (.80)	4.72 (1.21)	4.26 (1.07)	2.41 (.84)	2.35 (1.02)

Note: * $p < .05$, ** $p < .01$, *** $p < .001$.
[†] Labels included Nationality (e.g., Cambodian, Portuguese, Dominican, etc.), Hyphenated (e.g., Dominican-American, etc.), Panethnic (e.g., Southeast Asian, Latino, etc.), American, Racial (e.g., Hispanic, Asian, black, white), and Ethno-linguistic (e.g., Spanish, English, Khmer).

TABLE 9 Cultural Identification

	Cambodian n = 115		Dominican n = 101		Portuguese n = 107		Statistical Test
	M	(SD)	M	(SD)	M	(SD)	
Ethnic pride (−2 low to 2 high)	1.47[f]	(.63)	1.57	(.75)	1.72[f]	(.56)	$F_{(2,317)} = 4.0$*
Centrality (0 low to 8 high)	4.50	(2.29)	4.33	(2.1)	4.03	(2.14)	ns
Salience (0–1)	.47	(.34)	.37	(.33)	.22[c]	(.29)	$F_{(2,303)} = 15.75$***
Stability (0–1)	.80	(.17)	.76[e]	(.12)	.81[e]	(.11)	$F_{(2,305)} = 4.07$*
Ethnic label satisfaction	%		%		%		
Selects ethnic minority label as happiest label	40.0		35.8		24.2		$\chi^2_{(2,318)} = 7.77$*
Would get rid of a label	44.3		34.7		27.0		$\chi^2_{(2,304)} = 6.8$*
Skin color satisfaction	%		%		%		
Would like to change skin color	28.6		30.9		13.7		$\chi^2_{(2,311)} = 9.588$**

Note: $p < .05$, ** $p < .01$, *** $p < .001$.
[a] Cambodians significantly different from other groups.
[b] Dominicans significantly different from other groups.
[c] Portuguese significantly different from other groups.
[d] Cambodians and Dominicans significantly different from one another.
[e] Portuguese and Dominicans significantly different from one another.
[f] Cambodians and Portuguese significantly different from one another.
[g] All three groups significantly different.

TABLE 10 In- and Out-Group Preferences

Year 2	Cambodian $n = 115$	Dominican $n = 99$	Portuguese $n = 106$	Test Statistic
Comfort at home (Scale 1–7)	M (SD)	M (SD)	M (SD)	
In-group	5.35 (1.9)[a]	6.16 (1.4)	5.81 (1.5)	$F_{(2,319)} = 6.720$**
Out-group	3.42 (1.4)	4.74 (1.4)[b]	4.34 (2.0)	$F_{(2,319)} = 19.083$***
Comfort at school (Scale 1–5)	M (SD)	M (SD)	M (SD)	
In-group	4.05 (.95)[a]	4.48 (.69)	4.27 (.85)	$F_{(2,318)} = 6.961$**
Out-group	3.18 (1.14)[a]	3.61 (1.21)	3.5 (1.16)	$F_{(2,319)} = 4.088$*

Year 3	Cambodian $n = 103$	Dominican $n = 98$	Portuguese $n = 90$	Test Statistic
Comfort at home (Scale 1–7)	M (SD)	M (SD)	M (SD)	
In-group	5.33 (1.83)[d]	6.05 (1.44)[d]	5.83 (1.30)	$F_{(2,290)} = 5.839$**
Out-group	3.41 (1.34)[a]	4.49 (1.57)	4.57 (1.98)	$F_{(2,291)} = 15.694$***
Comfort at school (Scale 1–5)	M (SD)	M (SD)	M (SD)	
In-group	4.24 (.77)	4.44 (.76)	4.17 (.94)	Ns
Out-group	3.52 (.98)[c]	3.94 (1.06)	4.29 (.94)	$F_{(2,291)} = 14.485$***

Note: * $p < .05$, ** $p < .01$, *** $p < .001$, ns not significant.
[a] Cambodians significantly different from other groups.
[b] Dominicans significantly different from other groups.
[c] Portuguese significantly different from other groups.
[d] Cambodians and Dominicans significantly different from one another.
[e] Portuguese and Dominicans significantly different from one another.
[f] Cambodians and Portuguese significantly different from one another.
[g] All three groups significantly different.

TABLE 11 Detection of Discrimination

Percent detecting any discrimination	Cambodian		Dominican		Portuguese		Statistical Test
	n	%	n	%	n	%	
Year 2	$n = 106$	32.1	$n = 89$	56.2	$n = 95$	41.0	$\chi^2(2,290) = 13.66$**
Year 3	$n = 95$	32.4	$n = 88$	33.1	$n = 87$	45.1	ns
Rate of detection	n	$M\,(SD)$	n	$M\,(SD)$	n	$M\,(SD)$	
Year 2	$n = 106$	.122[a] (.21)	$n = 89$	.292 (.32)	$n = 95$	.227 (.26)	$F(2,289) = 10.61$***
Year 3	$n = 95$	.186[f] (.22)	$n = 88$	.229 (.26)	$n = 87$	.308[f] (.29)	$F(2,269) = 5.1$**

Note: * $p < .05$, ** $p < .01$, *** $p < .001$.
[a] Cambodians significantly different from other groups.
[f] Cambodians and Portuguese significantly different from one another.

TABLE 12 Children's Attitudes and Practices

	Cambodian			Dominican			Portuguese			Statistical Test
	n	M	(SD)	n	M	(SD)	n	M	(SD)	
Perceptions of teachers (1 low–5 high)	142	3.79^g	(.69)	140	3.95^g	(.69)	122	4.32^g	(.55)	$F_{(2,403)} = 22.531$***
School engagement (1 low–5 high)	142	4.33^a	(.46)	140	4.49	(.37)	122	4.48	(.33)	$F_{(2,403)} = 14.37$***
School values (1 low–5 high)	142	4.54	(.51)	140	4.63	(.44)	122	4.66	(.49)	ns
Wants to go to college (1 low–7 high)	114	6.04	(1.2)	99	6.37	(1.0)	105	6.09	(1.0)	ns
Expects to go to college (1 low–5 high)	115	4.30^d	(.78)	99	4.53^d	(.68)	105	4.46	(.57)	$F_{(2,318)} = 3.15$*
Absences (3 year average)	119	7.22	(9.21)	123	11.03^b	(7.56)	107	7.44	(8.03)	$F_{(2,348)} = 7.96$***
Child-reported time on homework (min/day)	140	22.13^d	(26.96)	137	33.18^d	(33.18)	121	26.39	(24.87)	$F_{(2,397)} = 4.33$*
Child-reported time spent watching TV (hours/day)	34	2.49	(1.7)	42	2.90	(1.93)	25	2.0	(1.37)	ns

Note: * $p < .05$, ** $p < .01$, *** $p < .001$.
[a] Cambodians significantly different from other groups.
[b] Dominicans significantly different from other groups.
[c] Portuguese significantly different from other groups.
[d] Cambodians and Dominicans significantly different from one another.
[e] Portuguese and Dominicans significantly different from one another.
[f] Cambodians and Portuguese significantly different from one another.
[g] All three groups significantly different.

TABLE 13   Experiences With School-Related Stress (School Situation Survey)

School Stress (1 low–5 high)	Cambodian n = 103 M (SD)	Dominican n = 99 M (SD)	Portuguese n = 90 M (SD)	Statistical Test
Teacher-interaction stress	1.89 (.76)	1.89 (.88)	1.70 (.71)	ns
Academic stress	2.86 (1.87)	2.75 (1.10)	2.94 (0.95)	ns
Academic self-concept stress	2.07 (.67)	2.14 (.77)	2.08 (.81)	ns
Emotional manifestation of stress*	2.05 (.70)^f	1.93 (.83)	1.76 (.68)^f	$F(2,291) = 3.68$*
Behavioral manifestation of stress	1.56 (.66)	1.62 (.62)	1.50 (.69)	ns
Physical manifestation of stress	2.14 (.97)	2.26 (.99)	2.02 (1.03)	ns

Note: * $p < .05$.
^{f} Cambodians and Portuguese significantly different from one another.

TABLE 14 Grades and Teacher Reports

	Cambodian			Dominican			Portuguese			Statistical Test
	n	M	(SD)	n	M	(SD)	n	M	(SD)	
GPA (3 year average) ($F = 1$, $A = 8$)	133	7.9	(1.7)	131	7.47	(1.8)	112	7.43	(2.0)	ns
Average teacher rating (1 low–5 high)	86	3.73[a]	(.81)	83	3.40	(.78)	84	3.40	(.71)	$F(2,252) = 5.2^{**}$
Percent on academic pathway		$n = 129$			$n = 126$			$n = 111$			ns
Excelling		20.9			10.3			9.9			
Positive		34.9			33.3			34.2			
Mixed		23.0			23.0			24.3			
Negative		14.0			23.8			25.2			
Abysmal		6.2			9.5			6.3			

Note: ** $p < .01$.
[a] Cambodian children significantly different from both the Portuguese and Dominican children.

203

TABLE 15 Comparing Excelling versus Negative and Abysmal Student
Pathways (Within-Group Analyses)

	Excelling M (SD)	Abysmal M (SD)	
Cambodians			
English language preference	4.92 (0.28)	4.53 (0.74)	$F(1,37) = 5.25^*$
Teacher-interaction stress	1.46 (0.62)	2.07 (0.97)	$F(1,31) = 4.84^*$
Behavioral manifestation of stress	1.28 (0.39)	1.81 (0.77)	$F(1,31) = 6.70^{**}$
School engagement	4.48 (0.36)	4.08 (0.64)	$F(1,51) = 7.93^{**}$
School values	4.68 (0.48)	4.22 (0.69)	$F(1,51) = 8.04^{**}$
Perceptions of teachers	4.09 (0.66)	3.60 (0.48)	$F(1,51) = 7.22^{**}$
Absences	4.3 (3.54)	14.6 (17.0)	$F(1,49) = 9.19^{**}$
Ethnic identity: pride	1.56 (0.58)	1.07 (0.82)	$F(1,37) = 4.85^*$
Comfort outside group (home)	3.97 (1.10)	2.8 (1.09)	$F(1,31) = 8.73^{**}$
Mother's year of immigration	1985 (3.45)	1982 (3.03)	$F(1,37) = 4.62^*$
Dominicans			
Teacher interaction stress	1.49 (.043)	2.29 (1.02)	$F(1,40) = 4.14^*$
Academic self-concept stress	1.75 (0.52)	2.32 (0.63)	$F(1,40) = 4.91^*$
Behavioral manifestation of stress	1.26 (0.38)	1.78 (0.63)	$F(1,40) = 4.15^*$
Ethnic identity: centrality	3.5 (1.84)	5.37 (1.94)	$F(1,40) = 7.24^{**}$
Absences	8.23 (5.26)	13.75 (8.89)	$F(1,52) = 4.47^*$
Mother's year of immigration	1972 (21.9)	1983 (7.3)	$F(1,34) = 5.76^*$
Proportion of working parents	1.0 (.46)	0.59 (0.47)	$F(1,36) = 4.91^*$
Portuguese			
Teacher interaction stress	1.36 (0.30)	1.95 (0.69)	$F(1,33) = 6.20^*$
Academic self-concept stress	2.59 (0.89)	3.27 (0.93)	$F(1,33) = 8.45^{**}$
Physical manifestation of stress	1.41 (0.57)	2.26 (1.15)	$F(1,33) = 4.44^*$
Absences	3.63 (4.88)	10.42 (10.03)	$F(1,43) = 4.61^*$

Note: $^* p < .05$, $^{**} p < .01$.

TABLE 16   Children's Language Use/Preference

	Cambodian N = 114		Dominican N = 106		Portuguese N = 102		Statistical Test
	M	(SD)	M	(SD)	M	(SD)	
English language preference (0 low–5 high)	4.68	(.75)	4.70	(.71)	4.59	(.80)	ns
Bilingual preference (0 low–1 high)	.32	(.73)	.23	(.54)	.34	(.78)	ns

	Cambodian n = 115	Dominican n = 108	Portuguese n = 107	Statistical Test
Percent who say they speak another language	99.1	98.1	94.4	ns

Note: * $p < .05$, ** $p < .01$, *** $p < .001$.

Appendix A ∷

Selected Measures

CI = Children's Interview
PI = Parent's Interview
TQ = Teacher Questionnaire
IW = Rhode Island Information Works

	Alpha	Anchors and Range	Items and Information
I. School Context			
Teacher Characteristics			
Teacher race/ethnicity (TQ)			What is your race/ethnicity?
Teacher pedagogy (TQ)	Overall α = .91 Cambodian α = .92 Dominican α = .92 Portuguese α = .90	1 (strongly disagree) to 9 (strongly agree)	Children do better in school if I make learning fun. Children do better in school if I relate materials to their culture or cultural backgrounds. Children do better in school if I make materials appear relevant to real life. Children do better in school if they are divided into groups according to their abilities. Children do better in school if their families are involved in their education. Children do better in school if they come to school well rested. Children do better in school if they are well-groomed. Children do better in school if they come from intact families. Children do better in school if they come from families of higher socioeconomic status. Children do better in school if they come from families where English is regularly spoken. Children do better in school if their teachers come from the same cultural background. Children do better in school if they come from a hardworking family.

continued

Continued

	Alpha	Anchors and Range	Items and Information
			Children do better in school if their parents are educated.
			Children do better in school if their parents read to them.
			Children do better in school if their parents help them with their homework.
Teacher grievances (IW)			This information was collected by the Rhode Island Department of Education. Number of grievances filed by teachers in each school each school year recorded; grievances were filed for five categories: insufficient materials, too many students, physical environment, administrative decisions and other grievances. *Analysis Note:* *Rate reported in Table 3 reflects an average for teacher grievances across individual schools and across the three years of the study.*
School Characteristics			
School size (IW)			This information was collected and processed by the Department of Education in Rhode Island (RIDE) for each school in Rhode Island. *Analysis Note:* *Scores appearing in Table 3 represent the average of the reported school size for across the three years of the study.*
Class size in the school: Average (IW)			Class size recorded as the average of the figures reported by the core academic teachers on the SALT survey for each school. The survey asks, "What is the average class size in the primary content classes that you teach at this school?" "Core" academics include: math, science, language arts, and social studies—areas in which the "subjects spend more than 50 percent of their learning time." (Information Works, 1999)

	Analysis Note: *Scores appearing in Table 3 represent the average of the reported class size, averaged across schools and across the three years of the study.*
Student attendance in the school (IW)	This information was collected and processed by the Department of Education in Rhode Island (RIDE) for each school in Rhode Island. This is the average percentage of time that students are present within the 180 instructional days per year. *Analysis Note:* *Rate reported in Table 3 reflects the average attendance rate, averaged across schools and across the three years of the study.*
Total number of suspensions in the school (IW)	This information was collected and processed by the Department of Education in Rhode Island (RIDE) for each school in Rhode Island. This is the total number of suspensions per school. Reasons for suspensions include assault, fighting, weapons, sale of controlled substance, possession of controlled substance with intent to sell, being under the influence of a controlled substance, disorderly conduct, threat/intimidation, tobacco possession or use, vandalism, larceny/theft, other. *Analysis Note:* *Rate reported in Table 3 reflects the average of the number of suspensions, averaged across schools and across the three years of the study.*

continued

Continued

	Alpha	Anchors and Range	Items and Information
Percent of students in ESL (IW)			This information was collected and processed by the Department of Education in Rhode Island (RIDE) for each school in Rhode Island. Percent of students who received content area instruction solely in English, while learning English as a second language. *Analysis Note:* *Rate reported in Table 3 reflects the average of percent of students in ESL, averaged across schools and across the three years of the study.*
Percent of students who are black (IW)			This information was collected and processed by the Department of Education in Rhode Island (RIDE) for each school in Rhode Island. Percent of students in school having origins in any of the African-American racial groups, not including people of Hispanic origins. *Analysis Note:* *Rate reported in Table 3 reflects the average percent of students who are black, averaged across schools and across the three years of the study.*
Percent of students in school who are white (IW)			This information was collected and processed by the Department of Education in Rhode Island (RIDE) for each school in Rhode Island. Percent of students having origins in any of the original peoples of Europe, North Africa, the Middle East or the Indian Sub-Continent. Add who collected it. *Analysis Note:* *Rate reported in Table 3 reflects the average percent of students who are white, averaged across schools and across the three years of the study.*

Percent of students in school who are Hispanic (IW)

This information was collected and processed by the Department of Education in Rhode Island (RIDE) for each school in Rhode Island. Percent of students having Mexican, Puerto Rican, Cuban, Central or South American or other Spanish culture or origin, regardless of race.

Analysis Note:
Race reported in Table 3 reflects the average percent of students who are Hispanic, averaged across schools and across the three years of the study.

Percent of students in school who are Asian (IW)

This information was collected and processed by the Department of Education in Rhode Island (RIDE) for each school in Rhode Island. Percent of students having origins in any of the original peoples of the Far East, Southeast Asia or the Pacific Islands, e.g., China, Japan, Korea, the Philippine Islands and Samoa.

Analysis Note:
Rate reported in Table 3 reflects the average percent of students who are Asian, averaged across schools and across the three years of the study.

Percent of students who are eligible for free/reduced price meals (IW)

This information was collected and processed by the Department of Education in Rhode Island (RIDE) for each school in Rhode Island. Students whose family incomes fell below certain income (poverty or near poverty) guidelines were eligible for a free/reduced price lunch. This reflects the percent of students eligible for free/reduced price lunch in October of each school year tested.

continued

Continued

	Alpha	Anchors and Range	Items and Information
			Analysis Note:
			Rate reported in Table 3 reflects the average percent of students who are eligible for free/reduced price meals, averaged across schools and across the three years of the study.
Percent of students severely below proficiency in math (IW)			This is the percentage of students in school who placed severely below proficiency on the New Standards Reference Examination's (NSRE).
			Analysis Note:
			Rate reported in Table 3 reflects the average percent of students placing severely below proficiency in math, averaged across schools and across the three years of the study.
Percent of students who are below proficiency in math (IW)			This is the percentage of students in school who placed below proficiency for the math component of the New Standards Reference Examination (NSRE).
			Analysis Note:
			Rate reported in Table 3 reflects the average percent of students placing below proficiency in math, averaged across schools and across the three years of the study.
Percent of students who are severely below proficiency in writing (IW)			Percent of students in school who scored severely below proficiency on the Rhode Island Writing Assessment. This level was defined as students who "are not able to demonstrate skills in applying concepts and processes. Students have difficulty communicating ideas." (Information Works, 1999)

Analysis Note:

Rate reported in Table 3 reflects the average of the percent of students scoring severely below proficiency in writing, averaged across schools and across the three years of the study.

Percent of students below proficiency in writing (IW)

Percent of students that placed below proficiency in writing on the Rhode Island Writing Assessment. At this level "students demonstrate some skills in applying concepts and processes. Students communicate some idea effectively" (Information Works, 1999).

Analysis Note:

Rate reported in Table 3 reflects the average of the percent of students placing below proficiency in writing, averaged across schools and across the three years of the study.

II. Family Context

Household Characteristics and Demographics

Household size (PI)

Please name the people living with (child) starting with yourself.

Analysis Note:

Figure in Table 4 reflects the total number of people residing in household as reported by the parent.

continued

Continued

	Alpha	Anchors and Range	Items and Information
			For each person specified following the question above, the following questions were asked:
Education (PI)			How many years of schooling have (has) you/s/he had?
Percent of families with two working parents (PI)			Are you working now? Is he/she [spouse] working now? *Analysis Note:* *Percentage reported in Table 4 reflects the percent of families for whom two parents were working.*
Skilled workers (PI)			If so, what is your position right now? If so, what is his/her position right now? *Analysis Note:* *Responses to the question above were grouped into "skilled labor" vs. "unskilled labor" categories. These categories were based on white-collar vs. blue-collar labor categories. Percent reported in Table 4 represents the percent of families for who one or more parent was in a "skilled labor" position.*
Mobility (PI)			How many places have you lived since (child) began school?

Family Cultural Socialization

Language

Comfort with English Language (PI)	Cambodian $\alpha = .93$ Dominican $\alpha = .90$ Portuguese $\alpha = .95$	0 (little to no comfort with the English language) to 3 (high comfort with the English language)	Do you communicate in English with neighbors who were born in the United States? Do you talk to people at work in English? Do you talk to strangers on the phone in English? Do you speak English with people at your child's school? *For all questions, if yes:* How comfortable are you doing this? (1 = not Comfortable, 2 = comfortable, 3 = very Comfortable) *Analysis Note:* *Scores reported in Table 5 are averaged across the four questions to get an overall Comfort with the English Language Score. Answering that they did not speak English, was given a score of 0.*
Degree of English Spoken to Child (PI)		1 (speaks only non-English) to 5 (speaks only English)	What languages do you speak to (child)? (1 = only non-English, 2 = more non-English than English, 3 = both equally, 4 = more English than non-Eng., 5 = all English)

Cultural Practices

Frequency of Parent Cultural Practices (PI)	Overall $\alpha = .69$		How many times a week do you eat [ethnicity] food? How many times a week do you watch [ethnicity] TV/Videos?

continued

Continued

	Alpha	Anchors and Range	Items and Information
	Cambodian $\alpha = .66$ Dominican $\alpha = .61$ Portuguese $\alpha = .74$		How many times a week do you read [ethnicity] printed material (e.g. newspaper)? How many times a week do you listen to [ethnicity] music? How many times a week do you go to church/temple? How many times a week do you sing/play [ethnicity] songs/games? *Analysis Note:* *Figure reported in Table 5 is the sum of yeses (yes = 1, no = 0) for the questions above.*
Frequency of Child Cultural Practices (PI)	Overall $\alpha = .61$ Cambodian $\alpha = .53$ Dominican $\alpha = .61$ Portuguese $\alpha = .66$		How many times a week does your child eat [ethnicity] food? How many times a week does your child watch [ethnicity] TV/Videos? How many times a week does your child read [ethnicity] printed material (e.g. newspapers)? How many times a week does your child listen to [ethnicity] music? How many times a week does your child go to church/temple? How many times a week does your child sing/play [ethnicity] songs/games?[i] *Analysis Note:* *Figure reported in Table 5 is the sum of yeses (yes = 1, no = 0) for the question above.*

Parent Educational Values and Practices

Aspirations and Expectations for the Future

Parent's educational aspirations for child (PI)	What is the highest level of schooling you would like child to have? (1 = graduate from high school, 2 = go to vocational school for job training after high school, 3 = get some college, 4 = graduate from college, 5 = get a graduate or professional degree [e.g. M.A., M.D., Ph.D.])
	What could prevent your child from completing this level of schooling?

Parental Involvement

Beliefs regarding parental involvement: Education (PI)	0 (not at all involved) to 7 (very involved)
	How involved should parents be in their child's education?
Rules for the child (PI)	0 (no rules) to 2 (consistent home-based rules)
	Do you have any rules about what time your child has to be home? (1 = yes, 0 = no)
	Do you have any rules about who your child can spend time with? (1 = yes, 0 = no)
	Analysis Note:
	Figure in Table 6 represents the sum of the yes responses for the questions above.

continued

Continued

	Alpha	Anchors and Range	Items and Information
Someone checks the child's homework (PI)			Does anyone check the child's homework before child turns it in? (1 = yes, 0 = no)
Literacy Activities in the Household			
How often parent reads for pleasure (PI)		0 (never reads) to 5 (reads everyday)	Do you read for pleasure—how often? (0 = doesn't read, 1 = once a year, 2 = few times a year, 3 = few times a month, 4 = few times a week, 5 = everyday)
How often child reads for pleasure (PI)		0 (never reads) to 5 (reads everyday)	Does your child/do you read for pleasure—how often? (0 = doesn't read, 1 = once a year, 2 = few times a year, 3 = few times a month, 4 = few times a week, 5 = everyday)
Reading together (PI)			Do you currently read to your child? (yes = 1, no = 0) Did you read to you child in the past? (yes = 1, no = 0) Did you read to you child in the past? (yes = 1, no = 0)
Children's books in the home (PI)		1 (no books in home) to 4 (many in home books)	How many children's books do you have in your home? (1 = 0 books, 2 = <10, 3 = 10–50, 4 = >50)

Other books in the home (PI)	1 (no books in home) to 4 (many books in home)	How many other books do you have in your home? (1 = 0 books, 2 = < 10, 3 = 10–50, 4 => 50)
III. Child Cultural Attitudes and Identification		
Language preference (CI)	Overall $\alpha = .61$ Cambodian $\alpha = .60$ Dominican $\alpha = .56$ Portuguese $\alpha = .64$	Which language do you like to speak more? Do you like to have people speak to you in… Do you like to watch TV and movies in… Would you like to have you teachers teach in… When people read or tell you stories, what do you like more: to hear stories in… (1 = English, 2 = Other language, 3 = Both the same) *Analysis Note:* *English preference figure reported in Table 16 represents the number of times participant selected "English" when answering the preceding questions. Bilingual preference figure represents the proportion of times participants selected "Both the same".*

continued

Continued

Labels (CI)	Alpha	Anchors and Range	Items and Information
			See Appendix B for complete list.
Ethnic pride (CI)	Overall: α = .62 Cambodian α = .72 Dominican α = .54 Portuguese α = .48	1 (not at all proud) to 4 (extremely proud)	Statements are read using highest ranked ethnic descriptor and children are asked to choose the group that most resembles them and then indicate how true of them this statement is: These kids feel good about [ethnic descriptor] people **BUT** These kids do not feel good about [ethnic descriptor] people. These kids are happy that they are [ethnic descriptor] **BUT** These kids are sad that they are [ethnic descriptor]. These kids feels that [ethnic descriptor] people are important in America **BUT** These kids do not feel [ethnic descriptor] people are important in America These kids are proud to be [ethnic descriptor] **BUT** These kids are not proud to be [ethnic descriptor]. *(Participants choose a group that was most like them [those with negative feelings about their ethnic identity or those with positive feelings about their ethnic identity]; they then rated whether the statement they chose was 1 = Really true of me (negative), 2 = Sort of true of me (negative), 3 = Sort of true of me (positive), 4 = Really true of me (positive))* *Analysis Note:* *Figure reported in Table 9 reflects this score averaged across questions.*

| Centrality (CI) | Overall
$\alpha = .72$
Cambodian
$\alpha = .78$
Dominican
$\alpha = .61$
Portuguese
$\alpha = .81$ | 0 (little/no centrality) to 8 (high centrality) | Would you want the class to know your name?
Would you want the class to know your last name?
Would you want the class to know what religion you are?
Would you want the class to know what country you come from?
Would you want the class to know what country your parents come from?
Would you want the class to know what language you speak at home with your parents? Would you want the class to know what kind of food you eat at home?
Would you want the class to know the holidays that you celebrate at home?

Analysis Note:
Figure reported in Table 9 is the sum of yeses for the questions listed above. |
| Salience (CI) | | 1 (not important) 2 (important), 3 (very important) | You picked (##) words. "Which of these words is the most important to who you are?" Tell me which word would be #1, #2, etc. No ties allowed

Analysis Note:
Salience values reported in Table 9 represent the proportion of time (out of the three years of the study) that the child picked an ethnic descriptor as the label that is "most important to who you are." Other possible labels included those pertaining to gender, family role, etc. (see Appendix B). |

continued

Continued

	Alpha	Anchors and Range	Items and Information
Stability (CI)		0 (not stable) to 1 (very stable)	*Analysis Note:* *Stability was measured by looking at how many times a child picked a ethnic descriptor as being most important (see items listed for Salience measure) over the three years. Figure in Table 9 is the proportion of time over the three years that they chose ethnic descriptor as most important.*
Happiest label (PI)			Of all these words about you which one makes you the happiest?
Ethnic label satisfaction (CI)			Of all these words about you, are there any that you wish you could get rid of? *If yes,* • Which ones would you get rid of? • Why would you get rid of that word?
Skin-color satisfaction (CI)			If you could have another skin color, would you want it?
In/Out group comfort Home (CI)	In-Group Cambodian $\alpha = .73$ Dominican $\alpha = .75$ Portuguese $\alpha = .89$	1 (not at all comfortable) to 7 (very much comfortable)	How comfortable would you feel if one of these White kids came over to your house to play? How comfortable would you feel if one of these Black kids came over to your house to play? How comfortable would you feel if one of these Asian kids came over to your house to play? How comfortable would you feel if one of these Spanish or Latino kids came over to your house to play?

	Out-Group Cambodian: $\alpha = .74$ Dominican: $\alpha = .77$ Portuguese: $\alpha = .88$	How much would you want to be friends with White kids? How much would you want to be friends with Black kids? How much would you want to be friends with Asian kids, like Cambodian or Chinese kids? How much would you want to be friends with Spanish or Latino kids? *(For all questions participants gave their response by pointing to a number on a scale from 1, under which was written "not at all, to 7, under which was written "very much").*
In Group Comfort School (CI)	Overall $\alpha = .62$ Cambodian $\alpha = .62$ Dominican $\alpha = .47$ Portuguese $\alpha = .65$	1 (not at all comfortable) to 5 (very much comfortable) situation	When you are on the playground with [descriptor] kids, which face shows how you would feel? When you are in a classroom with a teacher who is [descriptor] which face shows how you would feel? When you are with your family doing [descriptor] things, which face shows how you would feel? When you are in the lunchroom with kids who are [descriptor], which face shows how you would feel? *Children were asked to point to a number along a number scale used to depict saddest to happiest (signified by smiley/frowny faces on either end—see below)* :(1 2 3 4 5 :)

continued

Continued

	Alpha	Anchors and Range	Items and Information
Out-Group comfort School (CI)	Overall $\alpha = .73$ Cambodian $\alpha = .68$ Dominican $\alpha = .75$ Portuguese $\alpha = .74$	1 (not at all comfortable) to 5 (very much comfortable)	When you are on the playground with kids who are not [descriptor] which face shows how you would feel? In a classroom with a teacher who is not [descriptor], which face shows how you would feel? When you are in the lunchroom with a bunch of kids who are not [descriptor], which face shows how you would feel? *Children were asked to point to a number along a number scale used to depict saddest to happiest (signfied by smiley/"frowny" faces on either end)* : (1 2 3 4 5 :)
Perceptions of discrimination (CI)			Let's pretend you are Bopha/Sam nang, Ramona/Raymon, Joao/Manuela and I am Pat. We are both [ethnic descriptor] girls/boys. One day I come up to you and say, "Hi Bopha/Sam nang, Ramona/Raymon, Joao/Manuela. I was talking to my friends yesterday, and we decided that we don't want to play with you anymore because you go to a school where most of the kids are White (but not Portuguese), and you like your friends who are White (but not Portuguese) better than you like us." • Tell me what you would do about this problem? • Why did I (Pat) say this to you?

2. Now, here is another story. This time, let's pretend that you are Chamnap/Sam nang, Rosa/Luis, Tiago/Clarissa and you are the only [ethnic descriptor] person in your classroom. When you raise your hand to answer a question in class, the teacher almost never calls on you even though you almost always know the answer.

- Tell me what you would do about this problem?
- Why does the teacher always pick someone else?

3. Let's pretend that you are Sophy/Lom orng, Pablo/Vanessa, Raphael/Theresa. You are a [ethnic descriptor] boy/girl. You just started a new school this year where most of the kids are not [ethnic descriptor], and you haven't made friends yet. One day you are on the playground, and someone who is not [ethnic descriptor] comes up to you and says,

Portuguese: Euw... Portuguese, you are really ugly
Asians: Your eyes are really funny and you're really ugly.
Latino: You speak funny and you're really stupid.
Black: You are really dark and really ugly.

- Tell me what you would do about this problem?
- Why does this kids say that you were ugly or stupid?

4. Let's now pretend that you are Sothea/Sophal, Carmen/Tito, Jose/Isabel. You are a [ethnic descriptor] girl/boy. All the students in your school are [ethnic descriptor]. Your classmates tease you because they say that you act proper and are trying to act like you are not [ethnic descriptor].

continued

Continued

	Alpha	Anchors and Range	Items and Information

			• Tell me what you would do about this problem.
			• Why do your classmates say you are trying to act like you are not [ethnic descriptor]?
			5. Finally, let's pretend that you are Phally/Sopheap, Hector/Marilyn, Eduardo/Lourdes, and you were born in Rhode Island. Your new best friend just moved here from (ethnic descriptor's country of ancestry: Dominican Republic, Cambodia, or Portugal). Other kids say that you shouldn't hang out with him/her.
			• Tell me what you would do about this problem.
			• Why don't your friends want you to hang out with the new kid?
			(0 = does not perceive discrimination, 1 = does perceive discrimination)
			Analysis Notes:
			If participants detected discrimination in any of the four scenarios they were included in "Percent detecting any discrimination" (see Table 11).
			Rate of detection presented in Table 11 represents the proportion of scenarios for which the participant detected discrimination.

V. Child Academic Attitudes and Expectations

| Perceptions of teachers (CI) | Overall: $\alpha = .71$ Cambodian: $\alpha = .68$ | 1 (low perception of teacher support) to 5 (high perception of teacher support) | How many of your teachers: • Believe you can do well in school? • Are willing to help you if you need extra help on school work? • Would be willing to help you with a personal problem if you had one? |

226

	Dominican: α = .71 Portuguese: α = .67	• Care if you get bad grades? • Care whether you do your school work? (1 = none, 2 = a few, 3 = half, 4 = most, 5 = all) *Analysis Note:* *Responses were averaged across the five questions to get a composite score.*
Engagement (CI)	Overall: α = .59 Cambodian: α = .55 Dominican: α = .59 Portuguese: α = .60	1 (low engagement) to 5 (high engagement) How important is it to you that you get good grades? How important is it to you that you stay out of trouble at school? How important is it to you that your teachers like you? How important is it to you that you do your homework? How important is it to you that you go to school every day? How important is it to you that you graduate from high school? How important is it to you that you have friends at school? How important is it to you that you try hard in school? (1 = not important at all, 2 = not as important, 3 = in between, 4 = pretty important, 5 = very important) *Analysis Note:* *Engagement score reported in Table 12 is the average of the responses given* *to the questions above.*

	Alpha	Anchors and Range	Items and Information
School values (CI)	Overall $\alpha = .66$ Cambodian $\alpha = .65$ Dominican $\alpha = .61$ Portuguese $\alpha = .71$	1 (low endorsement of school values) to 5 (high endorsement of school values)	How often do you feel it is okay to skip school for a day? How often do you think it is okay to cheat on tests? How often do you feel it is okay to talk back to teachers? How often do you feel it is okay to disobey school rules? How often do you feel it is okay to copy someone's homework? (1 = never, 2 = hardly ever, 3 = sometimes, 4 = often, 5 = always) *Analysis Note:* *Figure reported in Table 12 is the average of the responses given to the questions above (reverse coded).*
Aspirations: Wants to go to college (CI)	Overall $\alpha = .77$ Cambodian $\alpha = .77$ Dominican $\alpha = .79$ Portuguese $\alpha = .77$	1 (low aspirations) to 7 (high aspirations)	How much do you want to go to college? (1 = not at all to 7 = very much).
Expects to go to college (CI)		1 (low expectations) to 7 (high expectations)	How much do you expect to go to college? (1 = not at all to 7 = very much).

Daily Practices		
Absences (ST)		Obtained from school transcripts—averaged over 3 years of study.
Homework (PI)		How many minutes does your child usually work on homework a day?
School Stress: School Situation Survey (CI)		
Academic self-concept Stress (CI)	Overall $\alpha = .66$ Cambodian: $\alpha = .61$ Dominican: $\alpha = .68$ Portuguese: $\alpha = .7$	I do well in school and get good grades. I feel that I learn things easily. I do good work in school. School work is easy for me. (1 = never, 2 = rarely, 3 = sometimes, 4 = often, 5 = always) *Analysis Note:* *Responses were reverse coded, then averaged across the questions to get a composite score.*
Teacher interaction stress (CI)	Overall $\alpha = .65$ Cambodian $\alpha = .60$ Dominican $\alpha = .75$ Portuguese $\alpha = .57$	I feel that some of my teachers don't like me very well. Some of my teachers call on me when they know I am not prepared just to embarrass me. I feel that some of my teachers don't really care about what I think or how I feel. I feel that my teachers treat me fairly. Some of my teachers yell at me for no reason. (1 = never, 2 = rarely, 3 = sometimes, 4 = often, 5 = always) *Analysis Note:* *Response to question 4 was reverse coded. Responses were averaged across the questions to get a composite score.*

continued

	Alpha	Anchors and Range	Items and Information
Peer interaction stress (CI)	Overall $\alpha = .64$ Cambodian $\alpha = .56$ Dominican $\alpha = .78$ Portuguese $\alpha = .43$		I enjoy doing things with my classmates at school Other students make fun of me at school. I get along well with my classmates. I enjoy talking to my classmates at school. I have many friends at school. ($1 = never$, $2 = rarely$, $3 = sometimes$, $4 = often$, $5 = always$) *Analysis Note:* *Response to questions 1 and 3 through 5 were reverse coded. Responses were averaged across the questions to get a composite score.*
Academic stress (CI)	Overall $\alpha = .60$ Cambodian $\alpha = .67$ Dominican $\alpha = .60$ Portuguese $\alpha = .48$		I worry about not doing well in school. I am afraid of getting poor grades. I worry about taking tests at school. ($1 = never$, $2 = rarely$, $3 = sometimes$, $4 = often$, $5 = always$) *Analysis Note:* *Responses were averaged across the questions to get a composite score.*

Emotional manifestation of stress (CI)	Overall $\alpha = .74$	I feel upset at school.
	Cambodian $\alpha = .69$	I feel mixed up at school.
	Dominican $\alpha = .80$	I feel frustrated at school.
	Portuguese $\alpha = .70$	I feel like crying at school.
		I feel nervous at school.
		I feel angry at school.
		($1 = never$, $2 = rarely$, $3 = sometimes$, $4 = often$, $5 = always$)
		Analysis Note:
		Responses were averaged across the questions to get a composite score.

Behavioral manifestation of stress (CI)	Overall $\alpha = .69$	I talk in class when I should be quiet.
	Cambodian $\alpha = .69$	I pick on other students at school.
	Dominican $\alpha = .62$	I yell at my classmates at school.
	Portuguese $\alpha = .76$	I talk back to my teachers.
		I try to get attention by acting silly in class.

continued

Continued

	Alpha	Anchors and Range	Items and Information
Physical manifestation of stress (CI)	Overall $\alpha = .73$ Cambodian $\alpha = .72$ Dominican $\alpha = .72$ Portuguese $\alpha = .75$		I get headaches at school. I feel sick to my stomach at school. I get stomach aches at school. (1 = never, 2 = rarely, 3 = sometimes, 4 = often, 5 = always) *Analysis Note:* *Responses were averaged across the questions to get a composite score.*
VI. Academic Outcomes			
Teacher reports: third year (TQ)			Compared to his/her classmates, how hard does [student] try to do well in school? Compared to his/her classmates, how well does [student] pay attention in class? Compared to his/her classmates, how regularly and carefully does [student] complete homework? Compared to his/her classmates, how actively does [student] participate in class? Compared to his/her classmates, how much does (student) seem to like the academic aspects of school (i.e., homework, class work, projects)?

Compared to his/her classmates, how much does [student] seem to like the other aspects of being in school (i.e. anything besides academic work)?

Compared to his/her classmates, how much does [student] seem to get along well and be comfortable with his/her classmates?

Compared to his/her classmates, how well behaved is [student] in class?

Compared to his/her classmates, how actively involved and encouraging do [student]'s parents seem in his/her education?

Relative to other Dominicans/Portuguese/Cambodians, how important does it seem to [student] that he/she is Dominican/Portuguese/Cambodian?

Compared to his/her classmates, does [student] seem on a good track to develop well socially and emotionally over the next few years?

(1 = significantly below average, 2 = below average, 3 = about average, 4 = above average, 5 = significantly above average)

Analysis Note:

Although teachers' scale was reliable, raters coded based on individual responses.

Appendix B ::
Social Identity Labels

Key
[1] Year 1 only   [3] Year 3 only
[2] Year 2 only   [4] Years 2 & 3
[3] Years 1 & 2

Roles
boy
girl
child[1]
son[4]
daughter[4]
parent
student[4]

Religion (everyone)
Jewish
Christian
Catholic
Evengelical[4]
Muslim
Buddhist
Jehovah's Witness
Protestant[1]
Pentecostal[1]
Hindu[1]
Mormon[1]
Seventh Day Adventist[1]

Ethnicity (everyone)
Racial Labels
White
Black
American-Indian[4]
Native American[1]
Multi-racial
Bi-racial
Mixed

American Label
American
Panethnic Labels
Asian
Latino
Hispanic
African
European[4]
Southeast Asian
Hyphenated Labels
Asian-American
Hispanic-American
Spanish-American
African-American
European-American[4]
Black-American
Ethno-linguistic Labels
Spanish
English
Khmer

*Asked if subject is
Cambodian or picked
Asian, South East Asian,
or Asian-American above*
Chinese
Chinese-American
Chinese-Cambodian[4]
Korean[3]
Korean-American[3]

Laotian[4]
Laotian-American[4]
Cambodian
Cambodian-American
Khmer
Khmer-American[4]
Thai
Thai-American
Vietnamese
Vietnamese-American
Hmong
Hmong-American
Laos[1]
Laos-American[1]
Japanese[1]
Japanese-American[1]
Filipino[1]
Filipino-American[1]
Indian[1]
Indian-American[1]
Pakistani[1]
Pakistani-American[1]

*Asked if subject is
Dominican or if they
picked Latino,
Latino-American,
Spanish,
Spanish-American,*

Hispanic,
Hispanic-American above
Chicano
Quisqueyano[4]
Boricua
Puerto Rican
Puerto Rican-American
Guatemalan
Guatemalan-American
Dominican
Dominican-American
Colombian
Colombian-American
Ecuadorian
Ecuadorian-American
Mexican
Mexican-American
Cuban
Cuban-American
Caribbean
Caribbean-American
Costa Rican[3]
Costa Rican-American[3]

Indio[1]
Salvadorean[1]
Salvadorean-American[1]
Haitian[3]
Haitian-American[3]
Jamaican[3]
Jamaican-American[3]
Nigerian[1]
Nigerian-American[1]
Liberian[1]
Liberian-American[1]
West Indian[1]
West Indian-American[1]
Caribbean[1]
Caribbean-American[1]
Bahamian[1]
Bahamian-American[1]
Trinidadian[1]
Trinidadian-American[1]
Guyanese[1]
Guyanese-American[1]
Barbadian[1]
Barbadian-American[1]

Asked if subject is
Portuguese or if they
chose White, European, or
European-American above
Portuguese
Portuguese-American
Azorean
Azorean-American
Cape Verdean
Cape
Verdean-American
Irish[4]
Irish-American[4]
Italian[4]
Italian-American[4]
French[4]
French-American[4]
Brazilian[4]
Brazilian-American[4]
British[2]
British-American[2]
British-American[2]

Notes ❖

1. Starting in the late nineteenth century and continuing until World War I, there were massive waves of immigration to the United States, primarily from Southern and Eastern Europe. Although there was diversity among these immigrants, they were, for the most part, European-born agriculturalists and laborers who filled the needs of a growing industrial economy and were largely concentrated in the lowest economic and social strata (Portes, 1996, pp. 96–102). Immigration resumed after the war but was shortly halted legislatively, and until this situation was reversed by the Immigration Act of 1965, the United States ceased to be "a nation of immigrants." After the Immigration Act of 1965, the waves of immigrants entering the United States were far more diverse than those that had come before, with the largest numbers coming from Latin America, the Caribbean, Europe, and East and Southeast Asia (Rumbaut & Portes, 2001). This wave of immigrants contained "increasing proportions of refugees, highly skilled professionals, undocumented laborers, and people entering on nonimmigrant visas" (Rumbaut, 1994a, pp. 591–592).

2. Portes and Rumbaut, 2001, p. xvii.

3. Portes and Rumbaut (2001) chronicle the different adaptational paths of families in Miami and San Diego. For example, they retell the story of a Haitian woman and her ailing husband who came to Miami as "boat people" and now live in the Haitian section of Miami. Despite their minimal resources, their sons are excelling in school—one has been recruited by Yale and the other plans to be a lawyer. In contrast is the story of a Cuban woman who came to the United States in the 1970s and received her green card immediately. She and her family initially settled in the suburbs of Chicago but faced such discrimination there that they moved to Miami. Now settled in Miami, they live in a comfortable house in a good part of town and are supported by a sizeable income, but despite this financial stability, their daughter lacks ambition and doesn't study hard in school.

4. According to Portes and Rumbaut (2001, p. xvii), "immigration begets ethnicity."

5. Recent research suggests that an immigrant group's incorporation into the larger society may take different forms, depending on conditions, contexts, and resources, a phenomenon known as "segmented assimilation" (Portes, 1995; Portes & Rumbaut, 2001; Portes & Zhou, 1993; Zhou, 1997b). As Rumbaut (1994a) explains, there is not one uniform path of assimilation but many; "one path may follow the relatively straight-line theory ... of assimilation into the white middle-class majority; an opposite type of adaptation may lead to downward mobility and assimilation into the inner-city underclass; yet another may combine upward mobility and heightened ethnic awareness within solidary immigrant communities" (p. 753–754).

6. Polls conducted by the *New York Times* or *CBS* in 1986 (Pear, 1986) and 1993 (Mydans, 1993) and by the Gallup organization more recently asked Americans, "In your view, should immigration be kept at its present level, increased or decreased?" In his speech to the 2004 Republican National Convention, Governor Schwarzenegger spoke to and about immigrants in America as though their experience was a universal one. Again, the public discourse talks about immigrants and immigration as a monolithic concept.

7. The developmental niche framework examines "the physical and social settings, the historically constituted customs and practices of child care and child rearing, and the psychology of the caretakers, particularly parental ethnotheories which play a directive role and are, by definition, shared with the community" (Super & Harkness, 2002, p. 271).

8. We define middle childhood as the years between 6 and 12, which is consistent with Sanders' (1985) definition and similar to Eccles' (1999) description of middle childhood as approximately ages 6 to 10.

9. See Fuligni (1998), Suárez-Orozco and Suáarez-Orozco (1995), Portes and Rumbaut (2001), Rumbaut and Portes (2001) and Rumbaut (1994a).

10. In their book on middle childhood, Huston and Ripke argue that "although the preschool years establish the base for future development, experiences in middle childhood can sustain, magnify, or reverse the advantages or disadvantages that children acquire in the preschool years. At the same time, middle childhood is a pathway to adolescence, setting trajectories that are not easily changed later" (2006, p. 2).

11. In his 1919 commentary on public education in the United States, Elwood Cubberley wrote, "the problem which has faced and still faces the United States is that of assimilating these thousands of foreigners into our national life and citizenship. We must do this or lose our national character"(1947, p. 488). In their history of U.S. school reform, Tyack and Cuban (1997) further explain, "Educational leaders have tried to transform immigrant newcomers and other 'outsiders' into individuals who matched their idealized image of what 'American' should be...[to] create model citizens through schooling"(p. 2).

12. See Stipek (2005) and Entwistle, Alexander, Pallas, and Cadigan (1987).

13. The notion of choice here refers to the "choosing" of an ethnic/racial identity by groups that because of their phenotypic racial features, language, religion, and/or other cultural practices, are labeled by the dominant culture

as minorities. The notion of choice does not imply that the child is able to pick any ethnicity, but that society ascribes various labels from which they can exercise some choice. The work by Waters (1994) exemplifies this process the best by illustrating the resistance displayed by some West Indian youth to the labels of black or African-American. Because their racial features are black, these youth are labeled as such by the society at large; yet, they themselves make a distinction between been West Indian and black. Rumbaut (1994a) also finds a range of labels that children from immigrant backgrounds pick. For example, among children whose parents were born in Latin-American countries, children would choose labels that described their national origin (Mexican), their ascribed panethnicity (Latino or Hispanic) or their hybrid background (Mexican-American). Finally, Bailey (2002) describes how Dominican youth maintain an ethno-linguistic separation between themselves and others, reflected in their usage of Spanish and their own self-identification as Dominican, Spanish, or Hispanic.

14. For example, strong ethnic pride has been related to lower drug use among adolescents (Marsiglia, Kulis, & Hecht, 2001) and higher academic achievement among African-American youth (Smith, Atkins, & Connell, 2003). In adults, a strong ethnic identity has been shown to act as a buffer against perceived racial discrimination (Mossakowski, 2003).

15. Although in this volume we focus on its applications in child and young adult samples, the term "immigrant paradox" has been used to describe puzzling health, academic, and behavioral outcomes across the age span. For example, studies have found that compared to native-born mothers, foreign-born women have lower rates of infant mortality (Markides & Coreil, 1986; Singh & Yu, 1996) and lower rates of low-birthweight babies (Acevedo-García, Soobader, & Berkman, 2005; Landale, Oropesa, Llanes, & Gorman, 1999; Scribner & Dwyer, 1989; Singh & Yu, 1996). Immigrants have a lower risk of mortality than those born in the United States and are at lower risk of death from many diseases (Singh & Siahpush, 2001).

16. Segregation is also a reflection of individual agency as exemplified by the phenomenon of "white fly," when white parents take their children out of schools as the number of minority students increase.

CHAPTER 2

1. Puerto Ricans are not officially considered immigrants (although they are considered involuntary minorities by Ogbu (1978)) as they are part of the United States as a function of an initial military occupation and annexation by the United States as a consequence of the Spanish-American War and their being considered American citizens by birth.

2. They are called voluntary because they are not considered refugees, but many immigrants migrate because they have (or perceive) no other choice because of the limited opportunities for education, employment, and escaping poverty in their country of origin. In that respect, even if they are here "voluntarily," they would stay in their country of origin if opportunities for a good life were available.

3. A transnational community can be described as a community "by which immigrants forge and sustain multi-stranded social relations that link together their societies of origin and settlement" (Basch, Glick Schiller, & Szanton Blanc, 1994, p. 6).

4. As one *New York Times* reporter noted, "The tenor of public conversation about immigration has changed, with emphasis shifting from romantic rhapsodies about the melting pot to anxiety attacks about the dwindling resources of an economically strapped nation" (Sontag, 1992, p. E5). Changing public attitudes have consistently informed policy change concerning immigration and immigrants (for review on policy change, see Fix & Zimmerman, 1997). Economic reasons as well as more racial attitudes and xenophobic fears have been cited as creating shifts in public opinion and the resulting policies (see Burns & Gimpel, 2000).

5. Fears of immigrant labor are especially strong in times when the economy is facing trouble and most pronounced in communities where mostly low- to middle-class workers feel that their jobs may be the ones at risk. As one African-American man voiced in a recent *Boston Globe* article, "[Employers will] let you go, and get one of these happy immigrants in your spot. . .They wont be late, they wont get sick and they wont complain. They will work every unhappy American citizen out of their grass cutting trash hauling, floor sweeping jobs" (Abraham, 2006). The magnitude of fear that has spread in some communities was most clearly evidenced by the recent passing of aggressive anti-immigration measures in Farmers Branch, Texas.

6. For reviews of the negative consequences of poverty on children's development, see Duncan & Brooks-Gunn (1999, 2000) Duncan, Brooks-Gunn & Klebanov (1994) and Huston (1991).

7. See a similar set of analyses and findings in Jensen (2001).

8. Portes and Rumbaut (2001) define *downward assimilation* as the alternative path children of immigrants take as they face the challenge of the "social context they encounter in American schools and neighborhoods [which] may promote a set of undesirable outcomes such as dropping out of school, joining youth gangs, or participating in the drug subculture. This alternative path has been labeled *downward assimilation* because the learning of new cultural patterns and entry into American social circles does not lead in these cases to upward mobility but to exactly the opposite" (p. 59).

9. Recent reports by the Harvard Civil Rights project, point out the high level of segregation observed in urban schools, which are now overwhelmingly nonwhite, poor and with limited resources and social and health problems of many types (See Frankenberg, Lee, & Orfield, 2003; Orfield & Lee, 2005).

10. Although Ogbu and colleagues posit that immigrants are voluntary minorities and therefore they do not adopt oppositional identities (involuntary minorities, those who are here because of slavery, conquest, and/or colonization, are the ones expected to adopt such identities), Rumbaut, C. Suárez Orozco and M. Suárez Orozco, Portes, Waters and their colleagues have observed such identities developing in more acculturated children of immigrants; thus this theoretical stance is useful to understand individual differences amongst children of immigrants as a function of acculturation and generation.

11. For examples, see Akom, 2003; Carter, 2003; Flores-Gonzalez, 1999; Spencer, Noll, Stoltzfus, & Harpalani, 2001; Tyson, 2002.

12. Perhaps this is a result of this work being done primarily with adolescents, for whom identity exploration is a fundamental developmental task; but the consistency across all these studies which represent approaches from distinct disciplines such as sociology, psychology, and anthropology is remarkable.

13. For a review of the literature on the associations between acculturation and health outcomes see Lara, Gamboa, Kahramanian, Morales, & Bautista, 2005.

CHAPTER 3

1. We are using race/ethnicity to emphasize the social construction nature of both constructs (see Cooper et al., 2005) Also, racial features (skin color, facial features) are a major component of the definition of the ethnicities of the post-1965 immigrant wave.

2. Refers to the process by which ethnic groups such as Jews, Irish, and Italians become "white" over successive generations (e.g., Kivisto & Blanck, 1990; Alba, 1985).

3. Ethnic constancy is "the consistent identification of one's ethnic group despite the passage of time or change in appearance" (Aboud, 1988, p. 15).

4. See Chapter 4 for a more extensive description of *cultural socialization* in immigrant families.

5. See Aboud and Ruble (1987) and Aboud and Amato (2001) for a clear example of research establishing a linkage between cognitive development and ethnic identity development, though the data to support this association is controversial (i.e., Ocampo, Knight, & Bernal, 1997; Semaj, 1980).

6. When we mention the theoretical frameworks for adolescent and adults, we are referring to Atkinson, Morton, & Sue, 1989; Cross, 1995; Phinney, 1993; and Helms, 1995.

7. Grindstaff, Galloway, and Nixon (1973) reproduced these results with Canadian-Indian children, Gregor and McPherson (1966) with South African Bantu, and Vaughan with Maori children in New Zealand (as cited in Morland, 1969).

8. All reports of discrimination to a certain degree are "perceptions" in that they are self-reports (not observed and reported by others). The difference in the literature is that "perception" is assessed by hypothetical vignettes including self or others as targets of discrimination, while "objective" experiences of discrimination refer to actual instances.

9. Ethnic/racial socialization refers to "parental practices that communicate messages about race or ethnicity to children" (Hughes & Chen, 1997), which can be verbal, nonverbal, explicit, and implicit.

10. Biculturalism refers to the experience of living in or at the junction between two cultures and requires the (a) knowledge of cultural beliefs and values, (b) positive attitudes toward both majority and minority groups, (c) bicultural efficacy, (d) communication ability, (e) role repertoire, and (f) a sense of being grounded (LaFromboise, Coleman, & Gerton, 1993).

CHAPTER 4

1. As described by Cooper (1999), in parallel design, one "frames their questions in terms of potentially universal processes" and defines "constructs and develops measures within each cultural community studied" (p. 4). These culture-specific research materials reap culturally meaningful results. These results can be looked at individually or in conjunction with others to determine within culture and across culture variation.

2. There are some exceptions in the literature, notably the work of Portes and Rumbaut, 2001.

3. Our model is a simplified version of the true view of development in context, where individuals at the same time that are influenced by context (i.e., school curriculum influences academic outcomes in children of immigrants), they are influencing their context (i.e., the presence of children of immigrants with particular language needs might lead to the creation of ESL or bilingual programs). However, this study concentrated on the first part of this equation.

4. Most children of immigrants, like most children in this country, attend public schools. However, public schools are not the only schools serving this role; an increasing number of minority children are attending parochial or independent schools. According to the Broughman and Swaim, 2006, minorities (all groups combined) made up 23.8% of those enrolled at private schools. Catholic school attendance, in particular, is associated with higher educational attainment as well as higher math and reading scores in high school for minority students (Keith & Page, 1985; Neal, 1995).

5. This means that these variables by themselves do not explain the mechanisms, structures, or processes of development, but they are distal indicators or marker for such processes.

6. From our informal knowledge of the communities, we knew that some immigrant parents chose to send their children to parochial schools and other independent schools that were within the area. In order to not skew our sample toward the poorest end of the immigrant population (those who are in public schools because their parents have no resources to send their children to independent schools), we recruited students in both public and independent schools. This was an important aspect of our design as we wanted to avoid the pitfall of most studies of minority and immigrant children where most samples are composed of families living in poverty (confounding ethnicity and poverty) but their findings are generalized to all members of the group.

7. In 1999, less than 2% of children in the United States were home-schooled, given the target age of interest (Bielick, Chandler, & Broughman, 2001).

8. In a comparative analyses of four studies conducted under the auspices of the McMCN (See García Coll, Thorne, Cooper, & Orellana, 1997), we found how variably and rather arbitrarily these categories are employed across the nation, reflecting both the local presence of particular immigrant groups (e.g., Latinos can mean mostly Mexican-Americans and Central Americans in one place or Puerto Rican and Dominican in another) or the blurring of important political

and linguistic differences (e.g., the practice of labeling as Southeast Asians such diverse groups as Laotians, Cambodian, Vietnamese, and Hmong).

9. Copies of all questionnaires are available from the author, in both English and Spanish; many of the Cambodian parents and interviewers and all of the Cambodian children did not read Khmer; therefore, the questionnaires were either read in English (for most Cambodian children) or translated simultaneously into Khmer if necessary (for most Cambodian parents), by bilingual interviewers.

10. Permission for conducting the study in the Cambodian community had to be obtained by the author from the senior monks in the local Cambodian temple prior to commencing the study.

11. Studies have found generation and acculturation to matter in identity and academic achievement (e.g., Bernal & Knight, 1993; Fuligni, 1997; Phinney, 1990; Portes & Rumbaut, 2001; Suárez-Orozco & Suárez-Orozco, 2001)

12. That is, Connell, Spencer, and Aber, 1994; Fuligni, 1997.

13. See Weisner (2005) for exploration of the advantages of using a mixed methods approach in the study of children's development.

14. During the 3 years of preliminary work, many investigators were consulted in this regard, most notably Ruben Rumbaut and Robin Jarret, as well all other members of the McMCN.

15. See unpublished summaries by Benjamin Bailey, 2000a, 2000b, and 2000c.

16. See Bronfenbrenner, 1986 and García Coll et al., 1997.

17. These hyphenated American derivatives come from Portes and Rumbaut (1996).

18. The values children place on school-related issues were measured through an adaptation from a survey created and employed by the Consortium on Chicago School Research.

CHAPTER 5

1. The local characterization of the three communities represented in this book is based on the ethnographic studies conducted by Benjamin Bailey, PhD, linguistic anthropologist for this project. The ethnographies were conducted by Dr. Bailey while performing his post-doctoral research at Brown University in 1999.

2. Cambodians, Laotians (including Hmong), and Vietnamese are considered in the United Sates, Southeast Asians. This is the label most used by local schools in the Providence area, including school census, which masks language and historical differences amongst the groups. Teachers, in particular, are usually unaware of which particular group the children in their classroom belong to.

3. Ogbu (1991) defines voluntary migrants as those individuals who were not forced to move to another country, but rather chose to move on the basis of finding better, more beneficial opportunities whether related to education, work, or freedom and rights (p. 436).

4. Many, including Rumbaut and Portes (2001), have found that these early governmental supports provided for refugee communities in the Untied States provided a benefit in beginning a new life in America. Rumbaut and Portes

note the importance of being received favorably and how it has influenced positive developmental outcomes for refugee children (p. 242). It was also found by Rumbaut and Portes that economically Cambodians who have lower education than other immigrant communities have faired well economically because of the government assistance they received when they first came to the United States (pp. 78–80).

5. Khmer, the language spoken in Cambodia, is primarily an oral language in this state. We had our consent forms translated into Khmer just to find out that most parents were illiterate and most of the younger generation could speak but not read or write Khmer.

6. Studies have documented the ways in which segregation is resurfacing in school systems. Inner-city schools are predominantly made up of poor, nonwhite students (Lee, 2004; Frankenberg, Lee, & Orfield, 2003).

7. In the 1998 Information Works reports, students were tested in math, writing, and health through the Regents Exam, while reading abilities were assessed by the MAT (Metropolitan Achievement Test) which was a norm-based exam. The Regents performance levels included exemplary, proficient, below proficient, and considerably below proficient performance levels. Exemplary students showed exceptional ability to apply and interpret concrete and abstract ideas or concepts. They were also able to communicate in a highly effective, clear, and organized way. Proficient students were able to apply ideas and concepts effectively and were able to communicate it clearly. Those performing below proficiency level had some skills in applying concepts and processes. They communicated some ideas clearly. Those performing considerably below proficiency level were not able to apply concepts and processes and had difficulty communicating ideas. Reading scores were assessed through the MAT tests which RIDE (Rhode Island Department of Education) had set an "at risk" benchmark at the 40th percentile or below. So those who were categorized as "high" scored between the 77th and 99th percentile. Those who scored between the 40th and 76th percentile were categorized as "middle," and those who scored at the 39th percentile and below were categorized in the "low" performance level. The MAT test was a norm-based test in which there were no proficiency standards, but rather students were ranked against one another in reference with a national sample group of students. In the 1999 reports, math, reading, and health had transitioned to being assessed through the New Standards Reference Exams, while the Writing Exam remained tested through the Regents Exams. The New Standard Reference Exams tested students' abilities to apply knowledge rather than testing their knowledge or memorization ability alone. Five performance levels were set: Achieved the standard with honors, achieved the standard, nearly achieved the standard, below the standard, and little evidence of achievement. The percentage of students scoring in the higher performance levels (achieved the standard with honors and achieved the standard) represent those students who met or surpassed the standards set by the state. The New Standards Reference Exams were created in collaboration with other states coordinated by the National Center on Education and the Economy. The Rhode Island Health and Writing exams were created by teachers, administrators, and RIDE's Office of Assessment with contractor assistance (Advanced

Systems, Inc.). By the 2000 Information Works reports, students were given New Standard Reference Exams in all four areas: reading, writing, health, and math (Information works, 1999, 2000, 2001).

8. Human capital is defined as the skill set and abilities one has obtained through education that contributes to productivity and economic advancements. Cultural capital can be defined as the cultural aspects of individuals and families that aids in the formation of social power hierarchies. Finally, social capital can be defined as the networks and relationships individuals belong to including the norms of those networks and social cohesion (Schuller, 2001).

9. For a child, having two parental figures has been considered a protective factor given the extensive research that shows single parenting is detrimental to child development (Astone & McLanahan, 1991; McLanahan & Carlson, 2002; McLanahan & Booth, 1989; Thomson, Hanson, & McLanahan, 1994).

10. Studies have shown that children in larger families have lower academic achievement (Downey, 1995; Kuo & Hauser, 1997; Parcel & Menaghan, 1994).

11. Several studies have shown strong correlations between parents' education and children's educational attainment (Belzil & Hansen, 2003; Ermisch & Francesconi, 2001; Mata, 1997 Oreopoulos, Page, & Stevens, 2003).

12. Hernandez (2004) categorizes parents from Indochina (including Cambodians) as characteristically of low education, and Yang (2004) reports that only 6.9% of Cambodian parents have bachelor degrees, placing this parents at a great distance from other Asian groups who are characterized by higher level of parental education.

13. In many indicators, like size of household, number of families living in poverty, and educational levels, our sample looks more high-risk than the Rhode Island and National populations (U.S. Census Bureau, 2000b, 2000c)

14. The 1999 poverty threshold was $17,029.00 (U.S. Census Bureau, 1999).

15. Growing up in poverty is associated with developmental problems (Brooks-Gunn & Duncan, 1997; Brooks-Gunn, Klebanov, & Duncan, 1996; Brooks-Gunn, Duncan, Klebanov, & Sealand, 1993; Duncan & Brooks-Gunn, 2000; Duncan, Brooks-Gunn, & Klebanov, 1994).

16. For example, see literature on racial/ethnic socialization and cultural maintenance (Hughes & Chen, 1997; Hughes & Johnson, 2001; Phinney, Romero, Nava, & Huang, 2001).

17. Studies have shown that strong ethnic socialization and identity lead to better developmental outcomes (Caughy, O'Campo, Randolph, & Nickerson, 2002; Hughes et al., 2006; Taylor, Casten, Flickinger, Roberts, & Fulmore, 1994).

18. See Portes and Rumbaut, 2005; Suárez-Orozco & Suárez-Orozco, 2001.

19. The high percentage of Dominican families who have returned to their country of origin is congruent with other findings (Gilbertson & Singer, 2003; Itzigsohn, Cabral, Medina, & Vazquez, 1999; Levitt & Dehesa, 2003) that categorize this population in the United States as transnational.

20. Research shows that parents differ in their educational aspirations and their actual involvement in their children's formal education in immigrant communities due to communication barriers (Dyson, 2001; Sosa, 1997).

21. Studies have shown that parents' educational aspirations and their actual involvement are related to their children's academic outcomes (Hill et al., 2004; Jodl, Michael, Malanchuk, Eccles, & Sameroff, 2001; Sosa, 1997).

22. Studies show that Khmer culture and families (similarly to other immigrant families) value high educational attainment (Fuligni et al., 1999; Smith-Hefner, 1993; Zhou, 1997a).

23. Parents' aspirations and expectations for their children have been found to be a protective factor in increasing children's own aspirations (Bandura, Barbaranelli, Caprara, & Pastorelli, 2001; Fuligni, 1997; Wentzel, 1998).

24. Studies have shown that having books at home (children and adults), reading yourself, and reading to your child matters for children's development (Golova, Alario, Vivier, Rodriguez, & High, 1999; McHale, Crouter, & Tucker, 2001; Senechal & LeFevre, 2002; Senechal, LeFevre, Thomas, & Daley, 1998).

25. Studies have shown that ethnic identity is an adolescent developmental occurrence (Phinney, 1989; Rumbaut, 1994a; Rosenthal & Hrynevich, 1985).

26. Studies have shown that children are aware of ethnic and racial categories starting in the preschool years (Clark & Clark, 1947; Kowalski & Lo, 2001; Bernal & Knight, 1997, 1997).

27. For work on other aspects of identity in children such as gender see Martin and Ruble, 2004; Ruble et al., 2004.

28. In their review article of the literature on children's collective identities, Ruble et al. (2004) argue that ethnic identity has implications for children's perceptions of their own groups and others.

29. For in-group and out-group examples in children, see Aboud, 2003; Nesdale and Flesser, 2001; Tropp & Wright, 2003, and for a review of the larger body of research on adults, see Kunda, 1999.

30. Studies have documented perceptions of discrimination in middle childhood (Brown & Bigler, 2005; Romero & Roberts, 1998; Verkuyten, 2002).

31. "Model minority" refers to a stereotype of Asian children in U.S. schools as being exemplary students both academically and behaviorally. This "academic superstardom" is often attributed to their coming from cultures which stress hard work and the value of education (Lee, 1994).

32. Studies have shown that positive attitudes toward school and teachers are related to better grades, tests, and academic outcomes (Birch & Ladd, 1997; Blumenfeld et al., 2005; Wentzel & Wigfield, 1998).

33. These findings are in contrast to findings from other populations where academic engagement actually declines over time starting as early as elementary school (Alexander, Entwistle, & Horsey, 1997; Eccles, Midgley, & Adler, 1984). Students become bored over time or do not understand how their education will help them day to day (Graham, 1994; Mickelson, 1990). They often do not feel like their hard work in school will benefit them in the long run (Fordham, 1988; Fordham & Ogbu, 1986).

34. Studies show that having high aspirations for the future is predictive of good developmental outcomes (Khattab, 2003; Schoon, 2001; Schoon & Parsons, 2002).

35. Studies show there is a relationship between teacher perceptions of children and their academic achievement (Alvidrez & Weinstein, 1999; Hamre & Pianta, 2001).

36. Studies have shown that high achieving kids show more school-related stress (i.e., Crystal et al., 1994; Luthar & Becker, 2002). Other studies show that school environments are stressful for kids because of the pressure they feel in thinking about future career goals and doing well on homework assignments and tests (de Anda et al., 1997; Omizo, Omizo, & Suzuki, 1988).

37. Studies have shown that school absences are related to school failure (Garry, 1996; Ludwig, Ladd, & Duncan, 2001).

38. Studies have supported this finding that ethnic minority adolescents and immigrant children who perceive more discrimination have worse academic outcomes (Rumbaut, 1994a; Schmader, Major, & Gramzow, 2001; Wong, Eccles, & Sameroff, 2003).

CHAPTER 6

1. Several authors have pointed out that higher educational attainment does not always translate into higher incomes, especially for minority groups. Barringer, Takeuchi, and Xenos (1990) found that although many Asians groups are, on average, better educated than the white population, only Japanese individuals approach the same level of income. Portes and Rumbaut find large discrepancies between income levels across nationalities, even when controlling for education, knowledge of English, and profession; they write, "no matter how educated a Mexican or Haitian parent is, his or chances of moving ahead economically are significantly constrained by the social environment" (2001, p. 80).

2. This poverty rate is much higher than the 2000 Census rate for Dominicans of only 29% (Hernandez, 2004), but it is reflective of the Dominican population in Rhode Island where 42 percent of the Dominican population live below the poverty level (U.S. Census Bureau, 2000e).

3. This employment rate is comparable with the U.S. census 2000 rate for Dominican parents of 59% full time employment (Hernandez, 2004).

4. This single head of household figure is higher than the 2000 Census rate of 37% as reported by Hernandez (2004), but as in this study, Dominicans have the highest rates of all immigrant groups, more than double the national rate for all immigrant groups.

5. Studies have shown that children in single parent households have worse developmental outcomes (Astone & McLanahan, 1991; McLanahan & Carlson, 2002; McLanahan & Booth, 1989; Thomson, Hanson, & McLanahan, 1994).

6. In Rhode Island, children who moved at least once were more likely to be held back in school, perform lower on reading tests, and be absent from school a significant number of days (Providence Plan, 2004). For example, in their study of Rhode Island fourth graders, Providence Plan (2004) found that while 66% of children who had not moved met proficiency in reading on state tests, only 59% of who had moved *once* met proficiency. For kids who had moved three times, less than half met state reading standards.

7. See the following that attest to the transnational nature of Dominicans in the United States (Bailey, 2002; Gilbertson & Singer, 2003; Itzigsohn et al., 1999; Levitt & Dehesa, 2003)

8. See Rumbaut and Portes (2001).

9. Dominican parents are among the lowest educated immigrant parents in the United States; the 2000 U.S. Census reported that 41% of Dominican parents had not completed a high school education (as cited in Hernandez, 2004). Portes and Rumbaut also noted this trend in their analysis of the 1984 census (1990). According to the 2000 U.S. Census, median family income for Dominicans was far below the average, both in Rhode Island (on average $19,186 for Dominicans, $52, 781 for the RI population as a whole) and in United States at large ($28,397 for Dominicans, $50, 046 for the U.S. population as a whole; U.S. Census Bureau, 2000d, 2000e, 2000f).

10. According to the 2000 U.S. Census, 91% of Dominican children in the United States were living in a household where English was not the language spoken in the home (as cited in Hernandez, 2004).

11. So Spanish is being used frequently because interpreters (both professional and kin) and bilingual workers are been sought out by most social services organizations, hospitals, and schools aside from the local Latino organizations.

12. I am using the phrase "Spanish-American" instead of "Spanish" to delineate the cultural distinctions between Spanish Caribbean culture and Spanish Iberian culture. Although language and history roots ties these two cultures, there are many foods and customs that are seeing only in the Spanish Caribbean; namely Puerto Rico, Dominican Republic and Cuba's culture has also indigenous and African influences.

13. As Bailey (2002) contends, Dominicans do not have the choice of a white, American identity in the United States, because of their African descendent phenotype. They can be Dominican, Dominican-American, or black. Many of those who were considered white in their country of birth, could not choose this identity in the United States.

14. Although we find evidence for low acculturation in the parents, this is not so for the children. Most children in our study preferred to speak in English, as indicated by their stated language preferences.

15. Studies have stressed the greater emphasis on respect of authority and family obligation in Latino Families (see Fuligni, Tseng, & Lam, 1999). In addition, a greater use of, "unilateral decision making...[and] rules (especially regarding out-of-home behavior)" has been documented in Latino families (see Halgunseth, Ispa, & Rudy, 2006, p. 1284).

16. Studies have found that reading for pleasure leads to higher academic achievement (Flowers, 2003; Hofferth & Sandberg, 2001).

17. The word *Spanish* was added to our original list of labels during the extensive piloting that was conducted to develop the measures used in this study. Spanish was spontaneously given by many Latino children. When asked why they were Spanish (which usually connotes national origins to Spain), they said because they spoke the language. We realized that in this community of children, Spanish meant the language not the national origin. We therefore added this term to the list. The lesson: listen to the children's own social categories

and ask "why?" See Cooper et al. (2005) for a detailed discussion of children's construction of social categories.

18. Similar findings are reported by Bailey, 2001. In his study of Dominican high school students, Bailey writes, "Unlike non-Hispanic African descent immigrants, who generally identity themselves as 'black' in the second generation, Dominicans in the second generation identify themselves as 'Dominican,' 'Spanish,' or 'Hispanic.' Spanish language... helps preserve a distinct sense of Dominican origins" (Bailey, 2001a, p. 704).

19. Recent evidence suggests that in-group preference should not be confounded with out-group prejudice; that they are in fact distinct processes (Cameron et al., 2001).

20. Studies have shown that school absences are related to negative academic outcomes (Garry, 1996; Ludwig et al., 2001).

CHAPTER 7

1. Bailey (2000c) refers to a 1957 series of earthquakes of Faial (one of the Azores islands) and the supportive reaction of the local community as incentives for having the second massive migration start before the 1965 immigration reform.

2. Most of our families were from the Azores and would be considered "white." We excluded families from Cape Verde, who are usually racially considered "black" in this country because we were interested in having one of our groups represent the traditional European migration, where after several generations they become "white."

3. What we consider important is having some contact with the teacher; a higher number of visits could reflect academic problems and not necessarily interest in their child's education.

4. For examples of European immigrants "becoming white" in the U.S. social structure, see Alba (1985), Ignatiev (1995), and Kivisto & Blanck (1990).

5. We are not arguing that the identities observed at these ages are neither as stable nor necessarily as central to these children as they might be to adolescents and adults. What we are arguing is that the emphasis on ethnic identity as a solely an adolescent phenomenon is misleading, since children at much earlier ages are aware of these sources of differences and their social meanings (see Ruble et al., 2004).

6. The local Portuguese community embraces people who are born in the Azores, Portugal, and Cape Verde. The most recent immigrants who are racially white are not from Portugal per se but from the Azores. Thus our sample reflects the characteristics of the local Portuguese community.

7. For more details on how children of this age group learn, construct, and resist these dominant social categories see Cooper et al., 2005.

8. It is interesting to note that in all the three immigrant groups, the least popular choices are panethnic labels, such as Asian, Latino, or European, which are "a socially constructed grouping that categorizes people who have little in common yet are perceived to belong together in the mainstream American society" (Lopez & Espiritu (1997) as cited in Akiba et al., 2004, p. 13)

9. For example, there is evidence that in-group preference should not be confounded with out-group prejudice, that they are in fact distinct processes (Cameron et al., 2001).

10. Astone and McLanahan (1994) found that differences in residential mobility explained in part the higher rate of high school drop out among step families than in intact families. In addition, Tucker, Marx, and Long (1998) found that among children not living with both biological parents, those who moved more than once had significantly more school problems than those who had not.

11. See Chapter 1, pp. 11–12, and Chapter 2, pp. 30–32, for references and further information on the "immigrant paradox."

12. Since the correlation matrix was quite large given the number of variables, we only present those variables that showed a pattern of significant associations and not scattered significant associations.

13. See theoretical frameworks discussed in Chapter 4.

14. For descriptions of "symbolic ethnic identity," see Waters (1999).

CHAPTER 8

1. It is important to note that when interpreting causal models, the "fit" of a model speaks only to the sample of data collected. In other words, if a model fits *our* data, it does not mean it will fit all data collected in other samples of Cambodian, Dominican, and Portuguese immigrant groups. Furthermore, if a model does *not* fit the data, it may mean either that our theory does not fit our data or our data does not fit the theory—there can be alternate models that will fit the data as well.

2. A frequent critique of SEM procedures is the lack of consideration, on the part of the researcher, of alternate models. In building our models, alternate paths were added or constrained (i.e., eliminated), and fit statistics compared to ensure that the model we were building was not only theoretically driven, but also provided a statistically better fit to the data. For detailed information on procedures, critiques, and methods used, see Breckler (1990).

3. Structural Equation Modeling (SEM) is a statistical modeling approach based either on covariance or on correlation matrices. In our studies, a covariance approach is used. The defining characteristics of SEM that we use here include the capacity to build "latent variables" to measure indirectly observed concepts and the ability to test *structural* pathways that define a direction of effects from one variable to the next. In the end, an SEM model estimates the "fit" of observed data both at the measurement level (i.e., latent variable)and at the structural level (i.e., theoretically driven pathways between variables), see Bollen and Lennox (1991).

4. Latent variables are used to provide a measurement of a construct that can be captured only *indirectly*. For example, in our studies, Academic Attitudes are not measured directly—they are abstract ideas that can be measured indirectly by asking students a variety of questions about their academic engagement, aspirations, and values. Therefore, in building latent variables, we are estimating the strength of the combination of multiple "indicator variables" (e.g., engagement,

aspirations, values) that come together and represent our larger "Academic Attitudes" latent variable. In doing so, we examine both the overall model fit statistics and the parameter estimates are used to evaluate latent variables. For more information about latent variables, please see Borsboom, Mellenbergh, and Van Heerden, 2003; Cohen, Cohen, Teresi, Marchi, and Velez, 1990.

5. Commonly used SEM fit statistics such as the Normative Fit Index (NFI, values > .90 for adequate fit) and Root Mean Square Residual (RMSEA, values < .06 for adequate fit) were checked and met to ensure stability of parameter estimation. The χ^2 test also was used to gauge model fit. In SEM, the χ^2 tests the null hypothesis that the data *does* fit the theory, and therefore you want to accept the null hypothesis, with corresponding p values of > .05. For a description of these commonly used fit statistics and their origins, please see Maruyama, 1998; Hoyle, 1995.

6. During this model-building process, we initially intended to create a latent variable of the immigration context that would include parents' language use and preferences, cultural routines, year of immigration, perceptions of community support, and frequency of travel to the country of origin. However, we found that it was difficult to obtain an adequate fit for such a variable. In bivariate correlation analyses, we instead observed that the mothers' year of immigration was moderately correlated with many of these other aspects of immigration within each of the three immigrant groups and therefore used this variable as an indicator of the overall immigration context in our modeling analyses.

7. See Chapter 1, pp. 11–12, and Chapter 2, pp. 30–32, for specifics on the immigrant paradox.

References ⁑

Aboud, F. E. (1988). *Children and prejudice.* New York: Blackwell.

Aboud, F. E. (2003). The formation of in-group favoritism and out-group prejudice in young children: Are they distinct attitudes? *Developmental Psychology, 39*(1), 48–60.

Aboud, F. E., & Amato, M. (2001). Developmental and socialization influences on intergroup bias. In G. J. Fletcher & M. S. Clark (Series Eds.) & R. Brown & S. Gaertner (Vol. Eds.), *Blackwell handbook in social psychology: Vol. 4. Intergroup processes.* Oxford, England: Blackwell.

Aboud, F. E., & Doyle, A. B. (1993). The early development of ethnic identity and attitudes. In M. E. Bernal (Ed.), *Ethnic identity: Formation and transmission among Hispanics and other minorities.* SUNY series, United States Hispanic studies (pp. 47–59). Albany, NY: State University of New York Press.

Aboud, F. E., & Ruble, D. N. (1987). Identity constancy in children: Developmental processes and implications. In K. Yardley & T. Honess (Eds.), *Self and identity: Perspectives across the lifespan* (pp. 95–107). New York: Routledge.

Aboud, F. E., & Skerry, S. A. (1984). The development of ethnic attitudes. *Journal of Cross Cultural Psychology, 15*(1), 3–34.

Abraham, Y. (2006, April 16). Immigration hits home in Lynn: Blacks voice fear of a loss of jobs. *Boston Globe,* p. A1.

Ainsworth-Darnell, J. W., & Downey, D. B. (1998). Assessing the oppositional culture explanation for racial/ethnic differences in school performance. *American Sociological Review, 63,* 536–553.

Akiba, D., Szalacha, L. A., & García Coll, C. (2004). Multiplicity of ethnic identification during middle childhood: Conceptual and methodological considerations. *New Directions for Child and Adolescent Development,* (104)(Summer), 45–60.

Akom, A. A. (2003). Reexamining resistance as oppositional behavior: The nation of Islam and the creating of Black achievement ideology. *Sociology of Education, 76*(4), 305–325.

Alarcon, O., Szalacha, L. A., Erkut, S., Fields, J. P., & García Coll, C. (2000). The color of my skin: A measure to assess children's perceptions of their skin color. *Applied Developmental Science, 4*(4), 208–221.

Alba, R. D. (1985). *Italian Americans: Into the twilight of ethnicity.* Englewood Cliffs, NJ: Prentice Hall.

Alexander, K. L, & Entwistle, D. R. (1988). Achievement in the first 2 years of school: Patterns and processes. *Monographs of the Society for Research in Child Development, 53*(2, Serial No.218).

Alexander, K., Entwistle, D. R., & Horsey, C. S. (1997). From first grade forward: Early foundations of high school dropouts. *Sociology of Education, 70*(2), 87–107.

Alexander, K. L., Entwistle, D. R., & Kabbani, N. S. (2001). The dropout process in life course perspective: Early risk factors at home and school. *Teachers College Record, 103*(5), 760–822.

Anderson, E. M., & Maehr, M. L. (1994). Motivation and schooling in the middle grades. *Review of Educational Research, 64,* 287–309.

Annie E. Casey Foundation. (2005). *Annie E. Casey Foundation Kids Count Data Book.* Baltimore, MD: Annie E. Casey Foundation.

Arroyo, C. G., & Zigler, E. (1995). Racial identity, academic achievement, and the psychological well-being of economically disadvantaged adolescents. *Journal of Personality and Social Psychology, 69*(5), 903–914.

Asakawa, K. (2001). Family socialization practices and their effects on the internalization of educational values for Asian and White American adolescents. *Applied Developmental Science, 5*(3), 184–194.

Astone, N. M., & McLanahan, S. S. (1991). Family structure, parental practices and high school completion. *American Sociological Review, 56,* 309–320.

Astone N. M., & McLanahan S. S. (1994). Family structure, residential mobility, and school drop out: A research note. *Demography, 31,* 575–584.

Atkinson, D. R., Morton, G., & Sue, D. W. (Eds.). (1989). *Counseling American minorities: A cross-cultural perspective* (3rd ed.). Dubuque, IA: William C. Brown.

Au, T. K., & Harackiewicz, J. M. (1986). The effects of perceived parental expectations on Chinese children's mathematics performance. *Merrill-Palmer Quarterly, 32*(4), 383–392.

Acevedo-García, D., Soobader, M., & Berkman, L. (2005). The differential effect of foreign-born status on low birth weight by race/ethnicity and education. *Pediatrics, 115*(1), 20–30.

Azmitia, M., Cooper, C. R., García, E. E., & Dunbar, N. D. (1996). The ecology of family guidance in low-income Mexican-American and European-American families. *Social Development, 5*(1), 1–23.

Bailey, B. (1999). Language and ethnic/racial identity of Dominican American high school students in Providence, Rhode Island. Unpublished doctoral dissertation, Department of Anthropology, University of California-Los Angeles.

Bailey, B. (2000a). Description/background of Cambodian community: Refugee pathways and selection processes and the providence community. Unpublished manuscript.

Bailey, B. (2000b). The Providence Dominican community: Some aspects of immigration and ethnicity. Unpublished manuscript, Providence.

Bailey, B. (2000c). Some history and description of Portuguese immigration and the east providence/se New England Portuguese community. Unpublished manuscript.

Bailey, B. (2001a). Dominican American ethnic and racial identities and United States social categories. *International Migration Review, 35*(3), 677–708.

Bailey, B. (2001b). Language and negotiation of ethnic/racial identity among Dominican Americans. *Language and Society, 29,* 555–582.

Bailey, B. H. (2002). *Language, race, and negotiation of identity: A study of Dominican Americans.* New York: LFB Scholarly.

Bandura, A. (1993). Perceived self-efficacy in cognitive development and functioning. *Educational Psychologist, 28*(2), 117–148.

Bandura, A., Barbaranelli, C., Caprara, G. V., & Pastorelli, C. (2001). Self-efficacy beliefs as shapers of children's aspirations and career trajectories. *Child Development, 72*(1), 187–206.

Bali, V. A., & Alvarez, R. M. (2003). Schools and educational outcomes: What causes the race gap in student test sources? *Social Science Quarterly, 84,* 485.

Baron, R., & Kenny, D. (1986). The moderator-mediator variable distinction in social psychological research: Conceptual, strategic, and statistical consideration. *Journal of Personality and Social Psychology, 51*(6), 1173–1182.

Barringer, H. R., D. T. Takeuchi, & P. Xenos. (1990). "Education, Occupational Prestige, and Income of Asian Americans." *Sociology of Education, 63,* 27–43.

Basch, L., Glick Schiller, N., & Szanton Blanc, C. (1994). *Nations unbound: Transnational projects, postcolonial predicaments, and the deterriorialized nation states.* Basel, Switzerland: Gordon and Breach.

Belzil, C., & Hansen, J. (2003). Structural estimates of the intergenerational education correlation. *Journal of Applied Econometrics, 18,* 679–696.

Bempechat, J., Graham, S. E., & Jimenez, N. V. (1999). The socialization of achievement in poor and minority students: A comparative study. *Journal of Cross Cultural Psychology, 30*(2), 139–158.

Bernal, M. E., & Knight, G. P. (Eds.) (1993). *Ethnic identity: Formation and transmission: Among hispanics and other minorities.* New York: State University of New York Press.

Bernal, M. E., & Knight, G. P. (1997). Ethnic identity of Latino children. In J. G. García (Ed.), *Psychological interventions and research with Latino populations* (pp. 15–38). Needham Heights, MA: Allyn & Bacon.

Bernal, M. E., Knight, G. P., Garza, C. A., Ocampo, K. A., & Cota, M. K. (1990). The development of ethnic identity in Mexican-American children. *Hispanic Journal of Behavioral Sciences, 12*(1), 3–24.

Bernal, M. E., Knight, G. P., Ocampo, K. A., Garza, C. A., & Cota, M. K. (1993). Development of Mexican American identity. In M. E. Bernal (Ed.), *Ethnic identity: Formation and transmission among Hispanics and other minorities.*

SUNY series, United States Hispanic Studies (pp. 31–46). Albany, NY: State University of New York Press.

Bernal, M. E., Saenz, D. S., & Knight, G. P. (1995). Ethnic identity and adaptation of Mexican American youths in school settings. In A. M. Padilla (Ed.), *Hispanic psychology: Critical issues in theory and research* (pp. 71–88). Thousand Oaks, CA: Sage.

Berry, J. W. (1999). Emics and etics: A symbiotic conception. *Culture and Psychology, 5*(2), 165.

Berry, J. W., Phinney, J., Sam, D. L., & Vedder, P. (2006). *Immigrant youth in transition: Acculturation, identity, and adaptation across national contexts.* Mahwah, NJ: Lawrence Erlbaum Associates.

Bialystok, E. (1999). Cognitive complexity and attentional control in the bilingual mind. *Child Development, 70*(3), 636–644.

Bielick, S., Chandler, K., & Broughman, S. (2001 July) *Homeschooling in the United States: 1999.* (NCES publication 2001033) Washington, DC: National Center for Education Statistics.

Bigler, R. S., Brown, C. S., & Markell, M. (2001). When groups are not created equal: Effects of group status on the formation of intergroup attitudes in children. *Child Development, 72*(4), 1151–1162.

Bigler, R. S., Jones, L. C., & Lobliner, D. B. (1997). Social categorization and the formation of intergroup attitudes in children. *Child Development, 68*(3), 530–543.

Bigler, R. S., & Liben, L. S. (1993). A cognitive-developmental approach to racial stereotyping and reconstructive memory in European-American children. *Child Development, 64*(5), 1507–1518.

Billings, B. (1999). *Ethnicity and individual differences in achievement goals in kindergarten children.* Albuquerque, NM: Biennial Meeting of the Society for Research in Child Development. (ERIC Document Reproduction Service No. ED # 36288).

Birch, S. H., & Ladd, G. W. (1997). The teacher-child relationship and children's early school adjustment. *Journal of School Psychology, 35*(1), 61–79.

Black, M. M., Dubowitz, H., & Starr, R. H., Jr. (1999). African American fathers in low income, urban families: Development, behavior, and home environment of their three-year-old children. *Child Development, 70*(4), 967–978.

Blake, S. M., Ledsky, R., Goodenow, C., & O'Donnell, L. (2001). Recency of immigration, substance use, and sexual behavior, among Massachusetts adolescents. *American Journal of Public Health, 91,* 794–798.

Blakeslee, S. (2002, November 5). Brain power: The search for origins. *New York Times.* Retrieved December 18, 2008 from http://query.nytimes.com/gst/fullpage.html?res=9900EFD6153EF936A 35752C1A9649C8B63#, 2006

Blumenfeld, P., Modell, J., Bartko, T., Secada, W., Fredricks, J., & Friedel, J. (2005). School engagement of inner city students during middle childhood. In C. R. Cooper, C. García Coll, W. T. Bartko, H. M. Davis, & C. Chatman (Eds.), *Developmental pathways through middle childhood: Rethinking contexts and diversity as resources.* Mahwah, NJ: Lawrence Erlbaum.

Bollen, K., & Lennox, R. (1991). Conventional wisdom on measurement: A structural equation perspective. *Psychological Bulletin*, 110(2), 305–314.

Borsboom, D., Mellenbergh, G. J, & van Heerden, J. (2003). The theoretical status of latent variables. *Psychological Review*, 110(2), 203–219.

Bourdieu, P. (1986). The forms of social capital. In J. G. Richardson (Ed.), *Handbook of theory and research for the sociology of education* (pp. 241–248). New York: Greenwood.

Boykin, A. W., & Toms, F. D. (1985). Black child socialization: A conceptual framework. In H. P. McAdoo & J. L. McAdoo (Eds.), *Black children: Social, educational, and parental environments. Sage focus editions* (vol. 72, pp. 33–51). Thousand Oaks, CA: Sage Publications, Inc.

Bradley, R. H., & Corwyn, R. F. (2002). Socioeconomic status and child development. *Annual Review of Psychology*, 52, 372–399.

Breckler S. J. (1990). Applications of covariance structure modeling in psychology: Cause for concern. *Psychological Bulletin*, 107(2), 260–273.

Brewer, M. B. (1999). The psychology of prejudice: Ingroup love or outgroup hate? *Journal of Social Issues*, 55(3), 429–444.

Brewer, M. B. (2001). Ingroup identification and intergroup conflict: When does ingroup love become outgroup hate? In R. Ashmors, L. Jussim & D. Wilder (Eds.), *Social identity intergroup conflict, and conflict reduction*. New York: Oxford University Press.

Bronfenbrenner, U. (1979). *The ecology of human development: Experiments by nature and design*. Cambridge, MA: Harvard University Press.

Bronfenbrenner, U. (1986). Ecology of the family as a context for human development: Research perspectives. *Developmental Psychology*, 22(6), 723–742.

Brooks-Gunn, J., & Duncan, G. J. (1997). The effects of poverty on children. *Future of Children*, 7(2), 55–71.

Brooks-Gunn, J., Duncan, G. J., Klebanov, P. K., & Sealand, N. (1993). Do neighborhoods influence child and adolescent development? *American Journal of Sociology*, 99(2), 353–395.

Brooks-Gunn, J., Klebanov, P. K., & Duncan, G. J. (1996). Ethnic differences in children's intelligence test scores: Role of economic deprivation, home environment, and maternal characteristics. *Child Development*, 67(2), 396–408.

Broughman, S. P., & Swaim, N. L. (2006). *Characteristics of private schools in the United States: Results From the 2003–2004 private school universe survey* (NCES 2006-319). Washington, DC: U.S. Department of Education, National Center for Education Statistics.

Brown, S. B., & Bigler, R. S. (2002). Effects of minority status in the classroom on children's intergroup attitudes. *Journal of Experimental Child Psychology*, 83(2), 77–110.

Brown, C. S., & Bigler, R. S. (2004). Children's perceptions of gender discrimination. *Developmental Psychology*, 40(5), 714–726.

Brown, C. S., & Bigler, R. S. (2005). Children's perceptions of discrimination: A developmental model. *Child Development*, 76(3), 533–553.

Brown, E. R., Wyn, R., Yu, H., Valenzuela, A., & Dong, L. (1999). Access to health insurance and health care for children of immigrant families. In D. J. Hernandez (Ed.), *Children of immigrants: Health, adjustment, and public assistance*. Washington DC: National Academy Press.

Bui, H. N., & Thongniramol, O. (2005). Immigration and self-reported delinquency: The interplay of immigration status, gender, race and ethnicity. *Journal of Crime and Justice, 28*, 79–100.

Buriel, R. (1994). Immigration and education of Mexican Americans. In A. Hurtado & E. E. García (Eds.), *The educational achievement of Latinos: Barriers and successes* (pp. 197–226). Santa Cruz: Regents of the University of California.

Burns, P., & Gimpel, J. (2000). Economic insecurity, prejudicial stereotypes and public opinion on immigration policy. *Political Science Quarterly, 115*(2), 201–225.

Cachelin, F. M., Weiss, J. W., & Garbanati, J. A. (2003). Dieting and its relationship to smoking, acculturation, and family environment in Asian and Hispanic adolescents. *Eating Disorders, 11*(1), 51–62.

Canniff, J. G. (2001). *Cambodian refugees' pathways to success: Developing a bi-cultural identity*. New York: LFB Scholarly.

Cameron, J., Alvarez, J., Ruble, D. N., & Fuligni, A. (2001). Children's lay theories about ingroup: Reconceptualizing research on prejudice. *Personality and Social Psychology Review, 5*(2), 118–128.

Carlson, C. I., Wilson K. D., & Hargrave, J. L. (2003). The effect of school racial composition on Hispanic intergroup relations. *Journal of Social and Personal Relationships, 20*, 203–220.

Carter, P. (2003). Black cultural capital, status positioning, and schooling conflicts for low-income African American youth. *Social Problems, 50*, 136–155.

Carter, R. S., & Wojtkiewicz, R. A. (2000). Parental involvement with adolescents' education: Do daughters or sons get more help? *Adolescence, 35*(137), 29–44.

Caughy, M. O. B., O'Campo, P. J., Randolph, S. M., & Nickerson, K. (2002). The influence of racial socialization practices on the cognitive and behavioral competence of African American preschoolers. *Child Development, 73*(5), 1611–1625.

Chang, L., Morrissey, R., & Koplewicz, H. (1995). Prevalence of psychiatric symptoms and their relation to adjustment among Chinese-American youth. *Journal of the American Academy of Child & Adolescent Psychiatry, 34*(1), 91–99.

Chapa, J., & De La Rosa, B. (2004). Latino population growth, socioeconomic and demographic characteristics, and implications for educational attainment. *Education and Urban Society, 36*(2), 130–149.

Chao, R. K. (2000). Cultural explanations for the role of parenting in the school success for Asian-American children. In M. C. Wang & R. D. Taylor (Eds.), *Resilience across contexts: Family, work, culture, and community* (pp. xiii, 386 p.). Mahwah, NJ: Lawrence Erlbaum.

Chiu, M. L., Feldman, S. S., & Rosenthal, D. A. (1992). The influence of immigration on parental behavior and adolescent distress in Chinese families residing in two western nations. *Journal of Research on Adolescence*, 2(3), 205–239.

Clark, K. B., & Clark, M. P. (1939). Development of consciousness of self and the emergence of racial identification in negro preschool children. *Journal of Social Psychology*, 10, 591–599.

Clark, K. B., & Clark, M. P. (1947). Racial identification and preference in negro children. In L. T. Benjamin (Ed.), *A history of psychology: Original sources and contemporary research* (pp. 169–178). San Francisco: McGraw Hill.

Clark, A., Hocevar, D., & Dembo, M. H. (1980). The role of cognitive development in children's explanations and preferences for skin color. *Developmental Psychology*, 16(4), 332–339.

Coatsworth, J. H. (2004). Globalization, growth, and welfare in history. In M. M. Suárez-Orozco & D. B. Qin-Hilliard (Eds.), *Globalization: Culture and education for a new millennium*. Berkeley: University of California Press.

Cohen, P., Cohen, J., Teresi, J., Marchi, M., & Velez, C. N. (1990). Problems in the Measurement of Latent Variables in Structural Equations Causal Models. *Applied Psychological Measurement*, 14(2), 183–196.

Coleman, J. S. (1988). Social capital in the creation of human capital. *American Journal of Sociology*, 94, 95–120.

Collignon, F. F., Men, M., & Tan, S. (2001). Finding ways in: Community-based perspectives on Southeast Asian family involvement with schools in a New England state. *Journal of Education for Students Placed at Risk*, 6(1–2), 27–44.

Connell, J. P., Spencer, M. B., & Aber, J. L. (1994). Educational risk and resilience in African-American youth: Context, self, action, and outcomes in school. *Child Development*, 65(2), 493.

Connolly, P. (1998). *Racism, gender identities and young children: Social relations in a multi-ethnic, inner-city primary school*. New York: Routledge.

Cooper, C. R. (1999). Multiple selves, multiple worlds: Cultural perspectives on individuality and connectedness in adolescent development. In A. S. Master (Ed.), *Cultural processes in child development. The Minnesota symposia on child psychology* (Vol. 29, pp. 25–57). Mahwah, NJ: Lawrence Erlbaum Associates, Publishers.

Cooper, C. R., Dominguez, E., & Rosas, S. (2005). Soledad's dream: How immigrant children bridge their multiple worlds and build pathways to college. In C. R. Cooper, C. T. García Coll, W. T. Bartko, H. Davis, & C. Chatman (Eds.), *Developmental pathways through middle childhood: Rethinking contexts and diversity as resources*. Mahwah, NJ: Erlbaum.

Cooper, C. R., Jackson, J. F., Azmitia, M., & Lopez, E. M. (1998). Multiple selves, multiple worlds: Three useful strategies for research with ethnic minority youth on identity, relationships, and opportunity structures. In V. A. McLoyd & L. Steinberg (Eds.), *Studying minority adolescents: Conceptual, methodological, and theoretical issues* (pp. 111–125). Mahwah, NJ: Lawrence Erlbaum.

Cooper, C. R., García Coll, C., Thorne, B., & Orellana, M. F. (2005). Beyond demographic categories: How immigration, ethnicity, and "race" matter for children's identities and pathways through school. In C. R. Cooper, C. García Coll, W. T. Bartko, H. M. Davis, & C. Chatman (Eds.), *Developmental pathways through middle childhood: Rethinking contexts and diversity as resources*. Mahwah, NJ: Lawrence Erlbaum.

Corenblum, B., & Annis, R. C. (1993). Development of racial identity in minority and majority children: An affect discrepancy model. *Canadian Journal of Behavioral Science, 25*(4), 499–521.

Corenblum, B., & Wilson, A. E. (1982). Ethnic preference and identification among Canadian Indian and White children: Replication and extension. *Canadian Journal of Behavioral Science, 14*, 50–59.

Crocker, J., & Major, B. (1989). Social stigma and self-esteem: The self-protective properties of stigma. *Psychological Review, 96*(4), 608–630.

Crosnoe, R. (2005). The diverse experiences of Hispanic students in the American educational system. *Sociological Forum, 20*(4), 561–588.

Crosnoe, R. (2006a). Health and the education of children from racial/ethnic minority and immigrant families. *Journal of Health and Behavior, 47*, 77–93.

Crosnoe, R. (2006b). *Mexican roots, American schools.* Stanford, CA: Stanford University Press.

Cross, W. E., Jr. (1991). *Shades of black: Diversity in African-American identity.* Philedelphia: Temple University Press.

Cross, W. E., Jr. (1995). Oppositional identity and African American youth: Issues and prospects. In W. D. Hawley (Ed.), *Toward a common destiny: Improving race and ethnic relations in America* (pp. 185–204). San Francisco, CA: Jossey-Bass/Pfeiffer.

Cross, W. E., & Cross, B. T. (2002). Theory, research, and models. In P. B. Pedersen, J. G. Draguns, W. J. Lonner, & J. E. Trimble (Eds.), *Counseling across cultures* (Vol. 6, pp. 154–181). New York: Sage.

Crystal, D. S., Chen, C., Fuligni, A. J., Stevenson, H. W., Hsu, C.-C., Ko, H.-J., Kitamura, S., & Kimura, S. (1994). Psychological maladjustment and academic achievement: A cross-cultural study of Japanese, Chinese, and American high school students. *Child Development, 65*(3), 738–753.

Cubberley, E. (1947). *Public education in the United States: A study and interpretation of America educational history.* Boston: Houghton Mifflin Co.

Darling-Hammond, L. (1999). *Teacher quality and student achievement: A review of state policy evidence.* Center for the Study of Teaching and Policy: University of Washington.

Darling-Hammond, L. (2000). How teacher education matters. *Journal of Teacher Education, 51*(3), 166–173.

Dauber, S. L., Alexander, K. L., & Entwistle, D. R. (1996). Tracking and transitions through the middle grades: Channeling educational trajectories. *Sociology of Education, 69*, 290–307.

de Anda, D., & Riddel, V. A. (1991). Ethnic identity, self-esteem, and interpersonal relationships among multiethnic adolescents. *Journal of Multicultural Social Work, 1*(2), 83–98.

de Anda, D., Bradley, M., Collada, C., Dunn, L., Kubota, J., Hollister, V., et al. (1997, April). A study of stress, stressors, and coping strategies among middle school adolescents. *Social Work in Education, 19*(2) 87–98.

Dee, T. S. (2004). Teachers, race and student achievement in a randomized experiment. *Review of Economics and Statistics*, 86(1), 195–210.

Delgado-Gaitán, C. (1987). Parent perceptions of school: Supportive environments for children. In H. T. Trueba (Ed.), *Success or failure* (pp. 131–155). Cambridge, MA: Newbury House Publishers.

Delgado-Gaitán, C. (1991). Involving parents in the schools: A process of empowerment. *American Journal of Education*, 100(1), 20–46.

Delgado-Gaitán, C. (1992). School matters in the Mexican-American home: Socializing children to education. *American Educational Research Journal*, 29(3), 495–513.

Development and use of neighborhood health analysis: Residential mobility in context. (2002, October 31). Providence, RI: The Providence Plan.

Dickinson, D., Snow, C. E., Roach, K., Smith, M., & Tabors, P. (1998, April 18). *Home and preschool factors affecting language and literacy development in kindergarten*. Paper presented at the Annual Meetings for the Society for the Scientific Study of Reading, San Diego, CA.

Dolores, A.-G., Soobader, M., & Berkman, L. (2005). The differential effect of foreign-born status on low birth weight by race/ethnicity and education. *Pediatrics*, 115(1), 20–30.

Downey, D. B. (1995). When bigger is not better: Family size, parental resources and children's educational performance. *American Sociological Review*, 60, 746–761.

Doyle, A. B., & Aboud, F. E. (1995). A longitudinal study of white children's racial prejudice as a social-cognitive development. *Merrill Palmer Quarterly*, 41(2), 209–228.

Duany, J. (1998) Reconstructing racial identity: Ethnicity, color, and class among dominicans in the United States and Puerto Rico. *Latin American Perspectives*, 25(3), 147–172.

Duncan, G. J., & Brooks-Gunn, J. (2000). Family poverty, welfare reform, and child development. *Child Development*, 71(1), 188–196.

Duncan, G. J., Brooks-Gunn, J., & Klebanov, P. K. (1994). Economic deprivation and early childhood development. *Child Development*, 65(2), 296–318.

Duncan, G., & Brooks-Gunn, J. (1999). *Consequences of growing up poor*. New York: Russel Sage.

Dyson, L. L. (2001). Home-school communication and expectations of recent Chinese immigrants. *Canadian Journal of Education*, 26(4), 455–476.

Ebihara, M. (1985). Khmer. In D. Haines (Ed.), *Refugees in the United States*. Westport, CT: Greenwood.

Eccles, J. S. (1999). The development of children ages 6 to 14. *Future of Children*, 9(2), 30–44.

Eccles, J. S., Midgley, C., & Adler, T. (1984). Grade-related changes in the school environment: Effects on achievement motivation. In J. G. Nicholls (Ed.), *Advances in motivation and achievement* (Vol. 3, pp. 283–331). Greenwich, CT: IAI.

Eccles, J. S., Roeser, R., Wigfield, A., & Freedman-Doan, C. (1999). Academic and motivational pathways through middle childhood. In L. Balter & C. S.

Tamis-LeMonda (Eds.), *Child psychology: A handbook of contemporary issues* (pp. 287–317). Philedelphia, PA: Psychology Press.

Ensminger, M. E., & Slusarcick, A. L. (1992). Paths to high school graduation or dropout: A longitudinal study of a first-grade cohort. *Sociology of Education*, 65(2), 95–113.

Entwistle, D. R., Alexander, K. L., Pallas, A. M., & Cadigan, D. (1987). The emergent academic self-image of first graders: Its response to social structure. *Child Development*, 58(5), 1190–1206.

Erickson, E. H. (1963). *Childhood and society*. New York: Norton.

Erkut, S., Alarcón, O., & García Coll, C. T. (1998). *Normative study of Puerto Rican adolescents final report*. Special Report, Center for Research for Women, No. 23, Wellesley, MA.

Erkut, S., Szalacha, L. A., Alarcon, O., & García Coll, C. (1999). Stereotyped perceptions of adolescents' health risk behaviors. *Cultural Diversity and Ethnic Minority Psychology*, 5(4), 340–349.

Erkut, S., & Tracy, A. J. (2002). Predicting adolescent self-esteem from participation in school sports among Latino subgroups. *Hispanic Journal of Behavioral Sciences*, 24(4), 409–429.

Ermisch, J., & Francesconi, M. (2001). Family matters: Impacts of family background on educational attainment. *Economica*, 68, 137–156.

Feldlaufer, H., Midgley, C., & Eccles, J. S. (1988). Student, teacher, and observer perceptions of the classroom before and after the transition to junior high school. *Journal of Early Adolescence*, 8, 133–156.

Felix-Ortiz, M., Newcomb, M., & Myers, H. (1994). A multidimensional measure of cultural identity for Latino and Latina adolescents. *Hispanic Journal of Behavioral Sciences*, 16(2), 99–115.

Finn, J. D. (1993). *School engagement & students at risk*. Washington, DC: National Center for Education Statistics.

Finn, J. D., & Rock, D. A. (1997). Academic success among students at risk for school failure. *Journal of Applied Psychology*, 82(2), 221–234.

Fisher, C. B., Wallace, S. A., & Fenton, R. E. (2000). Discrimination distress during adolescence. *Journal of Youth and Adolescence*, 29(6), 679–695.

Fix, M., & Zimmermann, W. (1997). Immigrant families and public policy: A deepening divide. In A. Booth, A. C. Crouter, & N. Landale (Eds.), *Immigration and the family: Research and policy on U.S. Immigrants*. Mahwah, NJ: Lawrence Erlbaum Associates.

Flanagan, K. D., & West, J. (2004). *Children born in 2001: First results from the base year of the ECLS-B (No. NCES 2005-036)*. Washington, DC: U.S. Department of Education.

Flores-Gonzalez, N. (1999). Puerto Rican high achievers: An example of ethnic and academic identity compatibility. *Anthropology & Education Quarterly*, 30(3), 343–362.

Flowers, T. (2003). Exploring the influence of reading for pleasure on African American high school students' reading achievement. *The High School Journal*, 87(1), 58–62.

Fordham, S. (1988). Racelessness as a factor in black students' school success: Pragmatic strategy or pyrrhic victory? *Harvard Educational Review*, 58(1), 54–84.

Fordham, S., & Ogbu, J. (1986). Black students' school success: Coping with the burden of acting white. *Urban Review, 18*(3), 176.

Frankenberg, E., Lee, C., & Orfield, G. (2003). *A multiracial society with segregated schools: Are we losing the dream?* Cambridge, MA: Harvard University, Civil Rights Project.

Fuligni, A. (1997). The academic achievement of adolescents from immigrant families: The roles of family background, attitudes, and behavior. *Child Development, 68*(2), 351–363.

Fuligni, A. (1998). Adolescents from immigrant families. In V. C. McLoyd & L. Steinberg (Eds.), *Studying minority adolescents: Conceptual, methodological, and theoretical issues* (pp. 127–143). Mahwah, NJ: Lawrence Erlbaum Associates, Publishers.

Fuligni, A. (2001a). A comparative longitudinal approach to acculturation among children from immigrant families. *Harvard Educational Review, 71*(3), 566–578.

Fuligni, A. (2001b). Family obligation and the academic motivation of adolescents from Asian, Latin American, and European backgrounds. *New Directions for Child and Adolescent Development, 94*, 61–76.

Fuligni, A. J., Alvarez, J., Bachman, M., & Ruble, D. N. (2001). A comparative longitudinal approach to acculturation among children from immigrant families. *Harvard Educational Review, 71*(3), 566–578.

Fuligni, A. J., Alvarez, J., Bachman, M., & Ruble, D. N. (2005). Family obligation and the academic motivation of young children from immigrant families. In C. R. Cooper, C. García Coll, T. Bartko, H. Davis, & C. Chatman (Eds.), *Developmental pathways through middle childhood* (pp. 261–283). New Jersey: Lawrence Erlbaum Publishers Inc.

Fuligni, A. J., & Hardway, C. (2004). Preparing diverse adolescents for the transition to adulthood. *Children of Immigrant Families, 14*(2), 100–119.

Fuligni, A., & Pedersen S. (2002). Family obligation and the transition to young adulthood. *Developmental Psychology, 38*(5), 856–868.

Fuligni, A. J., Tseng, V., & Lam, M. (1999). Attitudes toward family obligations among American adolescents with Asian, Latin American, and European backgrounds. *Child Development, 70*(4), 1030–1044.

Fuligni, A., Witkow, M., & García, C. (2005). Ethnic identity and the academic adjustment of adolescents from Mexican, Chinese, and European backgrounds. *Developmental Psychology, 41*(5), 799–811.

Furrer, C., & Skinner, E. (2003). Sense of relatedness as a factor in children's academic engagement and performance. *Journal of Educational Psychology, 95*(1), 148–162.

García Coll, C. (1990). Developmental outcome of minority infants: A process-oriented look into our beginnings. *Child Development, 61*(2), 270–290.

García Coll, C., Akiba, D., Palacios, N., Bailey, B., Silver, R., DiMartino, L., et al. (2002). Parental involvement in children's education: Lessons from three immigrant groups. *Parenting: Science and Practice, 2*(3), 303–324.

García Coll, C., & Magnuson, K. (1997). The psychological experience of immigration: A developmental perspective. In A. Booth, A. C. Crouter, & N. Landale (Eds.), *Immigration and the family: Research and policy on U.S. Immigrants* (pp. 91–131). Mahwah, NJ: Lawrence Erlbaum.

García Coll, C., & Magnusson, M. B. (1999). Cultural influences on child development: Are we ready for a paradigm shift? In A. S. Masten (Ed.), *The Minnesota symposia on child psychology: Vol. 29. Cultural processes in child development* (pp. 1–24). Mahway, NJ: Erlbaum.

García Coll, C., & Magnuson, K. (2000). Cultural differences as sources of developmental vulnerabilities and resources. In J. P. Shonkoff & S. J. Meisels (Eds.), *Handbook of early childhood intervention* (2nd ed.). Cambridge: Cambridge University Press.

García Coll, C., Lamberty, G., Jenkins, G., McAdoo, H. P., Crnic, K., Wasik, B. H., et al. (1996). An integrative model for the study of developmental competencies in minority children. *Child Development, 67*(5), 1891–1914.

García Coll, C., Thorne, B., Cooper, C., & Orellana, M. J. (1997). Beyond social categories: race, ethnicity, social class, gender, and developmental research, Society for Research in Child Development biennial meeting. Washington, DC.

García Coll, C., & Szalacha, L. S. (2004). The multiple contexts of child development. *Children of Immigrant Families, 14*(2), 80–97.

Garry, E. M. (1996). *Truancy: First step to a lifetime of problems.* Washington, DC: Department of Justice, Office of Juvenile Justice and Delinquency Prevention.

Gilbertson, G., & Singer, A. (2003). The emergence of protective citizenship in the USA: Naturalization among Dominican immigrants in the post-1996 welfare reform era. *Ethnic and Racial Studies, 26*(1), 25–51.

Gill, S., & Reynolds, A. J. (1999). Educational expectations and school achievement of urban African American children. *Journal of School Psychology, 37,* 403–424.

Glick, J. E., & White, M. J. (2003). The academic trajectories of immigrant youths: Analysis within and across cohorts. *Demography, 40*(4), 759–783.

Glick, J. E., & White, M. J. (2004). Post-secondary school participation of immigrant and native youth: The role of familial resources and educational expectations. *Social Science Research, 33,* 272–299.

Goodenow, C. (1993). The psychological sense of school membership among adolescents: Scale development and educational correlates. *Psychology in the Schools, 30*(1), 79–90.

Golova, N., Alario, A. J., Vivier, P. M., Rodriguez, M., & High, P. C. (1999). Literacy promotion for Hispanic families in a primary care setting: A randomized, controlled trial. *Pediatrics, 103,* 993–997.

Graham, L. H. (2000). Self-efficacy, motivation constructs, and mathematics performance of middle school students: A three-year longitudinal study. *Dissertation Abstracts International Section A: Humanities and Social Sciences, 61*(5-A), 1741.

Graham, S. (1994). Motivation in African Americans. Reviews of Educational Research, 64, 55–117.

Greene, J. C. (2001). Mixing social inquiry methodologies. In V. Richardson (Ed.), *Handbook of research on teaching* (4th ed.). Washington, DC: American Educational Research Association.

Greene, J. C., & Caracelli, V. J. (1997). *Advances in mixed-method evaluation: The challenges and benefits of integrating diverse paradigms*. San Francisco: Jossey-Bass Publishers.

Greenwood, C. R., Horton, B. T., & Utley, C. A. (2002). Academic engagement: Current perspectives in research and practice. *School Psychology Review*, 31(3), 328–350.

Gregor, A. J., & McPherson, D. A. (1966). Racial preference and ego-identity among white and Bantu children in the republic of South Africa. *Genetic Psychology Monographs*, 73(2), 217–253.

Grindstaff, C., Galloway, W., & Nixon, J. (1973). Racial and cultural identification among Canadian Indian children. *Phylon*, 34(4), 368–377.

Halgunseth, L., Ispa, J., & Rudy, D. (2006). Parental control in Latino families: An integrated review of the literature. *Child Development*, 77(5), 1282–1297.

Haller, A. O., & Portes, A. (1973). Status attainment processes. *Sociology of Education*, 46(Winter), 51–91.

Hamre, B. K., & Pianta, R. C. (2001). Early teacher-child relationships and the trajectory of children's school outcomes through eighth grade. *Child Development*, 72(2), 625–638.

Haubert, J., & Fussell, E. (2006). Explaining pro-immigrant sentiment in the U.S.: Social class, cosmopolitanism, and perceptions of immigrants. *International Migration Review*, 40(3), 489–507.

Harker, K. (2001). Immigrant generation, assimilation, and adolescent psychological well-being. *Social Forces*, 79(3) 969–1004.

Harkness, S., & Super, C. (1994). The developmental niche: A theoretical framework for analyzing the household production of health. *Social Science and Medicine*, 38(2), 217–226.

Harris, K. M. (1999). The health status and risk behavior of adolescents in immigrant families. In D. J. Hernandez (Ed.), *Children of immigrants: Health, adjustment and public assistance*. Washington, DC: National Academy Press.

Helms, J. E. (1995). An update of helms's white and people of color racial identity models. In J. Ponterotto, J. Casas, L. Susuki, & C. Alexander (Eds.), *Handbook of multicultural counseling* (pp. 181–198). Thousand Oaks, CA: Sage.

Hernandez, D. J. (1999). *Children of immigrants: Health, adjustment, and public assistance*. Washington, DC: National Academy Press.

Hernandez, D. J. (2004). Demographic change and the life circumstances of immigrant families. *Future of Children*, 14(2) 17–47.

Hernandez, D. J., & Charney, E. (1998). *From generation to generation: The health and well-being of children in immigrant families*. Washington, DC: National Academy Press.

Hernandez, D. J., & Darke, K. (1999). Socioeconomic and demographic risk factors and resources among children in immigrant families. In D. J. Hernandez (Ed.), *Children of immigrants* (pp. 19–126). Washington, DC: National Academy Press.

Hill, N. E., Castellino, D. R., Lansford, J. E., Nowlin, P., Dodge, K. A., Bates, J. E., et al. (2004). Parent academic involvement as related to school behavior, achievement, and aspirations: Demographic variations across adolescence. *Child Development,* 75(5), 1491–1509.

Hirschfeld, L. A. (1995). Do children have a theory of race? *Cognition,* 54, 209–252.

Hirschfeld, L. A. (1996). *Race in the making: Cognition, culture, and the child's construction of human kinds.* Cambridge, MA: MIT Press.

Hirschfeld, L. A. (1997). The inheritability of identity: Children's understanding of the cultural biology of race. *Child Development,* 66(5), 1418–1437.

Hofferth, S. L., & Sandberg, J. F. (2001). How American children spend their time. *Journal of Marriage and the Family,* 63(2), 295–308.

Hopkins, M. C. (1996). *Braving a new world: Cambodian (Khmer) refugees in an American city.* Westport, CT: Bergin Gasvey.

Hough, R. L., Hazen, A. L., Soriano, F. I., Wood, P., McCabe, K., & Yeh, M. (2002). Mental health care for Latinos: Mental health services for Latino adolescents with psychiatric disorders. *Psychiatric Services,* 53, 1556–1562.

Hoyle, R. H. (1995). *Structural equation modeling; concepts, issues, and applications.* Thousand Oaks, CA: Sage.

Hughes, D., & Chen, L. (1997). When and what parents tell children about race: An examination of race-related socialization among African American families. *Applied Developmental Science,* 1(4), 200–214.

Hughes, D., & Chen, L. (1999). The nature of parents' race-related communications to children: A developmental perspective. In L. Balter & C. Tamis-LeMonda (Eds.), *Child psychology: A handbook of contemporary issues.* Philadelphia: Taylor & Francis.

Hughes, D., & Johnson, D. J. (2001). Correlates in children's experiences of parents' racial socialization behaviors. *Journal of Marriage and Family,* 63, 981–995.

Hughes, D., Rodriguez, J., Smith, E. P., Johnson, D. J., & Stevenson, H. (2006). Parents' ethnic/racial socialization practices: A review of research and directions for future study. *Developmental Psychology,* 42(5), 747–770.

Hussey, J. M., Hallfors, D. D., Waller, M. W., Iritani, B. J., Halpern, C. T., & Bauer, D. J. (2007). Sexual behavior and drug use among Asian and Latino adolescents: Association with immigrant status. *Journal of Immigrant and Minority Health,* 9(2), 85–94.

Huston, A. (1991). *Children in poverty: Child development and public policy.* New York: Cambridge University Press.

Huston, A. C., & Ripke, M. N. (2006). *Developmental contexts in middle childhood: Bridges to adolescence and adulthood.* Cambridge: Cambridge University Press.

Ignatiev, N. (1995). *How the Irish became white.* New York: Routledge.

Information Works. (1999). *Information works! user guide.* (National Center for Public Education and Social Policy publication) Providence, RI Retrieved 2008, March 16 from: http://www.infoworks.ride.uri.edu/1999/guide/userguide.htm

Information Works. (2000). *Information Works! School District and State Reports:* 1999 (National Center for Public Education and Social Policy publication)

Providence, RI Retrieved 2008, March 16 from:
http://www.infoworks.ride.uri.edu/1999

Information Works. (2001). *Information works! school district and state reports:* 2000
(National Center for Public Education and Social Policy publication)
Providence, RI Retrieved 2008, March 16 from:
http://www.infoworks.ride.uri.edu/2000

Information Works. (2002). *Information works! school district and state reports:* 2001
(National Center for Public Education and Social Policy publication)
Providence, RI Retrieved 2008, March 16 from:
http://www.infoworks.ride.uri.edu/2001

Itzigsohn, J. (Spring 2005). The Dominican immigration experience. *Centro Journal,* 17(1), 270–281.

Itzigsohn, J., Cabral, C. D., Medina, E. H., & Vazquez, O. (1999). Mapping Dominican transnationalism: Narrow and broad transnational practices. *Ethnic and Racial Studies,* 22(2), 316–339.

Itzigsohn, J., Silvia, G., & Obed, V. (2005). Immigrant incorporation and racial identity: Racial self-identification among dominican immigrants. *Ethnic and Racial Studies,* 28(1), 50–78.

Jasinskaja-Lahti, I., & Liebkind, K. (2001). Perceived discrimination and psychological adjustment among Russian-speaking immigrant adolescents in Finland. *International Journal of Psychology,* 36(3), 174–185.

Jensen, L. (2001). The demographic diversity of immigrants and their children. In R. G. Rumbaut, & A. Portes (Eds.), *Ethnicities: Children of immigrants in America* (pp. 21–56). Berkeley: University of California Press.

Jodl, K. M., Michael, A., Malanchuk, O., Eccles, J. S., & Sameroff, A. (2001). Parents' roles in shaping early adolescents' occupational aspirations. *Child Development,* 72(4), 1247–1265.

Jordan, G. E., Snow, C. E., & Porche, M. V. (2000). Project ease: The effect of a family literacy project on kindergarten students' early literacy skills. *Reading Research Quarterly,* 35(4), 524–546.

Joyner, K., & Kao, G. (2000). School racial composition and adolescent racial homophily. *Social Science Quarterly,* 81(3), 810–825.

Jussim, L., Eccles, J. S., & Madon, S. J. (1996). Social perception, social stereotypes, and teacher expectations: Accuracy and the quest for the powerful self-fulfilling prophecy. *Advances in experimental social psychology,* 29, 281–388.

Jussim, L., & Harber, K. D. (2005). Teacher expectations and self-fulfilling prophecies: Knowns and unknowns, resolved and unresolved controversies. *Personality and Social Psychology Review,* 9(2), 131–155.

Jutte, D. P., Burgos, A., Mendoza, F., Ford, C. B., & Huffman, L. C. (2003). Use of the pediatric symptom checklist in a low-income, Mexican American population. *Archives of Pediatric Adolescent Medicine,* 157, 1169–1176.

Kao, G. (1999). Psychological well-being and educational achievement among immigrant youth. In D. J. Hernandez (Ed.), *Children of immigrants: Health, adjustment, and public assistance.* Washington, DC: National Academy Press.

Kao, G., & Tienda, M. (1995). Optimism and achievement: The educational performance of immigrant youth. *Social Science Quarterly,* 76(1), 1.

Kaplan, C. P., Erickson, P. I., & Juarez-Reyes, M. (2002). Acculturation, gender role orientation, and reproductive risk-taking behavior among Latina adolescent family planning. *Journal of Adolescent Research, 17*(2), 103–121.

Kasinitz, P., Mollenkopf, J. H., & Waters, M. C. (2004). *Becoming New Yorkers: Ethnographies of the new second generation.* New York: Russel Sage.

Katz, P. A. (1983). Developmental foundations of gender and racial attitudes. In R. L. Leahy (Ed.), *The child's construction of social inequality.* New York: Academic Press.

Katz, P. A. (2003). Racists or tolerant multiculturalists? How do they begin? *American Psychologist, 58*(11), 897–909.

Katz, P. A., & Downey, E. (submitted). *Infant categorization of race and gender cues. Child Development.* Unpublished manuscript.

Katz, P. A., & Kofkin, J. A. (1997). Race, gender, and young children. In S. S. Luthar, & J. A. Burack (Eds.), *Developmental psychopathology: Perspectives on adjustment, risk, and disorder* (pp. 51–74). Cambridge: Cambridge University Press.

Khattab, N. (2003). Explaining educational aspirations of minority students: The role of social capital and students' perceptions. *Social Psychology of Education, 6,* 283–302.

Keith, T. Z., & Page, E. B. (Autumn 1985). Do catholic high schools improve minority student achievement? *American Educational Research Journal, 22*(3), 337–349.

Kim, R. Y. (2002). Ethnic differences in academic achievement between Vietnamese and Cambodian children: Cultural and structural explanations. *Sociological Quarterly, 43*(2), 213–235.

Kinket, B., & Verkuyten, M. (1997). Levels of ethnic self identification and social context. *Social Research Quarterly, 60*(4), 338–354.

Kivisto, P., & Blanck, D. (1990). *American immigrants and their generations: Studies and commentaries on the Hansen thesis after fifty years.* Urbana: University of Illinois Press.

Knight, G. P., Bernal, M. E., Cota, M. K., Garza, C. A., & Ocampo, K. A. (1993). Family socialization and Mexican American identity and behavior. In G. P. Knight & M. E. Bernal (Eds.), *Ethnic identity: Formation and transmission among Hispanics and other minorities.* (Vol. viii, pp. 105–129). Albany, NY: State University of New York Press.

Knight, G. P., Bernal, M. E., Garza, C. A., & Cota, M. K. (1993). A social cognitive model of the development of ethnic identity and ethnically based behaviors. In M. E. Bernal & G. P. Knight (Eds.), *Ethnic identity: Formation and transmission among Hispanics and other minorities* (pp. 213–234). Albany: State University of New York Press.

Knight, G. P., Cota, M. K., & Bernal, M. E. (1993). The socialization of cooperative, competitive, and individualistic preferences among Mexican American children: The mediating role of ethnic identity. *Hispanic Journal of Behavioral Sciences, 15*(3), 291–309.

Knight, G. P., Bernal, M. E., Garza, C. A., Cota, M. K., & Ocampo, K. A. (1993). Family socialization and the ethnic identity of Mexican-American children. *Journal of Cross Cultural Psychology, 24*(1), 99–114.

Kohlberg, L. (1969). Stage and sequence: The cognitive-developmental approach to socialization. In D. A. Goslin (Ed.), *Handbook of socialization theory and research* (pp. 347–480). Chicago: Rand McNally.

Kowalski, K., & Lo, Y.-F. (2001). The influence of perceptual features, ethnic labels, and sociocultural information on the development of ethnic/racial bias in young children. *Journal of Cross Cultural Psychology, 32*(4), 444–455.

Kunda, Z. (1999). *Social cognition: Making sense of people.* Cambridge, MA: MIT Press.

Kuo, H.-H. D., & Hauser, R. M. (1997). How does size of sibship matter? Family configuration and family effects on educational attainment. *Social Science Research, 26,* 69–94.

LaFromboise, T., Coleman, H. L., & Gerton, J. (1993). Psychological impact of biculturalism: Evidence and theory. *Psychological Bulletin, 114*(3), 395–412.

Landale, N. S., Oropesa, R. S., Llanes, D., & Gorman, B. (1999). Does Americanization have adverse effects on health? Stress, health habits, and infant health outcomes among Puerto Ricans. *Social Forces, 78*(2), 613–642.

Lara, M., Gamboa, C., Kahramanian, M. I., Morales, L. S., & Bautista, D. E. H. (2005). Acculturation and Latino health in the United States: A review of the literature and its sociopolitical context. *Annual Review of Public Health, 26,* 367–397.

Lee, S. J. (1994). Behind the model-minority stereotype: Voices of high- and low-achieving Asian American students. *Anthropology & Education Quarterly, 25*(4), 413–429.

Lee, C. (2004). *Racial segregation and educational outcomes in metropolitan Boston.* Cambridge, MA: Harvard University.

Levitt, P., & Dehesa, R. d. l. (2003). Transnational migration and the redefinition of the state: Variations and explanations. *Ethnic and Racial Studies, 26*(4), 587–611.

Liebkind, K., Jasinskaja-Lahti, I., & Solheim, E. (2004). Cultural identity, perceived discrimination, and parental support as determinants of immigrants' school adjustments: Vietnamese youth in Finland. *Journal of Adolescent Research, 19*(6), 635–656.

Logan, J. R., J. Stowell & Oakley, D. (2002). Choosing segregation: Racial imbalance in American public schools, 1999-2000, Lewis Mumford Center for Comparative Urban and Regional Research, University of Albany: 1–25.

Lopez, D., & Espiritu, Y. (1997). Panethnicity in the United States: A theoretical framework. In D. Hamamoto, R. Torres, & R. D. Torres (Eds.), *New American destinies: A reader in contemporary Asian and Latino immigration* (pp. 195–218) New York: Routledge.

Lorenzo, M. K., Frost, A. K., & Reinherz, H. Z. (2000). Social and emotional functioning of older Asian American adolescents. *Child and Adolescent Social Work, 17*(4), 289–304.

Lorenzo, M. K., Pakiz, B., Reinherz, H. Z., & Frost, A. (1995). Emotional and behavioral problems of Asian American adolescents: A comparative study. *Journal of Child and Adolescent Social Work, 12*(3), 197–212.

Ludwig, J., Ladd, H. F., & Duncan, G. J. (2001). Urban poverty and educational outcomes. *Brookings-Wharton Papers on Urban Affairs, 2,* 147–201.

Luthar, S. S., & Becker, B. E. (2002). Privileged but pressured? A study of affluent youth. *Child Development, 73*(5), 1593–1610.

Macmillan, R., & Eliason, S. R. (2003). Characterizing the life course as role configurations and pathways: A latent structure approach. In J. T. Mortimer & M. J. Shanahan (Eds.), *Handbook of the life course.* New York: Kluwer Academic/Plenum.

Mansfield, C. (2001, December). *Contextual influences on student motivation in the first year of middle school.* Paper presented at the Annual Conference of the Australian Association for Research in Education, Fremantle, Western Australia.

Markides, K. S., & Coreil, J. (1986). The health of Hispanics in the Southwestern United States: An epidemiologic paradox. *Public Health Reports, 101*(3), 253–265.

Marks, A. K. (2008). Being bicultural: Developing ethnic identities in middle childhood and adolescence. (Doctoral dissertation: Brown University, 2008) *Dissertation Abstracts International: Section B: The Sciences and Engineering, 68*(7-B), 4867.

Marks, G. N., Fleming, N., Long, M., & McMillan, J. (2000). *Patterns of participation in year 12 and higher education in Australia: Trends and issues. (No. 17).* Melbourne: Australian Council for Educational Research.

Marks, A. K., & García Coll, C. (In preparation). Ethnic identities and school experiences among bicultural adolescents.

Marks, A. K., & García Coll, C. (2007). Early academic skill development among American Indian and Alaska native youth: A growth modeling study. *Developmental Psychology, 43*(3), 633–646.

Marks, G. N., McMillan, J., & Hillman, K. (2001). *Tertiary entrance performance: The role of student background and school factors (No. 22).* Victoria, Australia: Australian Council for Educational Research.

Marks, A. K., Powell, K., & García Coll, C. (in press). Ethnic identity. In R. Schweder(Editor-in-chief), *The Chicago Companion to the Child.* Chicago, IL: University of Chicago Press.

Marks, A. K., Szalacha, L. S., Boyd, M. J., & García Coll, C. (2007). Emerging ethnic identity and its relation to social group preferences in middle childhood: Findings from the Children of Immigrants Development in Context (CIDC) study. *International Journal of Behavioral Development, 31*(5), 501–513.

Marsiglia, F. F., Kulis, S., & Hecht, M. L. (2001). Ethnic labels and ethnic identity as predictors of drug use among middle school students in the southwest. *Journal of Research on Adolescence, 11*(1), 21–48.

Martin, C. L., & Ruble, D. (2004). Children's search for gender cues. *Current Directions in Psychological Science, 13*(2), 67–70.

Martinez, R. J., & Valenzuela, A. (2006). *Immigration and crime.* New York: New York Universtiy Press.

Maruyama, G. (1998). *Basics of structural equation modeling.* Thousand Oaks, CA: Sage.

Mata, F. (1997). *Intergenerational transmission of education and socio-economic status: A look at immigrants, visible minorities and aboriginals.* Ottawa, ON: Statistics Canada, Department of Canadian Heritage.

McHale, S. M., Crouter, A. C., & Tucker, C. J. (2001). Free-time activities in middle childhood: Links with adjustment in early adolescence. *Child Development, 72*(6), 1764–1778.

McLanahan, S., & Booth, K. (1989). Mother-only families: Problems, prospects, and politics. *Journal of Marriage and Family, 51,* 557–580.

McLanahan, S. S., & Carlson, M. J. (2002). Welfare reform, fertility, and father involvement. *The Future of Children, 12*(1), 147–165.

McLanahan, S., & Sandefur, G. (1994). *Growing up with a single parent.* Cambridge, MA: Harvard University Press.

McLaughlin, C. S., Chen, C., Greenberger, E., & Biermeier, C. (1997). Family, peer, and individual correlates of sexual experience among Caucasian and Asian American late adolescents. *Journal of Research on Adolescence, 7*(1), 21–54.

McLoyd, V. C. (1990). Minority children: Introduction to the special issue. *Child Development, 61,* 263–266.

McLoyd, V. C. (1998). Socioeconomic disadvantage and child development. *American Psychologist, 53*(2), 185–204.

McLoyd, V. C. (2005). Pathways to academic achievement among children from immigrant families: A commentary. In C. R. Cooper, C. T. G. Coll, W. T. Bartko, H. Davis, & C. Chatman (Eds.), *Developmental pathways through middle childhood: Rethinking contexts and diversity as resources.* Mahwah, NJ: Lawrence Erlbaum Associates.

McNeely, C. A., Nonnemaker, J. M., & Blum, R. W. (2002). Promoting school connectedness: Evidence from the national longitudinal study of adolescent health. *Journal of School Health, 72*(4), 138–146.

McQueen, A., Getz, J. G., & Bray, J. H. (2003). Acculturation, substance use, and deviant behavior: Examining separation and family conflict as mediators. *Child Development, 74*(6), 1737–1751.

Meier, K. J., & Wrinkle, R. D. (1999). Representative bureaucracy and distributional equity: Addressing the hard question. *Journal of Politics, 61*(4), 1025–1041.

Mendoza, F. S., & Dixon, L. B. (1999). The health and nutritional status of immigrant Hispanic children: Analyses of the Hispanic health and nutrition examination survey. In D. J. Hernandez (Ed.), *Children of immigrants: Health, adjustment and public assistance.* Washington, DC: National Academy Press.

Mickelson, R. A. (1990). The attitude-achievement paradox among black adolescents. *Sociology of Education, 63*(1), 44–61.

Midgley, C., Feldlaufer, H., & Eccles, J. S. (1989). Student/teacher relations and attitudes toward mathematics before and after the transition to junior high school. *Child Development, 60,* 981–992.

Modell, J. (2000). How may children's development be seen historically? *Childhood: A Global Journal of Child Research, 7*(1), 81–106.

Moll, L. C., Amanti, C., Neff, D., & Gonzalez, N. (1992). Funds of knowledge for teaching: Using a qualitative approach to connect homes and classrooms. *Theory into Practice*, 31(2), 132–141.

Moll, L. C., & Greenberg, J. B. (1992). Creating zones of possibilities: Combining social contexts for instruction. In L. C. Moll (Ed.), *Vygotsky and education: Instructional implications and applications of sociohistorical psychology* (pp. 319–348). New York: Cambridge University Press.

Morland, J. K. (1958). Racial recognition by nursery school children in Lynchburg, VA. *Social Forces*, 37(2), 132–137.

Morland, J. K. (1969). Race awareness among American and Hong Kong Chinese children. *The American Journal of Sociology*, 75(3), 360–374.

Morland, J. K., & Hwang, C. H. (1981) Racial/ethnic identity of preschool children: Comparing Taiwan, Hong Kong, and the United States. *Journal of Cross Cultural Psychology*, 12(4), 409–424.

Mossakowski, K. N. (2003). Coping with perceived discrimination: Does ethnic identity protect mental health? *Journal of Health and Social Behavior*, 44, 318–331.

Muller, C. (2001). The role of caring in the teacher-student relationship for at-risk students. *Sociological Inquiry*, 71(2), 241–255.

Mydans, S. (1993, June 27). A new tide of immigration brings hostility to the surface, poll finds. *New York Times*.

Nathenson-Mejia, S. (1994). Bridges between home and school: Literacy building activities for non-native English speaking homes. *Journal of Educational Issues of Language Minority Students*, 14, 149–163.

Neal, D. A. (1995). *The Effect of Secondary Schooling on (November)*. NBER Working Paper No. W5353.Available at SSRN: http://ssrn.com/abstract=225416

Nesdale, D., & Flesser, D. (2001). Social identity and the development of children's group attitudes. *Child Development*, 72(2), 506–517.

Newman, L. S., Liss, M. B., & Sherman, F. (1983). Ethnic awareness in children: Not a unitary concept. *The Journal of Genetic Psychology*, 14(3), 103–112.

Nightingale, D. S., & Fix, M. (2004). Economic and labor market trends. *Future of Children*, 14(2), 49–60.

Nord, C. W., & Griffin, J. A. (1999). Educational profile of 3- to 8- year old children of immigrants. In D. J. Hernandez (Ed.), *Children of immigrants*. Washington DC: National Academy Press.

Ocampo, K. A., Knight, G. P., & Bernal, M. E. (1997). The development of cognitive abilities and social identities in children: The case of ethnic identity. *International Journal of Behavioral Development*, 21(3), 479–500.

Ogbu, J. (1978). *Minority education and caste: The American system in cross-cultural comparison*. New York: Academic Press.

Ogbu, J. (1987). Variability in minority school performance: A problem in search of an explanation. *Anthropology and Education Quarterly*, 18, 312–334.

Ogbu, J. (1991). Minority coping responses and school experience. *Journal of Psychohistory*, 18(4), 433–456.

Ogbu, J. (1994). From cultural differences to differences in cultural frames of reference. In P. M. Greenfield & R. R. Cocking (Eds.), *Cross-cultural roots of minority child development* (pp. 365–391). Hillsdale, NJ: Erlbaum.

Ogbu, J. (2004). Collective identity and the burden "acting white" in black history, community, and education. *Urban Review, 36*(1), 1–35.

Ogbu, J., & Simmons, H. D. (1998). Voluntary and involuntary minorities: A cultural-ecological theory of school performance with some implications for education. *Anthropology and Education Quarterly, 29*(2), 155–188.

Okagaki, L. (2001). Parental beliefs, parenting style, and children's intellectual development. In E. L. Grigorenko (Ed.), *Family environment and intellectual functioning: A life span perspective* (pp. 141–172). Mahwah, NJ: Lawrence Erlbaum Associates, Publishers.

Okagaki, L., Frensch, P. A., & Dodson, N. E. (1996). Mexican American children's perceptions of self and school achievement. *Hispanic Journal of Behavioral Sciences, 18*(4), 469–484.

Okagaki, L., & Sternberg, R. J. (1993). Parental beliefs and children's school performance. *Child Development, 64*(1), 36–56.

Omizo, M. M., Omizo, S. A., & Suzuki, L. A. (1988). Children and stress: An exploratory study of stressors and symptoms. *The School Counselor, 3,* 267–275.

Orellana, M. F. (2003). Responsibilities of children in Latino immigrant homes. *New Directions for Youth Development, 2003*(100), 25–39.

Oreopoulos, P., Page, M. E., & Stevens, A. H. (2003). *Does human capital transfer from parent to child? The intergenerational effects of compulsory schooling (No. Working Paper 10164)*. National Bureau of Economic Research.

Orfield, G. (2001). *Schools more separate: Consequences of a decade of resegregation.* Unpublished manuscript.

Orfield, G., & Lee, C. (2005). *Why segregation matters: Poverty and educational inequality.* Boston, MA: Harvard University.

Parcel, T. L., & Menaghan, E. G. (1994). Early parental work, family social capital, and early childhood outcomes. *The American Journal of Sociology, 99*(4), 972–1009.

Patchen, M. (1982). *Black-white contact in schools.* West Lafayette, IN: Purdue University Press.

Paxton, P., & Mughan, M. 2006. What's to Fear from Immigrants? Creating an Assimilationist Threat Scale. *Political Psychology, 27*(4), 549–568.

Pear, R. (1986, July 1). New restrictions on immigration gain public support, poll shows. *New York Times.*

Peet, S. H., Powell, D. R., & O'Donnel, B. K. (1997). Mother-teacher congruence in perceptions of the child's competence and school engagement: Links to academic achievement. *Journal of Applied Developmental Psychology, 18,* 373–393.

Perea, F., & García Coll, C. (2008). The social and cultural contexts of bilingualism. In J. Altarriba & R. R. Heredia (Eds.), *An introduction to bilingualism: Principles and processes.* Mahway, NJ: Lawrence Erlbaum Publishers.

Perez, L. (2001). Growing up in Cuban Miami: Immigration, the enclaves, and new generations. In R. G. Rumbaut & A. Portes (Eds.), *Ethnicities: Children of immigrants in America* (pp. 91–125). Berkeley: University of California Press.

Phelan, P., Davidson, A. L., & Yu, H. C. (1993). Students' multiple worlds: Navigating the borders of family, peer and school cultures. In P. Phelan & A. L. Davidson (Eds.), *Renegotiating cultural diversity in American schools* (pp. 52–88). New York: Teacher College Press.

Phelan, P., Davidson, A. L., & Yu, H. C. (1998). *Adolescents' worlds: Negotiating family, peers and school.* New York: Teachers College Press.

Phinney, J. (1989). Stages of ethnic identity in minority group adolescents. *Journal of Early Adolescence, 9,* 34–39.

Phinney, J. (1990). Ethnic identity in adolescents and adults: Review of research. *Psychological Bulletin, 108*(3), 499–514.

Phinney, J. (1992). The multigroup ethnic identity measure: A new scale for use with diverse groups. *Journal of Adolescent Research, 7*(2), 156–176.

Phinney, J. (1993). A three-stage model of ethnic identity development in adolescence. In M. E. Bernal & G. P. Knight (Eds.), *Ethnic identity: Formation and transition among Hispanics and other minorities.* Albany: SUNY Press.

Phinney, J. S., Berry, J. W., Vedder, P. & Liebkind, K. (2006). The acculturation experience attitudes, identities and behaviors of immigrant youth. In J. Berry, J. Phinney, D. Sam, & P. Vedder (Eds.), *Immigrant youth in cultural transition.* Mahwah, NJ: Lawrence Erlbaum Associates.

Phinney, J. S., Romero, I., Nava, M., & Huang, D. (2001). The role of language, parents and peers in ethnic identity among adolescents in immigrant families. *Journal of Youth and Adolescence, 30*(2), 135–153.

Phinney, J. S., Ferguson, D. L., & Tate, J. D. (1997). Intergroup attitudes among ethnic minority adolescents: A causal model. *Child Development, 68*(5), 955–969.

Phinney, J., Horenczyk, G., Liebkind, K., & Vedder, P. (2001). Ethnic identity, immigration, and well-being: An interactional perspective. *Journal of Social Issues, 57*(3), 493–511.

Phinney, J. S., Madden, T., & Santos, L. J. (1998). Psychological variables as predictors of perceived ethnic discrimination among minority and immigrant adolescents. *Journal of Applied Social Psychology, 28*(11), 937–953.

Phoenix, A. (1998). Dealing with difference: The recursive and the new. *Ethnic and racial studies, 21*(5), 859–880.

Pong, S., & Hao, L. (2007). Neighborhood and school factors in the school performance of immigrants' children. *International Migration Review, 41*(1), 206–241.

Portes, A. (1995). Children of immigrants: Segmented assimilation and its determinants. In A. Portes (Ed.), *The economic sociology of immigration: Essays on networks, ethnicity, and entrepreneurship.* New York: Russell Sage.

Portes, A. (1996). Transnational communities: Their emergence and significance in the contemporary world-system. In R. P. Korzeniewicz & W. C. Smith (Eds.), *Latin America in the world-economy* (pp. xii, 280 p.). Westport, CT: Greenwood Press.

Portes, A. (1998). Social capital: Its origins and applications in modern sociology. *Annual Review of Sociology, 24*, 1–24.

Portes, A. (2000). The two meanings of social capital. *Sociological Forum, 15*(1) 1–12.

Portes, A., & Hao, L. (2005). La educación de los hijos de inmigrantes efectos contextuales sobre los logros educativos de la segunda generación. *Migraciones, 17*, 7–44.

Portes, A., & MacLeod, D. (1996). Educational progress of children of immigrants: The roles of class, ethnicity, and school context. *Sociology of Education, 69*(4), 255–275.

Portes, A., & MacLeod, D. (1999). Educating the second generation: Determinants of academic achievement among children of immigrants in the United States. *Journal of Ethnic & Migration Studies, 25*(3), 373.

Portes, A., & Rumbaut, R. G. (1990). *Immigrant America: A portrait.* Berkeley: University of California Press.

Portes, A., & Rumbaut, R. G. (1996). *Immigrant America: A Portrait.* Berkeley: University of California Press.

Portes, A., & Rumbaut, R. G. (2001). *Legacies: The story of the immigrant second generation.* Berkeley: University of California Press.

Portes, A., & Rumbaut, R. (2005). Introduction: The second generation and the children of immigrants a longitudinal study. *Ethnic and Racial Studies, 28*(6), 983–999.

Portes, A., & Zhou, M. (1993). The new second generation: Segmented assimilation and its variants. *The Annals of the American Academy of Political and Social Science, 530*, 74–96.

Providence Plan. (2004). *Student Mobility.* Retrieved from http://www.rikidscount.org/matriarch/documents/edu_student_mobility.pdf

Pumariega. (1986). Acculturation and eating attitudes in adolescent girls: A comparative and correlation study. *Journal of American Academy of Child Psychiatry, 25*(2), 276–279.

Quintana, S. M. (1994). A model of ethnic perspective-taking ability applied to Mexican-American children and youth. *International Journal of Intercultural Relations, 18*(4), 419–448.

Quintana, S. M. (1998). Children's developmental understanding of ethnicity and race. *Applied & Preventative Psychology, 7*, 27–45.

Quintana, S. M., & Vera, E. M. (1999). Mexican American children's ethnic identity, understanding of ethnic prejudice, and parental ethnic socialization. *Hispanic Journal of Behavioral Sciences, 21*(4), 387–404.

Ramsey, P. G. (1991). The salience of race in young children growing up in an all-white community. *Journal of Educational Psychology, 83*, 28–34.

Rice, J. K. (2003). *Teacher quality: Understanding the effectiveness of teacher attributes.* Washington, DC: Economic Policy Institute.

Rice, A. S., Ruiz, R. A., & Padilla, A. M. (1974). Person perception, self-identity, and ethnic group differences in Anglo, Black, and Chicano preschool children and third-grade children. *Journal of Cross Cultural Psychology, 5*(1), 100–108.

Rhode Island Kids Count. (2004). *Rhode Island Kids Count Factbook*. Providence, RI: Rhode Island Kids Count.

Roesser, R. W., Midgley, C., & Urdan, T. C. (1996). Perceptions of the school psychological environment and early adolescents' psychological and behavioral functioning in school: The mediating role of goals and belonging. *Journal of Educational Psychology, 88*(3), 408–422.

Rogoff, B. (1990). *Apprenticeship in thinking: Cognitive development in social context*. New York: Oxford University Press.

Rogoff, B. (2003). *The cultural nature of human development*. New York: Oxford University Press.

Rogoff, B., Paradise, R., Arauz, R. M., Correa-Chavez, M., & Angelillo, C. (2003). Firsthand learning through intent participation. *Annual Review of Psychology, 54*(1), 175–203.

Romero, A. J., & Roberts, R. E. (1998). Perception of discrimination and ethnocultural variables in a diverse group of adolescents. *Journal of Adolescence, 21*(6), 641–656.

Rosenberg, M., & Simmons, R. G. (1971). *Black and white self-esteem; the urban school child*. Washington, DC: American Sociological Association.

Rosenthal, D. A., & Hrynevich, C. (1985). Ethnicity and ethnic identity: A comparative study of Greek, Italian, and Anglo-Australian adolescents. *International Journal of Psychology, 20*, 723–742.

Rotheram-Borus, M. J., & Wyche, K. F. (1994). Ethnic differences in identity development in the United States. In S. L. Archer (Ed.), *Interventions for adolescent identity development* (pp. 62–83). Thousand Oaks, CA: Sage.

Ruiz-de-Velasco, J., & Fix, M. (2000). *Overlooked and underserved: Immigrant students in U.S. Secondary schools*. Washington, DC: The Urban Institute.

Ruble, D. N., Alvarez, J. M., Bachman, M., Cameron, J. A., Fuligni, A. J., García Coll, C. & Rhee, E. (2004). The development of a sense of "we": The emergence and implications of children's collective identity. In M. Bennett & F. Sani (Eds.), *The development of the social self*. East Sussex, England: Psychology Press.

Ruble, D. N., & Martin, C. L. (1998). Gender development. In N. Eisenberg (Ed.), *Handbook of child psychology: Social, emotional, and personality development* (Vol. 3, pp. 933–1016). New York: Wiley & Sons Inc.

Ruble, D. N., Martin, C. L., & Berenbaum, S. A. (2006). Gender development. In N. Eisenberg, W. Damon, & R. M. Lerner (Eds.), *Handbook of child psychology: Vol. 3, social, emotional, and personality development* (6th ed.). Hoboken, NJ: John Wiley & Sons Inc.

Rumbaut, R. G. (1994a). The crucible within: Ethnic identity, self-esteem, and segmented assimilation among children of immigrants. *International Migration Review, 28*(4), 748.

Rumbaut, R. G. (1994b). Origins and destinies: Immigration to the united states since world war ii. *Sociological Forum, 9*(4), 583–621.

Rumbaut, R. G. (1995). The new Californians: Comparative research findings on the educational process of immigrant children. In R. G. Rumbaut & W. A. Cornelius (Eds.), *California's immigrant children: Theory, research, and implications for educational policy* (pp. ix, 272 p.). San Diego, CA: Center for U.S.-Mexican Studies, University of California, San Diego.

Rumbaut, R. G. (1997). Assimilation and its discontents: Between rhetoric and reality. *International Migration Review*, 31(4), 923–960.

Rumbaut, R. G. (2000). *Children of immigrants and their achievement: The role of family, acculturation, social class, gender, ethnicity, and school contexts* Mimeograph. Michigan State University.

Rumbaut, R. G. (2005). Sites of belonging: Acculturation, discrimination, and ethnic identity among children of immigrants. In T. S. Weisner (Ed.), *Discovering successful pathways in children's development: Mixed methods in the study of childhood and family life* (pp. 111–163). Chicago, IL: The University of Chicago Press.

Rumbaut, R., & Ewing, W. (2007). *The myth of immigrant criminality and the paradox of assimilation: Incarceration rates among native and foreign-born men.* Washington, DC: Immigration Policy Center.

Rumbaut, R. G., & Portes, A. (2001). *Ethnicities: Children of immigrants in America.* Berkeley: University of California Press.

Ryan, A. M., & Patrick, H. (2001). The classroom social environment and changes in adolescents' motivation and engagement during middle school. *American Educational Research Journal*, 38(2), 437–460.

Sanders, C. (1985). The life cycle: III middle childhood 6–12 years. *Australian and New Zealand Journal of Family Therapy*, 6(2), 99–104.

Schmader, T., Major, B., & Gramzow, R. H. (2001). Coping with ethnic stereotypes in the academic domain: Perceived injustice and psychological disengagement. *Journal of Social Issues*, 57(1), 93–111.

Schoon, I. (2001). Teenage job aspirations and career attainment in adulthood: A 17-year follow-up study of teenagers who aspired to become scientists, health professionals, or engineers. *International Journal of Behavioral Developmental*, 25(2), 124–132.

Schoon, I., & Parsons, S. (2002). Teenage aspirations for future careers and occupational outcomes. *Journal of Vocational Behavior*, 60, 262–288.

Schuller, T. (2001). The complementary roles of human and social capital. *Canadian Journal of Policy Research*, 2(1), 89–106.

Schwartz, A. E., & Stiefel, L. (2006). *Is there a nativity gap? New evidence on the academic performance of immigrant students.* New York: American Education Finance Association.

Scribner, R., & Dwyer, J. (1989). Acculturation and low birthweight among Latinos in the Hispanic HANES. *American Journal of Public Health*, 79(9), 1263–1267.

Seidman, E., Aber, J. L., Allen, L., & French, S. E. (1996). The impact of the transition to high school on the self-esteem and perceived social context of poor urban youth. *American Journal of Community Psychology*, 24(4), 489–515.

Senechal, M., & LeFevre, J.-A. (2002). Parental involvement in the development of children's reading skills: A five-year longitudinal study. *Child Development*, 73(2), 445–460.

Senechal, M., LeFevre, J.-A., Thomas, E. M., & Daley, K. E. (1998). Differential effects of home literacy experiences on the development of oral and written language. *Reading Research Quarterly, 33*(1), 96–116.

Semaj, L. (1980). The development of racial evaluation and preference: A cognitive approach. *Journal of Black Psychology, 6*(2), 59–79.

Shields, M. K., & Behrman, R. E. (2004). Children of immigrant families: Analysis and recommendations. *Future of Children, 14*(2), 4–16.

Shumow, L., & Miller, J. (2001). Parents' at-home and at-school academic involvement with young adolescents. *Journal of Early Adolescence, 21*(1), 68–91.

Singh, G., & Siahpush, M. (2001). All-cause and cause-specific mortality of immigrants and native born in the United States. *American Journal of Public Health, 91*(3), 392–399.

Singh, G., & Yu, S. (1996). Adverse pregnancy outcomes: Differences between us- and foreign-born women in major us racial and ethnic groups. *American Journal of Public Health, 86*(6), 837–843.

Simmons, R. G., & Blyth, D. A. (1987). *Moving into adolescence: The impact of pubertal change and school context.* Hawthorne, NY: Aldine Transaction.

Simons, R. L., Murry, V., McLoyd, V., Lin, K., Cutrona, C., & Conger, R. D. (2002). Discrimination, crime, ethnic identity, and parenting as correlates of depressive symptoms among African American children: A multilevel analysis. *Developmental and Psychopathology, 14*, 371–393.

Sirin, S., & Rogers-Sirin, L. (2005). Components of school engagement among African American adolescents. *Applied Developmental Science, 9*(1), 5–13.

Skaalvik, E. M., & Hagtvet, K. A. (1990). Academic achievement and self-concept: An analysis of causal predominance in a developmental perspective. *Journal of Personality and Social Psychology, 58*(2), 292–307.

Skinner, E. A., & Belmont, M. J. (1993). Motivation in the classroom: Reciprocal effects of teacher behavior and student engagement across the school year. *Journal of Educational Psychology, 85*(4), 571–581.

Skinner, E. A., Zimmer-Gembeck, M. J., & Connell, J. P. (1998). Individual differences and the development of perceived control. *Monographs of the Society for Research in Child Development, 63*(2–3), 1–220.

Smith, E. P., Atkins, J., & Connell, C. M. (2003). Family, school, and community factors and relationships to racial/ethnic attitudes and academic achievement. *American Journal of Community Psychology, 32*(1–2), 159–173.

Smith-Hefner, N. J. (1993). Education, gender, and generational conflict among Khmer refugees. *Anthropology and Education Quarterly, 24*(2), 135–158.

Smith-Hefner, N. J. (1999). *Khmer American: Identity and moral education in a diasporic community.* Berkeley: University of California Press

Sontag, D. (1992, December 13). Calls to restrict immigration comes from many quarters. *New York Times*, p. E5.

Sosa, A. S. (1997). Involving Hispanic parents in educational activities through collaborative relationships. *Bilingual Research Journal, 21*(2 & 3), 103–111.

Spencer, M. B. (1984). Black children's race awareness, racial attitudes and self-concept: A reinterpretation. *Journal of Child Psychology and Psychiatry, 25*(3), 433–441.

Spencer, M. B. (1999). Social and cultural influences on school adjustment: The application of an identity-focused cultural ecological perspective. *Educational Psychologist*, 34(1), 43–57.

Spencer, M. B., & Markstrom, C. A. (1990). Identity processes among racial and ethnic minority children in America. *Child Development*, 61, 290–310.

Spencer, M. B., Noll, E., Stoltzfus, J., & Harpalani, V. (2001). Identity and school adjustment: Revisiting the acting white assumption. *Educational Psychologist*, 36(1), 21–30.

Steinberg, L., Lamborn, S. D., Dornbusch, S. M., & Darling, N. (1992). Impact of parenting practices on adolescent achievement: Authoritative parenting, school involvement, and encouragement to succeed. *Child Development*, 63(5), 1266–1281.

Steinberg, L., Brown, B. B., & Dornbusch, S. M. (1996). *Beyond classroom: Why school reform has failed and what parents need to do*. New York: Simon and Schuster.

Stepick, A., Grenier, G., Castro, M., & Dunn, M. (2003). *This land is our land: Immigrants and power in Miami*. Berkeley: University of California Press.

Steele, C. M. (1997). A threat in the air: How stereotypes shape the intellectual identities and performance of women and African Americans. *American Psychologist*, 52, 613–629.

Stipek, D. (2005). Children as unwitting agents in their developmental pathways. In C. R. Copper, C. García Coll, T. Bartko, H. M. Davis, & C. Chatman (Eds.), *Developmental pathways through middle childhood* (pp. 99–120). London: Lawrence Erlbaum Associates.

Suárez-Orozco, M. M. (1987). Becoming somebody: Central American immigrants in the U.S. inner-city schools. *Anthropology & Education Quarterly*, 18(4), 287–299.

Suárez-Orozco, M. M. (2004). Formulating identity in a globalized world. In D. B. Qin Hilliard & M. M. Suárez-Orozco (Eds.), *Globalization: Culture and education in the new millennium* (pp. 173–202). Berkeley: University of California Press.

Suárez-Orozco, C., & Suárez-Orozco, M. (1995). *Transformations: Migration, family life, and achievement motivation among Latino adolescents*. Stanford, CA: Stanford University Press.

Suárez-Orozco, C., & Suárez-Orozco, M. (2001). *Children of immigration*. Cambridge, MA: Harvard University Press.

Suárez-Orozco, C., & Todorova, I. (2003). *Understanding the social worlds of immigrant youth* (Vol. 2003). San Francisco: Jossey-Bass.

Suárez-Orozco, C., Suárez-Orozco, M., & Todorova, I. (2008). *Learning a new land: Immigrant students in American society*. Cambridge, MA: Belknap Press of Harvard University Press.

Super, C. M., & Harkness, S. (2002). Culture structures the environment for development. *Human Development*, 45(4), 270–274.

Suro, R., & Passel, J. (2003). *The rise of the second generation: Changing patterns in Hispanic population growth*. Washington, DC: Pew Hispanic Center.

Szalacha, L. A., Erkut, S., García Coll, C., Fields, J. P., Alarcon, O., & Ceder, I. (2003). Perceived discrimination and resilience. In S. S. Luthar (Ed.),

Resilience and vulnerability: Adaptation in the context of childhood adversities (pp. 414–435). New York: Cambridge University Press.

Tajfel, H. (1978). Social categorization, social identity, and social comparison. In H. Tajfel (Ed.), *Differentiation between social groups* (pp. 61–76). London: Academic Press.

Tajfel, H., & Turner, J. (1979). An integrative theory of intergroup conflict. In W. Austin & S. Wochel (Eds.), *The social psychology of intergroup relations* (pp. 33–47). Monterey, CA: Brooks/Cole.

Taylor, R. D., Casten, R., Flickinger, S. M., Roberts, D., & Fulmore, C. D. (1994). Explaining the school performance of African-American adolescents. *Journal of Research on Adolescence, 4*(1), 22–44.

Taylor, D. M., Wright, S. C., & Porter, L. E. (1993). Dimensions of perceived discrimination: The personal/group discrimination discrepancy. In M. P. Zanna & J. M. Olson (Eds.), *The psychology of prejudice: The Ontario symposium* (Vol. 7, pp. 233–255). Hillsdale, NJ: Erlbaum.

Thomson, E., Hanson, T. L., & McLanahan, S. S. (1994). Family structure and child well-being: Economic resources vs. Parental behaviors. *Social Forces, 73*(1), 221–242.

Thorne, B. (2005). Unpacking school lunchtime: Structure, practice, and the negotiation of differences. In C. R. Cooper, C. T. G. Coll, W. T. Bartko, H. Davis & C. Chatman (Eds.), *Developmental pathways through middle childhood: Rethinking contexts and diversity as resources.* Mahwah, NJ: Lawrence Erlbaum Associates.

Tolman, D. L., & Szalacha, L. A. (1999). Dimensions of desire: Bridging qualitative and quantitative methods in a study of female adolescent sexuality. *Psychology of Women Quarterly, 23*(1), 7–39.

Tropp, L. R., & Wright, S. C. (2003). Evaluations and perceptions of self, ingroup, and outgroup: Comparisons between Mexican-American and European-American children. *Self and Identity, 2*(3), 203–221.

Tucker, C. J., Marx, J., & Long, L. (1998). Moving on: Residential mobility and children's school lives. *Sociology of Education, 71*(2), 111–129.

Turner, J. C. (1982). Towards a cognitive redefinition of the social group. In H. Tajfel (Ed.), *Social identity and intergroup relations* (pp. 15–40). Cambridge: Cambridge University Press.

Tyack, D. B., & Cuban, L. (1997). *Tinkering toward utopia: A century of public school reform.* Cambridge, MA: Harvard University Press.

Tyson, K. (2002). Weighing in: Elementary-age students and the debate on attitudes toward school among Black students. *Social Forces, 80*(4), 1157–1190.

U.S. Census Bureau. (1990a). *Detailed Race Population Table, Providence, Rhode Island.* Retrieved October 2nd, 2008, from http://factfinder.census.gov/servlet/DTTable?_bm=y&-context=dt&-ds_name=DEC_1990_STF1_&-mt_name=DEC_1990_STF1_P006&-mt_name=DEC_1990_STF1_P007&-CONTEXT=dt&-tree_id=100&-redoLog=true&-all_geo_types=Y&-geo_id=01000US&-geo_id=16000US440400&-search_results=01000US&-format=&-_lang=en

U.S. Census Bureau. (1990b). *Detailed Race Population Table. Rhode Island.* Retrieved October 2nd, 2008, from http://factfinder.census.gov/ servlet/DTTable?_bm=y&-context=dt&-ds_name=DEC_1990_STF1_&-CONTEXT=dt&-mt_name=DEC_1990_STF1_P006&-mt_name=DEC_1990_STF1_P007&-tree_id=100&-redoLog=true&-all_geo_types=Y&-_caller=geoselect&-geo_id=01000US&-geo_id=04000US44&-search_results=16000US440400&-format=&-_lang=en

U.S. Census Bureau. (1999). *Poverty: 1999 Census Brief.* Retrieved October 2nd, 2007, from http://www.census.gov/prod/2003pubs/c2kbr-19.pdf

U.S. Census Bureau. (2000a). *Census 2000 Demographic Profile Highlights: Selected Population Group: Cambodian alone: Providence, RI.* Retrieved October 2nd, 2008, from http://factfinder.census.gov/servlet/SAFFIteratedFacts?_event=&geo_id=04000US44&_geoContext=01000US%7C04000US44&_street=&_county=&_cityTown=&_state=04000US44&_zip=&_lang=en&_sse=on&ActiveGeoDiv=&_useEV=&pctxt=fph&pgsl=040&_submenuId=factsheet_2&ds_name=DEC_2000_SAFF&_ci_nbr=015&qr_name=DEC_2000_SAFF_R1040&reg=DEC_2000_SAFF_R1040%3A015&_keyword=&_industry=

U.S. Census Bureau. (2000b). *Census 2000 Demographic Profile Highlights: Selected Population Group: Cambodian alone: Rhode Island.* Retrieved October 2nd, 2008, from http://factfinder.census.gov/servlet/SAFFIteratedFacts?_event=&geo_id=04000US44&_geoContext=01000US%7C04000US44&_street=&_county=&_cityTown=&_state=04000US44&_zip=&_lang=en&_sse=on&ActiveGeoDiv=&_useEV=&pctxt=fph&pgsl=040&_submenuId=factsheet_2&ds_name=DEC_2000_SAFF&_ci_nbr=015&qr_name=DEC_2000_SAFF_R1040&reg=DEC_2000_SAFF_R1040%3A015&_keyword=&_industry=

U.S. Census Bureau. (2000c). *Census 2000 Demographic Profile Highlights: Selected Population Group: Cambodian alone: United States.* Retrieved October 2nd, 2008, from http://factfinder.census.gov/servlet/SAFFIteratedFacts?_event=&geo_id=01000US&_geoContext=01000US&_street=&_county=&_cityTown=&_state=&_zip=&_lang=en&_sse=on&ActiveGeoDiv=&_useEV=&pctxt=fph&pgsl=010&_submenuId=factsheet_2&ds_name=DEC_2000_SAFF&_ci_nbr=015&qr_name=DEC_2000_SAFF_R1010&reg=DEC_2000_SAFF_R1010%3A015&_keyword=&_industry=

U.S Census Bureau. (2000d). *Census 2000 Demographic Profile Highlights: Selected Population Group: Dominican (Dominican Republic): Providence, RI* Retrieved on October 2nd, 2007, from http://factfinder.census.gov/servlet/SAFFIteratedFacts?_event=&geo_id=16000US4459000&_geoContext=01000US%7C04000US44%7C16000US4459000&_street=&_county=providence&_cityTown=providence&_state=04000US44&_zip=&_lang=en&_sse=on&ActiveGeoDiv=&_useEV=&pctxt=fph&pgsl=160&_submenuId=factsheet_2&ds_name=DEC_2000_SAFF&_ci_nbr=405&qr_name=DEC_2000_SAFF_R1160&reg=DEC_2000_SAFF_R1160%3A405&_keyword=&_industry=

U.S Census Bureau. (2000e). *Census 2000 Demographic Profile Highlights: Selected Population Group: Dominican (Dominican Republic): Rhode Island*. Retrieved on October 2nd, 2007, from http://factfinder.census.gov/servlet/SAFFIteratedFacts?_event=Search&geo_id=01000US&_geoContext=01000US&_street=&_county=&_cityTown=&_state=04000US44&_zip=&_lang=en&_sse=on&ActiveGeoDiv=geoSelect&_useEV=&pctxt=fph&pgsl=010&_submenuId=factsheet_2&ds_name=DEC_2000_SAFF&_ci_nbr=405&qr_name=DEC_2000_SAFF_R1010&reg=DEC_2000_SAFF_R1010%3A405&_keyword=&_industry=

U.S Census Bureau. (2000f). *Census 2000 Demographic Profile Highlights: Selected Population Group: Dominican (Dominican Republic): United States* Retrieved on October 2nd, 2007, from http://factfinder.census.gov/servlet/SAFFIteratedFacts?_event=&geo_id=01000US&_geoContext=01000US&_street=&_county=&_cityTown=&_state=&_zip=&_lang=en&_sse=on&ActiveGeoDiv=&_useEV=&pctxt=fph&pgsl=010&_submenuId=factsheet_2&ds_name=DEC_2000_SAFF&_ci_nbr=405&qr_name=DEC_2000_SAFF_R1010&reg=DEC_2000_SAFF_R1010%3A405 &_keyword=&_industry=

U.S Census Bureau. (2000g). *Census 2000 Demographic Profile Highlights: Selected Population Group: Portuguese: Providence, RI*. Retrieved on October 2nd, 2007, from http://factfinder.census.gov/servlet/SAFFIteratedFacts?_event=&geo_id=16000US4459000&_geoContext=01000US%7C04000US44%7C16000US4459000&_street=&_county=providence&_cityTown=providence&_state=04000US44&_zip=&_lang=en&_sse=on&ActiveGeoDiv=&_useEV=&pctxt=fph&pgsl=160&_submenuId=factsheet_2&ds_name=DEC_2000_SAFF&_ci_nbr=552&qr_name=DEC_2000_SAFF_A1160&reg=DEC_2000_SAFF_A1160%3 A552&_keyword=&_industry=

U.S Census Bureau. (2000h). *Census 2000 Demographic Profile Highlights: Selected Population Group: Portuguese: East Providence, RI*. Retrieved on October 2nd, 2007, from http://factfinder.census.gov/servlet/SAFFIteratedFacts?_event=Search&geo_id=01000US&_geoContext=01000US&_street=&_county=east+providence&_cityTown=east+providence&_state=04000US44&_zip=&_lang=en&_sse=on&ActiveGeoDiv=geoSelect&_useEV=&pctxt=fph&pgsl=010&_submenuId=factsheet_2&ds_name=DEC_2000_SAFF&_ci_nbr=552&qr_name=DEC_2000_SAFF_A1010&reg=DEC_2000_SAFF_A1010%3A552&_keyword=&_industry=

U.S. Census Bureau. (2003). *Educational Attainment in the United States*. Retrieved October 2nd, 2007, from http://www.census.gov/population/www/socdemo/education/cps2003.html

U.S. Department of Education. (1998). Partnership for Family Involvement in Education, and the GTE Foundation based on data from the National Opinion Research Center at the University of Chicago. *Family Involvement in Education: A Snapshot of Out-of-School Time*. Washington, DC: U.S. Department of Education.

Vandivere, S., Gallagher, M., & Moore, K. (2004). *Changes in children's well-being and family environments*. Washington, DC: Urban Institute.

Vaughan, G. M., Tajfel, H., & Williams, J. (1981). Bias in reward allocation in an intergroup and an interpersonal context. *Social Psychology Quarterly*, 44(1), 37–42.

Verkuyten, M. (1998). Perceived discrimination and self-esteem among ethnic minority adolescents. *The Journal of Social Psychology*, 138(4), 479–493.

Verkuyten, M. (2002). Perceptions of ethnic discrimination by minority and majority early adolescents in the Netherlands. *International Journal of Psychology*, 37(6), 321–332.

Verkuyten, M. (2003). Ethnic in-group bias among minority and majority early adolescents: The perception of negative peer behavior. *British Journal of Developmental Psychology*, 21(4), 543–564.

Verkuyten, M., & Brug, P. (2002). Ethnic identity achievement self-esteem and discrimination among Surinamese adolescents in the Netherlands. *Journal of Black Psychology*, 28, 122–141.

Verkuyten, M., & Brug, P. (2003). Educational performance and psychological disengagement among ethnic-minority and Dutch adolescents. *Journal of Genetic Psychology*, 164(2), 189–200.

Verkuyten, M., Kinket, B., & van der Wielen, S. (1997). The understanding of ethnic discrimination among preadolescents. *Journal of Genetic Psychology*, 158, 97–112.

Verkuyten, M., & Thijs, J. (2001). Peer victimization and self-esteem of ethnic minority group children. *Journal of Community & Applied Social Psychology*, 11(3), 227–234.

Verkuyten, M., & Thijs, J. (2004). Psychological disidentification with the academic domain among ethnic minority adolescents in the Netherlands. *British Journal of Educational Psychology*, 74(1), 109–125.

Walker, U. (2001). *A question of ethnicity—one word, different people, many perceptions: The perspectives of groups other than Māori, pacific peoples, and New Zealand Europeans*. New Zealand: Statistics New Zealand.

Waters, M. C. (1990). *Ethnic options: Choosing identities in America*. Berkeley: University of California Press.

Waters, M. C. (1994). Ethnic and racial identities of second-generation black immigrants in New York City. *International Migration Review*, 28(4), 795–820.

Waters, M. C. (1999). *Black identities: West Indian immigrant dreams and American realities*. New York: Russell Sage Foundation.

Weisner, T. S. (Ed.). (2005). *Discovering successful pathways in children's development: Mixed methods in the study of childhood and family life*. Chicago: University of Chicago Press.

Wenglinsky, H. (2000). *How teaching matters: Bringing the classroom back into discussions of teacher quality*. Princeton, NJ: Educational Testing Service, Policy Information Center.

Wentzel, K. R. (1994). Relations of social goal pursuit to social acceptance, classroom behavior, and perceived social support. *Journal of Educational Psychology*, 86(2), 173–182.

Wentzel, K. R. (1997). Student motivation in middle school: The role of perceived pedagogical caring. *Journal of Educational Psychology, 89*(3), 411–419.

Wentzel, K. R. (1998). Parents' aspirations for children's educational attainments: Relations to parental beliefs and social address variables. *Merrill-Palmer Quarterly, 44*(1), 20–37.

Wentzel, K. R., & Wigfield, A. (1998). Academic and social motivational influences on students' academic performance. *Educational Psychology Review, 10*(2), 155–175.

Whaley, A. L. (1993). Self-esteem, cultural identity, and psychosocial adjustment in African American children. *Journal of Black Psychology, 19*(4), 406–422.

Wong, C. A., Eccles, J. S., & Sameroff, A. (2003). The influence of ethnic discrimination and ethnic identification on African American adolescents' school and socioemotional adjustment. *Journal of Personality, 71*(6), 1197–1232.

Yang, K. Y. (2004). Southeast Asian American children: Not the model minority. *Future of Children, 14*(2), 127–133.

Yee, M. D., & Brown, R. (1992). Self-evaluations and intergroup attitudes in children aged three to nine. *Child Development, 63,* 619–629.

Zhou, M. (1997a). Growing up American: The challenge confronting immigrant children and children of immigrants. *Annual Review of Sociology, 23,* 63–95.

Zhou, M. (1997b). Segmented assimilation: Issues, controversies, and recent research on the new second generation. *International Migration Review, 31*(4, Special Issue: Immigrant Adaptation and Native-Born Responses in the Making of Americans), 975–1008.

Index ⚌

Note: The letter 'n' denotes note numbers and 'f' denotes figures.